THE
OLD
SOUTH
ILLUSTRATED

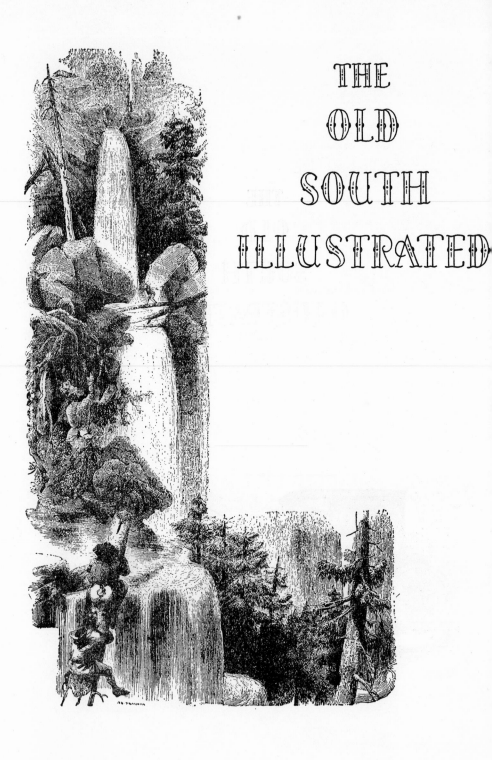

THE
OLD
SOUTH
ILLUSTRATED

BY PORTE CRAYON

[DAVID HUNTER STROTHER]

Profusely Illustrated
by the Author

Edited with an Introduction by

Cecil D. Eby, Jr.

Chapel Hill
The University of
North Carolina Press

Preface

THIS COLLECTION OF writings from the pen of "Porte Crayon" and of drawings from his pencil brings together for the first time the best of his travel narratives depicting the Old South. The text has been taken from his articles scattered in *Harper's Monthly* between 1853 and 1858, an interval when he wrote in succession three major series, *Virginia Illustrated* (reprinted in book form in 1857 and 1871), *North Carolina Illustrated,* and *A Winter in the South.* Also written before the War was *A Summer in New England,* a delightful companion piece to the others. Although it provides us with many illuminating and amusing insights into the temperament of the Northerner, considerations of space and purpose have decided against its inclusion in the present volume. For the same reason, all of David Strother's postwar writings have been omitted. For the serious student and the curious, the introduction and the appendix discuss the background of the articles in this anthology.

The reader will doubtless discover for himself that the illustrations of Porte Crayon are often as interesting as the writings. Such an opinion would accord well with the response of the public a century ago. Strother was a writer-artist—not one nor the other—and his total accomplishment cannot be measured with a one-dimensional criterion of art or literature alone. His first love and principal interest was the illustration, around which he wrote his literary sketch in such a way that the two complemented one another. The presentation of his literature without his art would be an injudicious distortion; the present book contains samples of both.

Strother's illustrated essays are highly eclectic. Descriptions of landscape, caricatures, reminiscences, anecdotes, historical excerpts, and scraps of poetry are often juxtaposed in his work. He was, after all, writing of travel—episodic by its very nature—rather than constructing a unified novel or a logical polemic. His purpose was to combine instruction with amusement, but there can be little doubt that he was more successful in accomplishing the latter. Today we are not interested in the temperatures of the Virginia springs, the depth of the mine at Gold Hill, or statistics of the Natural Bridge; but we are entertained by Squire Hardy, by Little Mice, and by Porte Crayon when he is himself rather than the antiquarian or cicerone. Most of the uninteresting digressions not relevant to a picture of the Old South have been cut from this book, but care has been taken not to delete sections which contain valuable or unusual social documentation.

The suggestion for preparing an edition of Strother's best work came to me from the University of North Carolina Press shortly after I had submitted a biography of Porte Crayon for its consideration. It is hoped that the present book will reveal to the public the writings and drawings of a man who a hundred years ago was one of our popular and well-known literary figures. My biography, scheduled for publication next year, will treat his life and career as artist, writer, soldier, and diplomat.

My principal debt, so far as materials are concerned, is to Porte Crayon's grandson, David H. Strother, who provided me with the originals of many illustrations used in *Harper's*. Some of these have been placed in the present text to supplement reproductions of the wood drawings. For his continued interest I wish to thank Professor Thomas P. Haviland of the University of Pennsylvania, under whose supervision I wrote the biography. I am also grateful to Professor Jay L. Curtis of Madison College for certain valuable suggestions and to my wife Patricia for her continued enthusiasm and support.

Contents

Preface   v

Introduction   ix

From *Virginia Illustrated*   1
  The Journey to Canaan   3
  Life in Canaan   23
  The Chimneys and the Warm Springs   37
  A Virginia Snow-Storm   49
  A Virginia Hostelry   59
  The Natural Bridge   69
  The Great Valley   84
  On the Road   105
  The University and Monticello   115

The Dismal Swamp   129

From *North Carolina Illustrated*   155
  The Fisheries   155
  The Piny Woods   180
  Guilford   200
  Picnic in the Gold Region   209

From *A Winter in the South*   217
  Third Paper   217
  Fifth Paper   245
  Sixth Paper   269

Bibliographical Appendix   293

Introduction

Lamenting the fact that Southern periodicals could not pay enough to keep their best writers at home, Dr. George W. Bagby, editor of the *Southern Literary Messenger,* particularly regretted the loss of "our own matchless, artist-writer, Porte Crayon,—the best contributor, by long odds, that Harper can boast." The *Messenger's* loss was *Harper's* gain, for David Hunter Strother, better known as "Porte Crayon," contributed to that magazine more than fifty illustrated essays during the quarter-century 1853-79. Certainly more than any other American writer, Strother possessed the "Harper touch," which was chiefly the gift of being able not only to write well but also to illustrate his articles with his own lively drawings. The age of illustration began in the eighteen fifties. No longer a pretentious adornment, the wood-engraving became a necessity for the successful magazine. When an editor found a writer trained in preparing the wood block for an engraver, he was likely to offer everything, even the staggering sum for a non-British writer of four or five hundred dollars per article. When the contributor was Porte Crayon, the House of Harper was prepared even to suggest, for certain pieces, a traveling account.

Porte Crayon was the country cousin of Irving's more urbane Geoffrey Crayon; he was the spade-bearded, garrulous interpreter of rural life and landscape for a generation of American readers. Two decades before the "local colorists" of the eighteen seventies, Strother scoured the highways and byways from New Hampshire to New Orleans in his search for the unusual and the picturesque. Although not averse to picturing cities like Boston or New Orleans, Strother preferred the back-country and the single-rutted hamlets of the provinces as proper subjects for his pen and pencil. He delighted in

drawing innyard loafers, Negro cooks, shabby country squires, and
village viragoes. In an age when the prevailing taste for rural description was Arcadian, Strother sought out Boeotian America; in an age
when sentimentality and romanticism were in vogue, he delineated
his subjects realistically. With an extraordinary disregard for belle-
tristic mannerisms, Strother scattered his characters throughout his
text, along with remarks on the landscape, historical digressions,
political and social satire, and rustic anecdotes. The results, although
eclectic, were highly successful, for there was a spice for every taste.
Unlike other travel writers of his day who combed the back alleys
of Timbuctu and explored the craters of Central American volcanoes
in their search for fresh materials, Strother found a wealth of materials
in the teeming America of his day. Although as an art student he
had rambled through Europe, he never drew upon these experiences
for a travel essay. The variety and the contrasts in the United States
were matter enough to satisfy any writer, as he knew.

Strother was a pioneer in delineating two regional types, the Southern Negro and the Appalachian mountaineer. In a period when the
Negro's rare appearance in literature was characterized by a one-
dimensional stereotype, Strother showed the ambivalent and variegated
qualities of flesh-and-blood colored folk like "Little Mice," "Uncle
Peter," and a host of others. His strain of realism was a shield against
the mawkish idealizing of the Negro which dominated so many other
Southern writers. And long before Mary N. Murfree, Strother caught
the ramshackle Allegheny "improvements" inhabited by proud moun-
taineers like Conway and Tim Longbow, who are not types but
differentiated characters. These two contributions alone should assure Porte Crayon a permanent place in American literature, but
when to these are added his panoramic view of the United States and
his unstrained revelations of American character, we see that his
work is valuable not only as literature but also as social history.

To estimate accurately how many Americans read *Harper's New
Monthly Magazine* each month is impossible, but a quarter of a
million would probably be a conservative figure. In 1852, only two
years after the first number of the magazine, a writer for the *Whig
Review* said of the *Monthly*, "There is not a village, there is scarcely
a township in the land into which your work has not penetrated."

Readers of the magazine were of nearly every class, high and low, from Newport to Virginia City. Editors of Southern magazines bewailed the fact that the New York magazine outsold all magazines in the South put together, but their appeals to pride and patriotism were to little avail in halting the rise in circulation of *Harper's Monthly*. Bagby put it well when he said, "Southern patriotism enables a man to abuse the Yankees, to curse the Yankees, to fight the Yankees, to do everything but quit taking the Yankee papers." *Harper's* went north and south, east and west; it was the first national magazine whose circulation department could prove the point by its figures. It was little wonder that the pay was so high and that Porte Crayon was so well known. In the decade preceding the Civil War, perhaps ten read his work for every one who had even heard of Hawthorne, Melville, or Whitman. Two weeks after the Battle of Gettysburg, Strother called upon the Secretary of War, Edwin Stanton, on official business. The Secretary wished to discuss three things: Meade's failure to destroy Lee, the New York draft riots, and the characters in *Virginia Illustrated*. At the other extreme was a private soldier who told Strother that he had carried that book through the arduous Tennessee campaigns in a knapsack already overloaded with government issue. It would be difficult to find better examples of enthusiasm from the great and the least about any other nineteenth-century American man of letters.

The first magazine article by Porte Crayon was "The Virginian Canaan," which was published in *Harper's New Monthly Magazine* in December, 1853. This was an illustrated narrative of a fishing trip made in 1852 to the Falls of the Blackwater near the present town of Davis, W. Va. Because Strother also illustrated a book called *The Blackwater Chronicle* (New York, 1853) which was written by his close friend and kinsman, Philip Pendleton Kennedy—the youngest brother of the Baltimore novelist, John Pendleton Kennedy —authorship of *The Blackwater Chronicle* has often mistakenly been attributed to Strother. Actually, *The Blackwater Chronicle,* a much longer work than "The Virginian Canaan," treated a sporting expedition made a year earlier, in 1851. There were, then, two separate trips to the Blackwater, and both were used by different writers as the subjects for narratives published in 1853.

Despite its limited scope, *The Blackwater Chronicle,* a mélange of travel, erudition, and effervescent romanticism, had a somewhat surprising popularity in the fifties; editions of it were brought out in London and Leipzig. Under the pen name of "Clerke of Oxenforde," Kennedy takes us on an expedition into a virtually uncharted wilderness of western Virginia, delights us with his amusing and realistic descriptions of the campers, and sometimes wearies us with his Shandyan virtuosity. Among the characters whom he describes is "Andante Strozzi," a caricature of Strother himself.

"The Virginian Canaan" is similar to *The Blackwater Chronicle* in its delineation of an expedition to the Falls of the Blackwater, but while Kennedy is more brilliant in style, Strother is more successful in creating a credible picture of travel in the mountains. The characters in Strother's essay are Porte Crayon, Mr. Penn (Kennedy), X.M.C. (ex-member of Congress Henry Bedinger, an early contributor of poetry to the *Southern Literary Messenger* and later the father of the Southern poetess Danske Dandridge), Mr. Jones (probably Frank Peters, a Martinsburg sportsman), Mr. Smith (probably Boyd Pendleton, the son of John P. Kennedy's favorite uncle, Philip Pendleton of Martinsburg), and Mr. Dindon (probably the younger Philip Pendleton, brother of Boyd).

After the success of "The Virginian Canaan," Strother wrote for *Harper's* five papers which he titled "Virginia Illustrated: Adventures of Porte Crayon and His Cousins." These treated a tour which he made in the autumn of 1853 up the Valley of Virginia and into the Piedmont. The characters, apparently, were real people. Little Mice was a Negro servant who went west after the Civil War, Fanny Crayon was Strother's sister Emily, Minnie May was doubtless a fictionalized portrait of Strother's first wife, Ann Doyne Wolff; Dora Dimple cannot be identified. From Martinsburg the excursion party visited most of the principal points of interest in the Valley, Weyer's Cave, the Alleghany springs, the Natural Bridge, and the Peaks of Otter. Crossing the Blue Ridge, they made their way to Lynchburg, Charlottesville, and finally to Berkeley Springs.

In the spring of 1856 Strother set out alone for a tour of the Carolinas and Georgia, but after spending a month at Suffolk, Va., he abandoned his intention to visit South Carolina and Georgia.

His article, "The Dismal Swamp," was followed by a series called "North Carolina Illustrated," which recorded impressions of fisheries on the Pamlico Sound, the piny woods, Guilford Court House, and Gold Hill. Late in 1856, Strother, accompanied by his wife and daughter, traveled to East Tennessee and thence to New Orleans in the spring following. The outcome of this trip was seven papers for *Harper's* called "A Winter in the South." Squire Broadacre, Bob Larkin, and the other characters described in this series appear to be almost entirely fictitious. Some of the drawings were done by David E. Henderson, an artist of Jefferson County, Va. Many of Henderson's originals are in the library at Princeton University. Only one more tour was made by Strother before the Civil War—to New England in the summer of 1859—but this is not relevant to the present book.

For the printing of illustrations in Strother's time, three processes were required in preparing a woodcut: drawing the sketch, transferring it to the wood block, and engraving the block. The artist first made his sketch, usually in pencil, on paper. A wood draughtsman took a seasoned block of boxwood, planed to the exact thickness of the type, and rubbed it with pumice stone and water to provide a clear background for the drawing, which was made directly on the block in either lead pencil or India ink washing. Finally, a wood engraver took the block and pasted a smooth piece of white paper over it. Using a lens fixed upon a permanent stand, he cut away small portions of the paper and engraved that part of the block so that he knew exactly what he had completed. This process of engraving was by far the most tedious, and no matter how excellent an artist's sketch was, it was at the mercy of the engraver. Strother was, of course, both an artist and a wood draughtsman, but there is no evidence that he ever engraved a block. His favorite engraver was Charles Edmonds, whose mark "C. Edmonds" or "Edmonds," followed by "SC" (sculpsit —"he has engraved"), can be seen on numerous illustrations. The firms of Richardson and Cox and J. W. Orr prepared others. Although no marks appear on the woodcuts for "North Carolina Illustrated" and "A Winter in the South," it is likely that one of the Orr brothers, Nathaniel or John William, engraved these, for the Orr firm was the center of illustration in New York for over forty years.

Engravers whose work was less known would doubtless never have missed such an opportunity for a bit of free advertising.

A century has passed since the heyday of Porte Crayon. No bibliography of his works or biography of his life has been published to help keep his fame alive. His many articles are scattered throughout odd volumes of *Harper's* and have never been collected into a single volume. These things in part explain why he is not better known, but there are also other reasons. The travel narrative as a literary *genre* has been relegated to a minor place in *belles lettres* of our generation. Had Strother written a series of romantic novels about Southern life, as did his cousin John Esten Cooke, he would doubtless be far better known. But Strother was not interested in romance. He wished to capture, before it vanished forever, the real South, as seen by one traveling through it. Because he put his creative energy into two channels, art and literature, rather than one, he became that distressing thing for cultural historians, the anomaly. In the pigeon-holing that so often accompanies evaluation of the arts, Strother's versatility has worked to his disadvantage. Was he an artist or a writer? The answer is that he was both. There are many signs, however, that augur favorably for a revival of interest in Porte Crayon. As the age which he described so minutely and so accurately becomes less familiar to us, his presentation of life and landscape before the Civil War becomes even more valuable. Recent years have seen a revival of interest in other *Harper's* artist-writers like Benson Lossing, Brantz Mayer, and John Ross Browne by those who wish to see the nineteenth century as it was rather than as it might have been; the re-evaluation of Porte Crayon—who was vastly their superior in range and depth—is inevitable. As a link between the vernacular tradition of the Southern humorists, most of whom were journalists, and the romantic tradition of the Southern novelists, Strother will eventually find his place in the canon of American literature.

David Hunter Strother was born in 1816 in Martinsburg, Virginia (now West Virginia), a thriving market town at the northern end of the Shenandoah Valley. His father, John Strother, was for years clerk of the circuit court of Berkeley County and a staunch Whig.

John Strother's dominant political ideology, a reverence for the principle of Federal Union, had been demonstrated during the War of 1812, when he resigned his commission in the Virginia militia in order to accept a lieutenancy in the army of the United States. David's mother, Elizabeth Hunter Strother, came from one of the most distinguished families of northern Virginia. Through her, Dave was a cousin of such literary figures as John Pendleton Kennedy, John Esten Cooke, and Philip Pendleton Cooke.

As a boy, Dave Strother was frail and sickly, and his inability to engage in the outdoor sports expected of most Virginia youths forced him into solitary pastimes—drawing, music, and reading. He devoured the novels of Scott, listened to his father's tales of bloody battles along the Canadian frontier, and acquired the rudiments of a classical education at the local academy. Art must have been his major interest, because in his thirteenth year he was sent to Philadelphia for study under Pietro Ancora, a well-known teacher. This step, however, was premature, for within a few months he returned to Martinsburg. Shortly thereafter he contracted a case of measles, which invigorated his physique in such a way that the pampered only son became overnight an *enfant terrible*. Books and sketching pads were thrown aside for guns and horses. Although small in stature, "Pidge," as he was called, developed into a fearless and reckless leader of a wild set of Martinsburg boys whose pranks were recalled (perhaps exaggerated) half a century later. Orchards were defruited, ferry boats on the nearby Potomac were "borrowed," and several gunpowder plots were carried out. Local legend-tellers avowed that it was "Pidge" who tied a jackass to the bell of a church steeple one memorable Sunday morning. When Colonel John found his son drilling and arming a militia company—a band of local academy boys —he was prepared to admit that Dave might become a better soldier than artist.

It is not surprising that in 1832 Dave made his first of three applications for West Point. Nor is it surprising that the son of Martinsburg's outspoken opponent of Andrew Jackson was turned down in those years of Democratic upheaval. Dave was shipped off instead to Jefferson College (now Washington and Jefferson) in Canonsburg, Pennsylvania, to await the return of the conservatives. His year at

Jefferson is a mystery. He never acquired much education there, but he was awarded the degrees of A.B. and M.A. (apparently retroactive and honorary) many years later. When Dave realized that a West Point appointment was out of the question, he tried in succession law, medicine, and engineering, but in each instance his ability apparently outran his enthusiasm. His most auspicious achievement during these years was a six-hundred-mile hike up the Valley of Virginia in mid-November, 1835, which was the first of many trips of exploration in his much-traveled career. The Natural Bridge, the Peaks of Otter, caroling Negroes on the James River—these caught his imagination in ways that patient study and diligent application could not.

Fortunately Strother did not lose his interest in art. In 1836 he enrolled with half a dozen other students in the drawing classes of Samuel F. B. Morse at Washington Square in New York. Although Morse seems to have been unimpressed by Strother's facility in oil painting, the Virginian's lively caricatures won his tutor's admiration. Morse, however, was not optimistic about the future of art in America. In a private chat which Strother never forgot, Morse said, "Strother, don't be an artist. It means beggary. . . . A house dog lives better." Advice of this kind from one of the foremost painters of the age was not calculated to kindle Strother's enthusiasm.

In 1838 Strother left New York for a trek into the wilderness of the Ohio Valley, where he spent two years, supporting himself by painting river-town merchants. He was so intrigued by the West that for a time he thought of abandoning civilization for a trapper's life on the upper Mississippi. A frantic letter from Colonel John, containing promises of supporting a trip to Europe, lured Dave back to Martinsburg in the spring of 1840.

For three years Strother rambled and occasionally studied in France and Italy. Arriving in Paris in time for the second funeral of Napoleon I, he wrote an account of the pageantry for the Martinsburg *Gazette* that was long remembered in his native town. In Florence he graduated from tourist to expatriate, moving in the circle of Horatio Greenough, Hiram Powers, and S. V. Clevenger. But Strother was more attracted by the mountain scenery of Italy than its art. On foot he penetrated distant passes of the Apennines and was a familiar guest at remote mountain monasteries. When visiting artists required a guide to out-of-the-way spots in the peninsula, Strother was never too busy with his art to refuse his services. His *tour de force,* a feat perhaps unique in the annals of American pedestrianism, was a November walk from Rome to Naples, with his ascent of Vesuvius on the following day. His efforts to make the volcano erupt, he told *Gazette* readers, were disappointingly unsuccessful.

Late in 1843 Strother returned to America with excellent sensibilities and a quite remarkable pair of legs but little notion of what he wished to do. He read Volney and Voltaire, was seized by a sense of cosmic futility, and filled his journal with self-depreciations. Painting straight-mouthed provincial merchants who settled about the fee in advance of the first sitting was neither dignified nor rewarding. Nor was he interested in helping his father develop the hotel constructed in the mid-forties at Berkeley Springs near the Potomac. A fellow Virginian and close friend of the New York days, John Gadsby Chapman, induced Strother to return to New York and to enter the booming profession of wood-engraving, which at that time was revolutionizing the book business. Chapman, who was also a fine painter, was well on his way to becoming the dean of wood-draughtsmen, and under his instruction Strother learned how to draw the sketch upon the wood block for the engraver. By 1850 he had all the work in this line he could conveniently manage. He illustrated books by S. G. Goodrich ("Peter Parley"), William Gilmore Simms, John Esten Cooke, and John Pendleton Kennedy, whose second edition of *Swallow Barn* contains the best specimens of Strother's work. His future as a craftsman seemed assured. In 1849 he married Ann Doyne Wolff, a nineteen-year-old Martinsburg girl, and with the birth of their daughter Emily in the following year, it seemed that Strother's career was about to level off upon a plateau of merely average accomplishment.

Strother's principal work, however, lay ahead of him. When he exhibited some sketches at the National Academy of Design during the spring of 1853, a friendly fellow artist induced him to take his portfolio over to the firm of Harper and Brothers, who were looking for indigenous sketches which could be used in their newly founded *Harper's New Monthly Magazine*. The interview was perhaps the greatest single event in Strother's life. The Harpers admired his drawings of a fishing trip into the mountains of western Virginia and commissioned him to write and to illustrate an article. The Strother-Harper alliance, born in an hour of conversation, lasted for a quarter-century, during which Porte Crayon prepared more than fifty essays for the magazine and gave it, said one editor, "a character of paper never furnished before or since." The often-made assertion that Strother was the best paid contributor to the American magazine during that period is probably true; in all, the Harpers paid him about $25,000 for his articles over the years.

While Strother was preparing his first article for *Harper's Monthly* during the summer of 1853, John Pendleton Kennedy brought Washington Irving to Berkeley Springs for a visit. Although Irving suffered in the ferocious Virginia heat, he was entertained by Strother's sketch book. No doubt the idea for "Porte Crayon," Strother's best-known pen name, was suggested by his meeting with "Geoffrey Crayon" at the Springs. His article, "The Virginian Canaan," was completed in the fall, submitted, and caught the fancy of editor and public alike. Harper gave him a roving commission to travel and to write whatever he liked. This generous arrangement was ideal for an adventurer like Strother, and during the next six years he made the most of it.

During the eighteen fifties Strother prepared four illustrated travel series—*Virginia Illustrated, North Carolina Illustrated, A Winter in the South,* and *A Summer in New England*—the results of excursions ranging from the White Mountains to the lower Mississippi. The first, brought out in book form in 1857 and 1871, remains his best-known work. The critical response to *Virginia Illustrated* is relevant here. It was reviewed in England and the United States, although, as might be expected, the New England periodicals ignored it entirely. *Graham's Magazine* called it "one of the most genial, whole-souled, amusing and descriptive works on local American scenery ever written" and praised its author as "a man of genius." The *Southern Literary Messenger* compared Strother's illustrations favorably with those of Doyle. Rather to his surprise, Porte Crayon was launched upon a career as a literary man.

The Civil War was the turning point in Strother's life. Up to this time he had been known as a Virginia writer publishing in the North, but after the War he was regarded by most Virginians as a renegade and apostate for his military service with the Union army. In order for us to separate fiction from fact, we should examine Strother's sentiments during the John Brown raid at Harpers Ferry. Living as he did less than twenty miles away, Strother was an eye-witness to the raid, the trial, and the execution. No abolitionist, Strother was re-pelled and baffled by what he felt were the fanatic objectives of John Brown. Hawthorne's remark, "Nobody was more justly hanged," would serve equally well to summarize the view of Strother. He could foresee that abolitionists would cause greater harm than they could ever cure. Yet from his father he had learned the necessity of the Union of states, from his own travels north and south he had seen the vast social and economic inequalities between the diverging sec-tions, and from his Italian experiences he had witnessed the anarchy in a country cut up into petty warring principalities. While his emotions were those of the Southerner, his reason had been disciplined by the realistic and pragmatic ideologies of the Northerner. As a curb for the ever-rising sectional hatred, he called for self-control and understanding, and when war finally broke out he referred to himself as "a sane man in a mad house." In the summer of 1861 shots were fired across the Potomac, and two armies converged upon Martins-burg. Under such exigencies neutrality was impossible. Strother joined the Federal army and left behind forever the friendships of forty-five years as a Virginian.

Because he was familiar with the topography of northern Virginia at a time when virtually no accurate maps were available, Strother was a valuable acquisition for Union commanders. He was made a captain of volunteers and served under General N. P. Banks during the disastrous Valley of Virginia campaign against Stonewall Jack-son in 1862. Promoted to lieutenant colonel, he joined General John Pope in time to participate as a staff officer in the second battle at Manassas. When Pope was relieved from command, McClellan called Strother to his staff just before Antietam. All of this was told in Strother's first postwar series, *Personal Recollections of the War by a Virginian,* which ran in *Harper's Monthly* from 1866 to 1868. His unpublished private notebooks record his subsequent service with Banks in Louisiana, with Kelley in West Virginia, and with Sigel and Hunter in the Valley of Virginia. Because he was chief of staff under General David Hunter, a distant cousin, during the plundering and burning of the Valley in 1864, many former friends blamed Strother for the unusual viciousness that characterized that campaign. Although he was never forgiven in many quarters, Strother was not involved in the depredations upon personal property. His journals show that he continually intervened to save both lives and property, often at great personal risk.

Late in 1864 Strother resigned from the army with the rank of colonel. After the death of his first wife in 1859, he had married Mary Hunter of Charles Town, Virginia (now West Virginia), in 1861. Since northern Virginia was still overrun with Confederate partisans, Strother lived with his family in Baltimore, watching the final activities of the War. When Richmond fell, he joined the staff of Governor Francis H. Pierpont and served as adjutant general of Virginia. In August, 1865, he was commissioned brigadier general by brevet and thereby became one of the few American artists ever to enjoy that high rank. It is ironical that as adjutant general Strother assisted in restoring to operation the Virginia Military Institute, which he had helped Hunter to destroy only a year previously.

Wearied with war, reconstruction, and politics, Strother returned to Berkeley Springs early in 1866 and entered a thirteen-year period of comparative leisure and quiet. Writing his military memoirs sapped his energy. For a time he made an effort to publicize the new state of West Virginia by editing the Charleston (West Virginia) *Herald* and by writing *The Mountains,* a travel narrative treating the West Virginia highlands. This last major literary effort added little to his fame, for Porte Crayon found that the American public had begun to lose its relish for his pictures of leisurely rural America. *Harper's Monthly* adapted its essays to please the "Gilded Age," and Porte Crayon seemed a little tarnished to the span-new generation. The late eighteen seventies were marked by his diminished reputation and fortune. Although Strother had been left a share of the Berkeley Springs Hotel by his father, that famous old inn never saw again the gay crowds of Southern gentry who had filled its rooms during the prewar summers. Strother was threatened by poverty until 1879, when he was appointed consul general to Mexico, a post he held with dignity and efficiency until 1885. Although his creative period had long since been at an end, his savings from Mexico permitted him to live in modest comfort at Berkeley Springs and Charles Town until his death at the latter on March 8, 1888. He was survived by his wife, his daughter Emily, and his son John, born in 1868.

VIRGINIA ILLUSTRATED

The Journey to Canaan

"Perlege Mæonio cantatas carmine ranas
Et frontem nugis solvere disce meis."—MARTIAL.

IN Randolph County, Virginia, there is a tract of country containing
from seven to nine hundred square miles, entirely uninhabited, and so
inaccessible that it has rarely been penetrated even by the most
adventurous. The settlers on its borders speak of it with dread, as
an ill-omened region, filled with bears, panthers, impassable laurel-
brakes, and dangerous precipices. Stories are told of hunters having
ventured too far, becoming entangled, and perishing in its intricate
labyrinths. The desire of daring the unknown dangers of this mysterious region stimulated a party of gentlemen, who were at Towers'
Mountain House on a trouting excursion, to undertake its exploration
in June 1851. They did actually penetrate the country as far as the
Falls of the Blackwater, and returned with marvelous accounts of the
savage grandeur of its scenery, and the quantities of game and fish to
be found there. One of the party wrote an entertaining narrative of
their adventures and sufferings, filling a stout volume—which every
body ought to read.

During the winter of 1852, several of the same party, with other
friends, planned a second trip, to be undertaken on the first of June
following. At that date, so fully was the public mind occupied with
filibustering and president-making, that the notes of preparation for
this important expedition were scarcely heard beyond the corporate
limits of the little town of M——, in the Valley of Virginia. Even
in this contracted circle the excitement was principally confined to the
planners themselves, while the public looked on with an apathy and
unconcern altogether unaccountable. Indeed, some narrow-minded
persons went so far as to say that it was nothing but a scheme of
idleness, and advised the young gentlemen to stick to their professions,

and let the bears alone. But, as may be supposed, all such met the usual fate of gratuitous counselors who advise people against their inclinations.

In the daily meetings which were held for five months previous to the date fixed for their departure, our friends discussed freely and at great length every thing that appertained, or that could in any way appertain, to the subject in view, from the elevation of the mountains and the course of rivers, down to the quality of a percussion-cap and the bend of a fish-hook. They became students of maps and geological reports; read Izaac Walton's "Complete Angler" and

EN GRANDE TENUE

"Le Guide et Hygiène des Chasseurs;" consulted Count Rumford and Doctor Kitchener, and experimented largely in the different kinds of aliments most proper for the sustenance of the human system. Mr. Penn, the author, copied at length a recipe for making cat-fish soup, assuring his friends that, when surfeited with venison and trout, this dish would afford them a delightful change. Mr. Porte Crayon, the artist, also furnished frequent designs for hunting-coats, caps, knapsacks, and leggins, modeled, for the most part, from those of the French army in Algiers. "For," said he, "the French are the most scientific people in the world; and as they have paid more attention to the equipment of their army than any other, every thing they adopt is presumed to be perfect of its kind."

The result of all this studying and talking was, that every one differed from his friend, and equipped himself after his own fashion. The commissary department suddenly concluded that biscuit and bacon were the most substantial, portable, and palatable articles of food known to the dwellers south of the Potomac, and accordingly made arrangements to have ample supplies of both ready for the occasion.

With the opening spring the buds began to swell and the blue-birds to warble, and the zeal of our adventurers kept pace with the season, so that by the first of April all were ready, fully equipped, "straining like greyhounds in the slip." The intolerable vacuum between this and the starting-day might be graphically illustrated by leaving half a dozen blank pages; but as such a procedure might be misunderstood, or characterized as clap-trap, it may be preferable to fill up the blank by introducing the *dramatis personæ* who are to figure in the following narrative.

Mr. PENN, an author of some distinction, has already been mentioned. He is gaunt and tall, with distinguished air and manners, flowing and graceful gestures, prominent and expressive eye, indicating, according to phrenology, a great command of language. In this case, however, the science was at fault, for when Penn got fairly started in discourse he had no command over his language at all. It poured forth in an irresistible torrent, carrying away the speaker himself, and overwhelming or putting to flight his audience.

Mr. DINDON, a fine, athletic sportsman, not a dandiacal popper at quails and hares, but a real Nimrod, a slayer of wild turkeys and deer, to whom the excitement of the chase was as the breath of his nostrils, and who sometimes forgot even that in his keen appreciation of the poetry of forest life. He was never known either to be wearied in a hunt or silenced in a debate.

Mr. JONES was somewhat inclined to be stout, not to say fat. Mr. J. was equally fond of rural sports and personal comforts. Ambitious of being considered a thoroughgoing sportsman, he kept the best dog and the most beautiful gun in the district. He frequently appeared covered with his hunting accoutrements, followed by his dog, and generally went out alone. Prying persons remarked that his game-bag was usually fuller when he went out than when he returned. Dindon, who was knowing in these matters, always said that J. was a humbug; that all this apparent fondness for the chase was a sham; that Jones, as soon as he got out of sight of town, found some shady place, ate the dinner that stuffed the game-bag, and went to sleep; when he woke, would drag himself through a thicket hard by, muddy his boots in a swamp, and return with the marks of severe fatigue and determined hunting upon him, and with whatever game he might be able to purchase from straggling urchins or old negroes who had been lucky with their traps. For the rest, Jones had some rare companionable qualities. He could give a joke with enviable point and readiness, and take one with like grace and good-humor.

The sprightly sketches which illuminate this unskillful narrative are the most appropriate and shall be the only introduction of our friend PORTE CRAYON. He has rendered the subjects with great truthfulness, and has exhibited even some tenderness in the handling of them. If he has nothing extenuated, he has, at least, set down naught in malice. Porte, indeed, modestly remarks that his poor abilities were entirely inadequate to do justice either to the sublimity of the natural scenery or the preposterous absurdity of the human species on that memorable expedition.

Mr. SMITH, a gentleman of imposing presence, of few words, but an ardent and determined sportsman, and a zealous promoter of the expedition, completes the catalogue.

Some time during the month of May, X. M. C. (for certain reasons his initials only are used), an accomplished and talented gentleman residing at a distance from M——, received a letter which ran as follows:

"DEAR X.,—We have fixed upon the 1st of June to start for the Canaan country. Our party will consist of Dindon, Jones, Smith, your old friend Penn, and myself. Can you join us? If so, give us immediate notice, and set about making your preparations without delay. I would recommend to you to procure the following equipments: a water-proof knapsack, fishing-tackle, and a gun; a belt with pistols—a revolver would be preferable, in case of a conflict with a panther; a hunting-knife for general purposes—a good ten-inch blade, sharp and reliable; it will be useful for cleaning fish, dressing game, and may serve you a turn when a bear gets you down in a laurel-brake. Store your knapsack with an extra pair of shoes, a change of raiment, such as will resist water and dirt to the last extremity, a pair of leggins to guard against rattlesnakes, and the following eatables: one dozen biscuits, one pound of ham, one pound of ground coffee, salt, pepper, and condiments. This will be the private store of each person; the public supplies will be carried out on horses.

"The place of rendezvous is the Berkeley Springs; the day the 31st of May.

     "Yours in haste,   PORTE CRAYON."

The corresponding committee had the gratification of receiving a favorable reply to the foregoing: "X. will certainly come." All right; the party is made up. The last May has come. Crayon, in full hunting costume, is standing on the portico of the great hotel at the Berkeley Springs. Messrs. Jones and Smith have arrived; their equipments have been examined and pronounced unexceptionable. Here comes X. What a pair of leggins! And there's Penn with him, in a blue jacket out at the elbows, with a rod like Don Quixote's lance.

"Ah, gentlemen! well met," shouted Penn, as they approached. "You see before you a personification of Prince Hal, at a time when he kept rather low company." Quoth Jones, "He looks more like Poins on a thieving expedition."

"Ah! my fat friend, are you there? glad to see you. I have a rod here, gentlemen, that will make you envious. See how superbly balanced! what a spring it has! the very thing for brook-fishing, for whipping the smaller streams. And then see how easily carried." Suiting the action to the word, he unjointed it, and slipped it into a neat case, portable, light, and elegant. "I procured one of the same sort for Smith when I was in New York. I will show you also a supply of artificial flies," continued Penn, drawing a leather case from his knapsack, "and a fine bug calculated for the largest sized trout."

Here he produced a bug, which renewed the astonishment and hilarity of the company.

A HUMBUG

"What is it for?" "What sort of creature is it?" "What does it represent?" shouted one and all.

"I have not dipped into entomology lately, but I have been assured that this bug is calculated to take none but the largest fish. No small fish will approach it, from personal apprehension; and no trout under two-and-twenty inches in length would venture to swallow it."

"If I were called upon to classify that bug," said Jones, "I would call it a *chimera;* in the vernacular, *humbug!*"

"Come to supper," said Porte. "We start at two o'clock tonight by the train."

The sun that rose fair and bright on the morning of the first of June found our fishermen just entering the United States Hotel in the town of Cumberland.

"Who the —— are they?" inquired one of the matutinal loafers in the bar-room.

"Oh! they be some o' these Hung'ry fellers, I reckon," replied a gaping stable-boy.

"Right, boy, right!" said Mr. Jones; "quite right; here's a dime. Landlord, let us have breakfast in the shortest time imaginable."

The route from Cumberland to the Oakland depôt, on the summit of the Alleghanies, and the trip from thence by wagon to Towers', was as barren of notable adventure as it was fruitful in jokes and hilarity. At Towers' they found their old comrade Dindon, who had gone ahead to procure guides, horses, etc.

"Well, what have you brought up?" asked Dindon.

"Eleven hundred and forty biscuit, twenty pounds of ground coffee, forty pounds of middling, and two hams; lard, salt, pepper, sugar, *et cetera;* all well packed and in good order. What have you done?"

"The eight loaves of bread are ready." "Good!" "The horses are ready." "Good!" "The guides are still to be looked after." "Hum! let us see the horses." "Andrew, bring out the animals."

Lame Kit and Old Sorry here made their first appearance on the stage, and were received with mingled laughter and indignation. Lame Kit's fore leg was as stiff as a ramrod; and old Sorry, among other defects, was blind and distempered.

"What an inhuman idea!" said Jones. "You don't really mean to afflict these wretched tackies with such loads of baggage as we have here?"

Dindon was aroused. "I'll bet a thousand dollars you haven't two such horses on your estate."

"No, I'll swear to it," responded Jones. "If I had, I'd have them shot within an hour."

No, sir," rejoined Dindon, with heat. "I mean that you can't produce their equals for strength and endurance."

"I won't take advantage of you," said Jones, "but will offer you a more equal bet: that, if you load them with this baggage, neither of them will live to reach the banks of the Cheat River."

"That shows your judgment in horseflesh. But what can be expected of a man educated north of the Potomac? What can he know about horses?"

Jones assumed an attitude confronting Dindon. "I'd like to know," said he, "if Northern horses are not universally conceded to be superior to Southern?"

"Gentlemen," interposed X., "I foresee an interminable wrangle. We'll adjourn. Cough them down."

The following day was spent in engaging guides. Thornhill, an intelligent, energetic, good-tempered fellow, agreed to undertake the business. His dwelling was a specimen of rural architecture not noticed by Downing, nor characterized by any of the writers on that subject. Porte declared it looked like the connecting link between a hut and a wood-pile; but, like the pearl in the oyster, the gem of disinterested hospitality is found as frequently in these humble abodes as in the proudest mansions of our good old State.

THORNHILL'S CABIN

All things being arranged at Towers' for an early start on the third, Crayon and X. M. C. shouldered their guns and knapsacks, and started for Conway's, nine miles distant, on the route to the Canaan country. They were to engage Conway to accompany the party, and to be in readiness to join the main body as they passed in the morning. Crayon had traveled the road on a former occasion, and, as he pretended to considerable skill in woodcraft, confidently took the lead, and struck into the forest by a blind path. For four or five miles all went well, until the declining sun was hidden by the tall crowns of the firs, and the path became more and more indistinct. Crayon became thoughtful, and dropped behind.

"Whose dogs are these?" quietly asked X.

Crayon looked up, and saw two wolves standing in the path, within thirty paces of them, staring with amazement at the strange intruders. In the twinkling of an eye his piece was leveled, but the wolves, with equal celerity, had betaken themselves to the bushes.

"Well, you don't say they were wolves? I supposed they were some of the neighbors' dogs. What a mortification! I might have shot them both."

"There are no neighbors hereabouts, X., and no dogs wandering about. The rule is to crack away at every four-legged creature you see, and the chances are that it is legitimate game. But we must be moving; night is coming rapidly on. Push on for Conway's."

Within the next mile Crayon came to a stand-still. "X.," said he, musingly, "at what hour does the moon rise to-night?"

"Don't know; haven't observed; are we not near Conway's?"

"My friend, it is useless to disguise matters. In fifteen minutes it will be pitch-dark. I have seen no trace of a path for the last half mile. This country looks strange to me. I couldn't go back if I would, I wouldn't go if I could; we should be laughed at."

"This life is all new to me," said X., with resignation; "but go on, and I'll follow till death."

"X., can you see a star, or any thing that might serve as a guide to prevent us from making circles?"

"No, I can see nothing but trees and bushes, and can hardly see them."

"Follow on, then; we'll try it."

As they trudged on, the forest grew murkier and darker, and the undergrowth more dense and tangled.

"Where are you, Porte?" "Here; come on." "Ho! I'm up to my knees in a marsh!" "Hist! did you hear that?" "Yes. Keep close, and don't shoot, or we may kill each other. Be careful of your fire-arms, and depend on your hunting-knife." "Good heaven! we are getting into a laurel-brake. Turn back, or we are gone."

On they struggled, torn by briers, throttled by wild vines, and tripped up by fallen timber.

"Porte! stop. I'm ready to perish with fatigue; let us rest a while on this log."

"X., did you ever sleep in the woods?"

"No, I never did."

"Have you any thing to eat in your knapsack?"

"Not a mouthful; to lighten my load, I tumbled mine into the general provision-bag."

"I did the same thing."

"How unlucky! I will take this impressive opportunity, Mr. X., to read you a lesson in woodcraft. Never leave the camp without a day's provision with you."

"But are we likely to get to Conway's to-night?"

"The probabilities seem to be against it; but let us try again."

Another hour of fruitless toil, and no hope.

"X., don't it seem to be getting lighter on our left hand?"

"Ho! by all that's jolly, I'm on open ground, and feel something like a beaten track under my feet."

A broad gleam of light shot across the wood like the sudden flash of a torch, revealing a long vista in the forest and the trodden and rutted surface of the highway.

"Whoop! whoop! hurrah! the moon and the big road—the big road and the moon. I knew it! I knew I couldn't be mistaken. Here's the stream. We're not a mile from Conway's."

The wanderers, notwithstanding their fatigue and knapsacks, indulged in a *pas de deux* and an embrace, then cheerily resumed their route. The moon rose higher and higher; anon they heard the bark of a dog—a long, welcome bow-wow. X. quoted Byron:

"'Tis sweet to hear the watch-dog's honest bark."

Then they came to a clearing, with a double cabin in the midst. The chorus of dogs was at its full.

"Get out, ye whelps! Who's there?"

"Hallo! old otter, come out of your den. Here are friends."

The old man stuck his weasel face out of the door, and after a short scrutiny recognized Porte Crayon. "Well done," said he; "but I'm glad to see ye. I heard ye were in the country, but I didn't expect to see ye at this time o'night. But come in; ye must be hungry. Gals, get up, and find the gentlemen some supper."

The old man's buxom daughters tumbled out of a bed in a dark corner of the room, and soon the fresh-heaped fire roared and sparkled in the chimney, and the table was spread with the best in the house —cold bread and meat, fragrant glades butter, rich milk, and maple beer. As they supped, they narrated their adventure with the wolves, at which their host chuckled greatly. A bed in the spare room of the cabin received the weary couple, who slept soundly until the morning.

"How delicious! What an invigorating atmosphere! What a magnificent forest is this that walls us round!" were their first ex- clamations on issuing from the cabin. When they had breakfasted, they took their seats upon a comfortable stump in front of the house, while Conway completed his simple arrangements for the journey.

"Is the fat gentleman in your company this time?" inquired he. "Well, I never expected to a-seed him agin. Is the big-eyed gentle- man coming too? he that writ a book, I disremember his name. And the one with spectacles?"

"Yes, they are all coming."

Anon, loud voices are heard issuing from the depths of the forest, which gradually approach, until those of Jones and Dindon are distinguishable, and the words, confusedly mingled, "Northern horses —Southern horses—trotters—thousand dollars—Eclipse;" then a long string of expletives. The head of the column emerges from the wood: this is no other than the fat man, stripped to his silk shirt and panta- loons, with a great pack on his back and a sapling in his hand; he was a good personification of Orson of the Wood. He presently halted and faced about.

"Dindon, I say, hush! you have the advantage of wind in this argument, but not of reason. You know I am short of breath; I can't

CONWAY

walk and discuss at the same time; it is ungenerous to press it now; wait until we halt for dinner. At present I say, peremptorily, hush!"

The detachment from Conway's now joined the march, and, whooping, laughing, singing, and wrangling, they wound along under the gloomy archway of the trackless forest. As they marched the party naturally fell into Indian file, with the baggage in the centre. Thornhill, with his tomahawk belted about him, led the van; Dindon, Crayon, and Penn followed; then came Lame Kit, led by Conway, and Old Sorry, conducted by Powell, a hunter who was engaged to go in with them to bring the horses out after they had reached their destination. Smith and X. M. C. formed the rear guard, and far behind lagged Mr. Jones, probably with the intention of avoiding useless discussions, and of managing his wind to the greatest advantage. After a march of six miles they entered a green glade of great beauty, watered by an amber rivulet, which they leaped with their packs and guns. This rivulet was the infant Potomac; that leap was from Maryland into Virginia. Now they breasted a mountain—a long, tiresome tug it was, that took the conceit out of more than one of the party who started fair that morning. On the summit they took a breathing-spell. This is the dividing ridge between the waters of the East and the West. In a short time they crossed another amber brook, a tributary of the Ohio, and one of the immediate sources of the Blackwater. About five o'clock in the afternoon they emerged from the dreary forest into another waving glade, and at the farther border Thornhill gave the welcome order to halt for the night.

Cheerfully our adventurers deposited their guns and knapsacks, and, after a brief repose, joined the hunters in heaping up dry logs and combustibles for the camp-fire. How the fire blazed and crackled! How grandly the smoke volumed up among the lofty tree-tops! The horses, relieved of their burdens, were tethered in the glade, up to their bellies in grass. While preparations for supper were going on, several of the party got out their fishing-tackle, and tried the little stream that watered the glade. It was alive with trout; and half an hour after, a hundred of the small fry were served up at supper with the biscuit and bacon. It was a meal that a monarch might envy. A good bed of hemlock branches was duly spread, the fire replenished with larger logs, and the weary party disposed itself to sleep as best it might, pillowed on log or knapsack. The excitement produced by the novelty of the situation kept X. awake. The gloom of the forest around was intense; the camp-fire blazed in the centre of a group of four lofty firs, whose straight and mast-like trunks were illuminated by its light for a hundred feet without the interruption of a limb, and whose tops interlaced and formed a lofty and almost impervious covering over the sleepers. X. raised himself upon his elbow and broke the silence:

"What a picturesque scene! What a couch! What a canopy! What sublime bed-posts!"

"Go to sleep, poet," growled a drowsy fellow, "or you'll be sorry for it to-morrow."

Presently a noise was heard in the forest—a wild, unearthly cry, an incomprehensible sound. Every body sprang up. "What the deuce is it?" inquired the sleepers, rubbing their eyes. "Gentlemen," said Dindon, deliberately cocking his rifle, "get your arms ready.

I know that sound well; it is the cry of a wolf." Again the terrible voice echoed through the wood, nearer and more distinct. There was a general clicking of gun-locks. Jones, who had made himself a comfortable nest at the foot of a tree, pitched into the centre of the group; Crayon sat the picture of deliberate valor, with hunting-knife in one hand, revolver in the other, and a rifle lying across his lap; X. crept on all-fours to get possession of his double-barrel; Penn, in whose poetic bosom the joy of meeting with an adventure over-balanced every personal consideration, with nervous haste drew forth his book, and began noting down the incident. Thornhill and Powell, however, so far from evincing any anxiety, seemed bursting with suppressed laughter, while Conway sat smoking his pipe with imperturbable gravity. Here is an extract from Mr. Penn's note-book:

"*Camp No. 1, 10 o'clock P.M.*—Disturbed by a terrible cry, somewhat resembling this: Too-too—too-hoo—too-too—too-hoo. Supposed to be wolves or panthers. In momentary expectation of an attack. If we perish. . . . *Half-past ten.*—Sounds ascertained to proceed from owls of the largest size, but not dangerous. Camp calm, and disposed to slumber."

Next morning our adventurers were stirring betimes—refreshed the half-extinct fire, dispatched a hasty breakfast, and resumed their march before sunrise. This was a hard day for most of them. The broken sleep and unusual beds had not done much to repair the fatigues of the previous day; the hills were steeper; and the fallen timber cumbered the route so greatly, that they were frequently obliged to make long *détours* to find a passage practicable for the horses.

The bodies of these fallen giants afforded quite a curious spectacle as they lay prone and supine, singly and in monstrous heaps, frequently a hundred and fifty feet in length and eighteen in girth, coated with a rich covering of moss, and their decayed wood affording a soil for thickets of seedlings of their own and other species. Sometimes they were seen spanning a ravine at a giddy height, like suspension bridges, the parasite growth forming a parapet or hand-rail, as if for the safety and convenience of the passer. Sometimes the faithless surface yielded to the tread, and the astounded hunter found himself imbedded to the armpits in what he had supposed to be solid wood. The climbing of these barricades was one of the principal items in the fatigue of the journey, and any one who happened to look back on that day would generally see Mr. Jones astride of one of them, beseeching the party to wait a while. It would be well for the venatical reputation of Mr. Jones if the events of this day could be effaced from the record, or covered by a black veil, like the face of Marino Faliero among the doges of Venice.

"Look at him," quoth Dindon, triumphantly; "he pretended to underrate that lame mare, and now he's glad to hang on her tail. He said she couldn't carry her load to the Cheat River, and now she is carrying his knapsack and himself into the bargain. I suppose, Jones, you'll now own you're no judge of horse-flesh?"

THROUGH THE WOODS

"It's too bad," said X. "Let go, Jones. Have you no greatness of soul? Don't you see the poor beast can hardly get along?"

But, deaf alike to satire or remonstrance, Jones kept his hold, until Kit, with a long-drawn breath, stood stock-still. "Thar', now," said the hunter, "I've been a looking for her to drop." The mare was released, and Jones attempted to seize Old Sorry by the same appendage. He, however, being too blind to see the justice of such a proceeding, relieved himself with a kick.

The hunters had been dodging the laurel-brakes all day. They

PASSING THE LAURELS

seemed to dread the passage, and would frequently go miles around to avoid it. They had stories of men who had spent days in them, wandering in circles, and who had finally perished from starvation;

and they say when once fairly in there is no calculating when you will get out. Some of these brakes extend for many miles, and are so dense that even the deer can not pass except by finding the thinnest places; and when the experienced woodman is forced to cross, he always seeks a deer-path. The ponderous strength of the bear enables him to traverse them more easily. In them he makes his lair; and our adventurers often found the laurel recently torn and broken by bears in going to and from their places of retreat. With the horses the passage could not even be attempted without a previous clearing of the way by the axe-men. Upon consultation, it was considered necessary to cross the brake before them, and the guides went into it lustily, while the rest of the company, one after another, dropped asleep. In about two hours the way was cleared, but it was with much difficulty that the horses could be induced to proceed. The guides swore like the army in Flanders; Kit's stiff leg would not yield to circumstances; and Sorry became several times so tangled that he had to be released by the axe. The footmen passed ahead of the horses, and soon found themselves in similar circumstances. They sank up to their knees in mud and water; they were throttled by the snake-like branches of the laurel, and were frequently obliged to resort to their hunting-knives to extricate a leg or an arm from its grasp. Ascending the stump of a riven hemlock, a striking picture presented itself. The laurel waved up and down as far as the eye could reach, like a green lake, with either shore walled by the massive forest, and out of its bed rose singly, or in groups of three or four, the tallest and most imposing of the fir species. The heads of our adventurers appeared and disappeared alternately as they struggled through; and, whether visible or invisible, the crackling of branches, the rustling of leaves, and a rolling fire of execrations marked their progress. All else was silent.

Toward evening a bear was seen, but so worn and spiritless were the adventurers that no one thought of pursuing it. All were anxious to reach the river that evening, as they had proposed. At length the ridge upon which they traveled seemed suddenly to terminate, and they heard, far below, the rushing of waterfalls. Here they came willingly to a halt, while the guides descended the mountain to ascertain their position. In the course of an hour they returned, reporting that the roaring was from the falls of the Blackwater, and that they now overlooked the site of the encampment of the last season. By this time it had grown so dark and rained so heavily that it became indispensable to look out for a place of encampment. The men dispersed to look for water, taking care, however, always to keep within calling distance of each other. Water was soon found on the border of a laurel-brake, a most cheerless spot for a bivouac. The rain fell in torrents. The horses were unloaded, and a young birch cut down for them to browse upon, in default of grass. While some tried, apparently without success, to get together dry combustibles for a fire, others endeavored to secure the provisions, arms, and ammunition from the rain; while others sunk down on the spot where they halted, and, wrapping their blankets about them, slept in spite of every thing. A more cheerless prospect for a night could scarcely be imagined. With garments soaked, blankets wet, every leaf dripping with water, and the earth covered with moss and dead leaves, like a sponge thoroughly saturated; with limbs stiff with fatigue and shivering with cold, there seemed to be little chance of obtaining either rest or fire. Conway's woodcraft, however, triumphed over all difficulties. With knife and hatchet he peeled the bark from a fir about four feet in circumference. With this he sheltered the fire until it got headway, and then heaping on such wood as was most combustible, there was soon a cheerful roaring blaze that defied the rain. He next, with forks, props, and cross-poles, erected the framework of a shed, twelve or fourteen feet long, which was speedily covered with bark, and afforded a complete shelter. The ground beneath was covered with hemlock branches, shaken and dried over the fire, to serve at once for seats and bedding. Fried middling and hot coffee were then served round, and from a most forlorn and unpromising beginning our adventurers found themselves in comparatively comfortable circumstances. Jones was, as usual, an object of peculiar attention. On their arrival at the halting-place Jones observed a large hemlock, which threw out its roots like the arms of a sofa. Between them a plump cushion of moss, which had hitherto escaped the rain, seemed to invite him to a seat. Mr. J. accepted the invitation, and set about making himself as comfortable as possible. Upon examining the ground about him, it occurred that just over his seat would be a very proper place to build the shed, and he gave orders accordingly. Whether from a malicious suggestion of some one else, or some sly waggery of his own, Conway took pains to locate the fire and shed at some distance off. Mr. Jones argued and remonstrated, but to no effect. The savor of supper enticed him from his lair for a short time, and he then found that the shed was so full there was not room for a ramrod. Mr. Jones was not a ramrod, nor was he to be outdone so easily. He took Conway aside in a mysterious manner, and whispered something in his ear. Conway went out, and soon returned with a superb piece of fresh-peeled bark, with which Jones was duly covered.

"Look here, gentlemen," said he, triumphantly, "you may now go to grass with your shed. I wouldn't change places with the man in the middle."

The shed replied with a shout of laughter and a storm of jokes.

"He's now fairly embarked in it," cried one.

"Looks more like he was embalmed," cried another.

"A mummy! or a mud-turtle lying on his back! Pharaoh the Fat! I'd like to see Gliddon unroll him before the Historical Society of Massachusetts."

"Rail on from your mud-hole, my good fellows; but take my advice, and reserve your wit, for it will require more than you have got among you to keep yourselves dry to-night. I am entirely impervious either to jokes or rain. Good-night."

THE MUMMY

Unfortunately for Jones's comfort, the wind changed, and the rain poured upon him in rivulets; and shortly afterward groans and lamentations were heard in the direction of the mummy.

"It seems to be in pain. Some one had better look after it," said X.

Conway good-naturedly took a chunk of fire and went to the assistance of the sufferer. It turned out that the acrid sap from the hemlock bark had got into his eyes; but it was soon over, and a deep sleep fell upon them all, which lasted until the wood-robin warbled a reveille on the following morning.

When they awoke it was still raining, and, from all appearances, had been raining hard all night. A thin vapory smoke rose from the extinguished embers, and all nature was dripping.

"By the beard of the Prophet!" exclaimed Porte Crayon, as he combed the leaves and sticks out of his own flowing appendage, "by the beard of Mohammed! I have been sleeping all night in a puddle of water."

"The hydrostatic bed," said Mr. Smith, "is preferable to any other for an invalid."

"Well done, Smith; this is the first time we've heard from you since night before last. You must be getting better."

"Thank you, I feel much better, and will hereafter be a believer in the water-cure."

"Look here!" said X., sticking his heels into the air, while a stream poured from each boot.

"Bless my soul!" quoth Mr. Penn, emphatically, as he gathered up his legs and arms like separate pieces of lumber, and scrutinized the covering of the shed, "there must be a leak in this roof. The water has been dribbling into my left ear until it is so full I can't hear." Just then a drop took him in the eye. "There! blast the thing, I was sure of it."

"Conway! Conway! my good friend, come here," cried a sepulchral voice.

"Hark from the tombs—the mummy desires to be uncased."

"No; stand back! I don't want any of your aid. Conway, good fellow, remove this confounded bark. Gently—there—now help me to bend my legs. Oh! ah! whew! thank you; let go now, I think I can stand alone;" and, after sundry efforts, Mr. Jones recovered the use of his legs sufficiently to carry him to breakfast, where, by a free use of fried middling and hot coffee, he lubricated his limbs into their usual condition of activity.

A council of war decided that the army was not in condition to move on that day; that they should remain under cover, and repose, while such as felt disposed should go out as scouts to explore thoroughly the surrounding country. Conway's talents were again called in requisition to extend and improve the comfort of their quarters. A pack of cards was introduced, and the day passed in careless jollity. During the forenoon, Porte Crayon, accompanied by Powell, went out to search for the Cheat River; but, after walking in idle circles for two hours, and becoming entangled in a laurel-brake, they were glad to get back to camp. Dindon, Thornhill, and Powell were more successful, and returned late in the evening with the report that they had found the Cheat, and had wounded an otter. This news gave great satisfaction; but their description of the stream differed so widely from the supposed location and size of that river, that the accuracy of the report was doubted by Mr. Penn and others who had been studying the geography of the country.

Life in Canaan

THE fourth morning proved a favorable one. The sun rose bright and clear, and our adventurers, refreshed in body and soul, resumed their journey with cheerful alacrity. After marching about a mile, an extensive laurel-brake seemed to offer an impassable barrier to their farther progress. Here the scouts of the previous evening informed them that the river flowed through the laurel some two or three hundred yards distant, upon which information a convenient spot was selected for a permanent encampment. Conway, Dindon, and Thornhill undertook to build the house, while the rest of the party started eagerly to explore the river and have a day's sport. After traversing the thicket, they reached a stream about forty-feet wide and of inconsiderable depth, completely hemmed in by laurel and beautifully arched with evergreens, so dense and dark that it had a cavernous look.

"This stream is certainly not the Cheat River," said Penn.

Powell suggested that it might be the Canaan Fork.

"There is no such stream known to geographers," said Penn.

"It is the same," rejoined Powell, "that we ignorant hunters have been accustomed to call by that name, and it empties into the Cheat not far from here, I should say."

"By the maps this stream has no right to be here at all," continued Penn. "Either the maps or the stream must be mistaken. My map is a very correct map; I don't like to doubt its authority, but I suppose I must defer to the actuality of the stream. Here it is. Now for the exploration."

The party, headed by Crayon, straggled down the bed of the stream, sometimes waist deep, sometimes ankle deep, climbing or dodging the enormous tree trunks that bridged it at short intervals. On turning a rocky bend, the stream, with its green archway, disappeared as if by some trick of magic, and a bright open landscape of mountain sides and distant hazy tops suddenly occupied its place. Beneath their feet yawned an unfathomable chasm, from whose misty depths rose a confused sound of rushing waters. The hemlocks below looked like shrubs. Into this abyss the wild stream leaped, falling into a black pool scintillating with foam and bubbles. Here it seemed to tarry for a moment to gather strength for another and more desperate plunge; then another and another, down! down! down! and down went the explorers, shouting, leaping, sliding, and tumbling, catching the spirit of the scene, until they seemed as wild and reckless as the torrent. Tarry upon this shelving platform of rock and look up. A succession of silvery cascades seem falling from the clouds. The pines which we saw beneath our feet now rise clear and diminutive against the blue sky. Below, the stream still pours down the yawning chasm. We can see it foaming far down, until rocks and trees are dim in the distance. Here's a clear leap of fifty feet; what's to be done? Can we go no farther? The trunk of a fallen hemlock has lodged against the rocky ledge. It stands at a perilous angle, and its decayed surface is covered with green and slippery ooze. Who cares! down we slide, one after another. What next? A shorter jump. On the opposite side is a tangled thicket of rhododendron; to reach it we must cross a bridge fearful as the arch of Al-Sirat, a slender trunk that has drifted across the furious current. Hurrah! the Ravels could not have done it better. Now swing down the laurels—not all at once, or they will break. Push on, boys! that great foaming caldron below us must be the river.

"There seems to be no way but this," said Porte, resolutely jumping upon a drifted trunk that projected full thirty feet over the ledge into the topmost branches of a lofty beech. He gained the tree in safety, and descended to the shore of the river. The others followed in rapid succession, although the dangerous bridge swayed and shook with each passenger.

"Jones, don't try it! Jones, you're too heavy. It shakes; it cracks; by heaven, he's gone!"

With a sullen crash the heavy
log fell into the pool below, while
the intrepid Jones slid down the
friendly beech, amid the bravos
and felicitations of his comrades.
Jones sat panting on a rock, red
with exertion, beaded with perspiration, all saturated with water,
and green with ooze. What a
miraculous change! Can that be
the same being that hung to old
Kit's tail, or that groaned so lustily when he got sap in his eye?
Jones, who crossed the bridge
with the step of a rope-dancer,
and who walked the drift-log
with the courage of a Delhi?

Oh Nature! how mighty are
thy influences upon the impress-
ible souls of men. How surely
do thy softer beauties woo to luxury and idolence the same spirits
who, amid thy rocks and thundering cataracts, are roused to energy
and active daring.

FALLS OF THE BLACK FORK OF CHEAT

The Black Fork of Cheat,* where our party stood, was about two hundred feet in width, and poured its amber flood, at an angle of some seven or eight degrees, over a bed of monstrous boulders, and between mountain walls a thousand or twelve hundred feet in height.

"It looks to me," said X., "like the bursting of Barclay and Perkins's big beer-tub, you remember, that flooded half London, and drowned so many people."

"I wish to heaven it was beer," said Jones; "I think I could drink a barrel of it on the spot."

FATE OF THE FANCY RODS

Such was the excitement and exhilaration produced by the discovery of these beautiful falls, that fishing became, for the time, a secondary object, and but few trout were caught. Penn and Smith, however, could not long resist the desire of trying their fine rods. Having uncased and fitted them up, they made a simultaneous throw. Smith's foot slipped, and he came down upon the point of his rod, splintering it to the last joint. Penn made a magnificent fling; but,

* More recent explorations have ascertained that the river referred to in this narrative is the main stem of the Blackwater, which empties into the Black Fork of Cheat some 9 miles below. The streams spoken of as the Blackwater and Canaan Fork are nameless tributaries of the Blackwater River hitherto unexplored and unknown. Our travelers, it seems, did not reach the Cheat River at all [Strother's note].

having forgotten to attach his line to the reel, three of the joints went over the falls, carrying with them the sea-grass line and that incredible specimen of entomology, the bug.

Having disposed of his rod to his complete satisfaction, Smith proposed to Crayon that they should make an exploration of the river, following its course downward toward the mouth of the Blackwater. They persevered in this undertaking until they had accomplished some two or three miles; but finding the route scarcely less difficult and hazardous than the descent of the falls, and having in the mean time emptied their haversacks, they concluded to return and rejoin their comrades. They found them waiting at the foot of the falls, tired of fishing, which had been unsuccessful, owing to the swollen condition of the stream.

The ascent of the falls was accomplished with more circumspection and with less danger than the descent. The precipices were avoided by scrambling up on the mountain sides through the laurel, and the explorers rejoined the building committee early in the afternoon. As they approached the spot, each one was big with the scenes and adventures of the day, and thirsting to begin the narrative of his personal experiences and exploits. They suddenly drew up, like men bewildered, and then gave a simultaneous shout of pleasure and admiration.

"Hurrah for Conway! Hurrah for Dindon! Hurrah for Thornhill! Well, this outdoes the wonders of the Canaan Fork!" exclaimed X.

Before them stood a neat and roomy cottage, complete at all points, with an open front, before which blazed a glorious fire; the baggage all securely and neatly bestowed, with shelves and fixtures for the cooking utensils, a rack at the fire for drying clothes, and, indeed, every comfort and convenience that could have been desired, and more than could have been reasonably hoped for. Conway sat philosophically smoking his pipe at the entrance; Thornhill was cooking supper; and Dindon, with a hospitable wave of the hand, desired them to walk in, make themselves at home, and take a bite of supper with him.

It was creditable to the exploring party that not a word was said in relation to their own adventures until the full meed of praise had been bestowed upon the builders for the ingenuity and industry which they had manifested in the accomplishment of their work. The enjoyment of the evening, however, was dampened by the unfavorable accounts of the condition of the river, and the diminished chances for sport. That night the mercury in Porte Crayon's pocket thermometer stood at 32°, and, notwithstanding the well-nourished fire and comfortable shelter, it was impossible to sleep on account of the cold. That night also finished Mr. Jones. The reaction from the enthusiasm of the previous day, combined with the cold and loss of rest, brought the mercury of his spiritual thermometer below zero. Powell was about to start that morning with the horses for the settlements. After partaking of a hearty breakfast, Jones formally announced his intention of accompanying them. Without regarding the exclamations of surprise which this announcement called forth, he proceeded as follows:

"A decent respect for the opinions of the world makes it necessary that I should give my reasons for this step. They are briefly these: I came out here for sport and pleasure; I have found neither. I have been out five days, and have not caught five trout. I have been tired to death, and unable to sleep—saturated, frozen, devoured by gnats and wood-ticks."

"And got sap in your eye," suggested Dindon.

"And besides, instead of venison and trout, I have been gorged with fried bacon and biscuit until I am sick of seeing them."

"Three times five makes fifteen," said X. "He has been gorged just fifteen times, to say nothing of snacks and odd biscuits. Poor fellow! how he must have suffered!"

"And," pursued Jones, in a louder key, "I pronounce the expedition a failure and a humbug, and, consequently, I will return with Powell."

Several hasty remarks were half uttered, when Porte Crayon rose and affectionately addressed Mr. Jones:

"In expressing my deep regret at your sudden departure, let me assure you that I am heartily seconded by every one here present; a regret that would have been felt under any circumstances, but which is doubly felt when we remember the gallant and spirited Jones of yesterday. And let me also express a hope that the acrimonious character of your remarks is the result of physical discomfort rather than of any unkind feeling toward this party or any member of it."

"Not a trace of it!" warmly responded Jones; "quite the contrary, I assure you all. I was wrong to say any thing against the enterprise; you all have enjoyed it, I have no doubt. But I will confess I'm not fit for this life. I'm—I am—friendship demands the sacrifice, and I'll out with the truth: I'm too confounded fat!"

A shout of approbation followed the avowal. "Jones, my dear fellow, your hand! Let's have a cordial embrace all round."

They started off—when Jones suddenly turned about. "Ah! X., my friend, come here. You were kind enough to make a calculation for me while I was speaking. It was civil of you. As I am going home, and you will probably have a great deal of walking to do before your return, I'll make you a present of my extra boots. Adieu!"

How Mr. Jones walked till he was out of sight, and then mounted Lame Kit; how he had a surprising adventure with a hen-pheasant; and how he got safe back to the settlements, have nothing to do with this narrative, and, consequently, will be considered as not having been alluded to at all.

The parties who went out to try the streams again soon returned unsuccessful and disappointed, and betook themselves to "all-fours" for the remainder of the day. Conway, however, who had gone over to the Blackwater, returned with about a hundred and fifty fine trout. This lucky forage afforded the company a couple of hearty meals, and determined them to leave their present location, and seek a more favorable one on the Blackwater; not, however, without many expressions of regret at deserting their fine cabin.

On the following morning they marched about four miles, and came upon the Blackwater Creek about a mile above the falls. As they followed down the bed of the stream, a deer was seen to cross a short distance from them, which so excited X. that he made a rush to get ahead of the main body, and, if possible, to get a shot. Just as he was about attaining his object, he set foot upon a slippery stone, and pitched head foremost into the water. As he emerged again, his gun spouting from both barrels, he was hailed with shouts of encouragement: "There goes the deer! shoot! bang away!" X. politely requested the company to go to a place where cold water was more of a rarity, and quietly took his position in the rear of the column.

The site chosen for the new encampment was on the brow of a cliff, within thirty paces of the great fall, a situation of unequaled beauty and savage grandeur. Surrounded by a tangled thicket of the rhododendron, canopied by the loftiest firs, the thunder of the cataract in their ears day and night, and its spray freshening the atmosphere they breathed, our adventurers passed the eight days that followed in the fullest enjoyment of the pleasures of forest life. Every day added to the treasures of Porte Crayon's sketch-book. The author reveled in a poetic existence, basking on moss-covered rocks, among foaming rapids and sparkling waterfalls; and if his haggard, unshaven countenance and dilapidated wardrobe presented a strong contrast to his mental beatitude, it only exemplified the more strikingly the predominance of mind over matter, and the entire disconnection that sometimes exists between the ideal and the material world.

On the first favorable day after their location, X. M. C., who had not yet fleshed his maiden hook in the gills of a trout, went out with Conway to try his luck. After many unsuccessful attempts, he at length hooked a fellow, and drew him out of the water with such a jerk (X. is possessed of great physical vigor) that rod, line, and fish were lodged in the overhanging branches of a tree. Here was a spite. The stream was wriggling with trout, and X. had just acquired the knack of hooking them; but his implements, and, worse than all, the first trophy of his skill, were hanging on the envious boughs. Now, if X. M. C. had any one trait that predominated over all others, it was determination. Missiles were plenty, and he straightway opened on the devoted fish a mingled shower of stones, sticks, and anathemas. At the end of an hour he succeeded in bringing him down, well dried, and slightly tainted.

"Well!" quoth Conway, who, from a short distance, had been the philosophical eye-witness of the proceeding, and who, during the time, had bagged some sixty of the finest trout, "well! I've seed fish catched in a great many different ways, but I never seed 'em chunked out of trees afore."

About four o'clock in the afternoon our sportsmen generally gathered in for dinner. There is a kind of seasoning found in these mountain countries which gives to the coarsest food a savor, compared with which Delmonico's *chefs de cuisine* are insipid. Would it not be possible for some of our chemists to make an extract from this sauce, and bottle it for city use? How would your truffles, your mushrooms, your *à la Marengo*'s be blotted from the list of delicacies, and their places filled with *sauce à l'Allegheine,* and fried middling, *sauté à l'air de le Montagne.* After dinner coffee and cards were introduced; and when it became too dark for all-fours, "the vaulted aisles of the dim wood rang" with songs, choruses, and recitations; and it is no more than just to mention that the neighboring bears had occasionally opportunities of hearing performances that would have challenged the admiration of the most gifted circles in the land.

On rainy days the camp had quite an air of domesticity. In the centre was the eternal party at "old sledge." The author, wearied with such trite amusement, conned his note-book in one corner; the artist, in another, arranged and retouched his sketches; while old Conway, with his jack-knife, passed his time in manufacturing wooden spoons, plates, and water-tight baskets of bark.

Conway was the most accomplished of woodsmen: small in stature, narrow-shouldered, and weasel-faced; insensible to fatigue, to hunger, or the vicissitudes or the weather; a shrewd hunter, a skillful fisher, unfailing in resources, he was ready in every emergency. He could build a comfortable house, and furnish it in a day, with no other material than what the forest afforded, and no other tools than his axe and jack-knife. Nor was he destitute of the arts of civilized life. He could mend clothes and cobble shoes with surprising dexterity; and any one who has visited his cabin may have observed an old fiddle hanging beside his powder-horn and pouch. When in camp his pipe was never out; he smoked before and after meals, when at work and when idle. He talked little, but occasionally told a quaint story of his hunting adventures, or cracked a dry joke; and the sharp twinkle of his gray eye, when any thing humorous was in question, showed the keenness of his appreciation of good-natured fun.

Rainy days were also fruitful in debates, which a discreet person might have characterized as noisy wrangles; and, as usual, the vehemence of the debaters was great in proportion to the littleness of the subject. It must be confessed the range of questions was a wide

one—any thing from the Constitution of the United States down
to the propriety of a play at "old sledge." The parties generally stood
arrayed, Dindon against the field, the field against Dindon. One
day Dindon was six in the game, and stood on the knave with another
trump. Two consecutive leads brought down his jack, and he lost
the game, but characterized his opponent's play as absurd and contrary
to Hoyle. The whole pack—not of cards, but of players—opened
upon him. The dispute waxed hotter and hotter, Dindon waxed
redder and redder, and finally lost all command of himself. He glared
about him like a baited bear. Suddenly rushing forward, he seized
Conway's axe. The debaters scattered and dodged like rats in a
pantry; but he deigned not to cast a look upon them, and strode out,
upsetting the water-bucket and knocking over the clothes-rack in his
progress. Presently he found himself *vis-à-vis* with an enormous
hemlock, full fifteen feet in girth. Without considering the size
and vigor of his opponent, he attacked him furiously. He knocked
out chips as large as dinner-dishes, and the earth around was soon
white with them. For a long time the combat seemed to be equal.
The perspiration stood on Dindon's forehead in drops as large as
kidney-beans. The inhabitants of the camp stood around at a respectful distance, dodging the chips, and wondering. Anon the lofty
crown of the hemlock was seen to waver, the blows of the axe
resounded with redoubled force, the trunk cracked and crackled, the
gigantic forest king began to sink, at first slowly, then with a rushing
sound, and, with a thundering crash like the broadside of a frigate, he
fell, crushing under him like shrubs a dozen trees, each of which
might have been the pride of a city park.

Dindon wiped his cheerful and unclouded brow, and with an
air of careless triumph slung the axe into a log. "There, now!" said
he; "some of you smart gentlemen may chop that fellow into fire-
sticks, and carry them to the camp."

"By the body of Hercules!" exclaimed X., as the green wood rang
with shouts of applause and triumph. "Shade of Milo! I here make a
vow never to dispute with Dindon again on any subject; the fate of
that hemlock has convinced me that he could never be wrong, and
that the rest of us are but poor feeble mortals, after all."

One afternoon the attention of the party in the shed was directed to the external world by the increasing roar of the cataract. It had been drizzling all day, but for an hour or more the rain fell by bucketsfull. Some apprehensions were expressed for the safety of Penn and Conway, who were absent on a fishing excursion. Accordingly, the party all went down to the banks of the stream to look out for the absentees. The Blackwater seemed to run mad; and the fall, swelled to treble its usual volume, made the very hills tremble. Quantities of drift were passing, and some shade of real anxiety clouded the faces of the watchers.

"Oh horror!" exclaimed X., "oh fatal day! there goes Penn's body! there! there! he's over the falls! he's gone!"

"Why," said Thornhill, "that looked to me like a forked stick."

"No," insisted X., "it was Penn. I recognized his legs. I can't be mistaken."

Many kindly regrets were expressed, and eulogies pronounced upon his virtues, talents, and amiable traits, some of which the defunct had the pleasure of overhearing as he crept out of a laurel thicket, and followed up the path to the shelter, all forlorn and dripping.

"Why, here comes the gentleman now," said Thornhill.

"Angels and ministers of grace, defend us!"

exclaimed X., throwing himself into a superb attitude;

"Be thou a spirit of health or goblin damned,
Thou com'st in such a questionable shape
That I will speak to thee. . . .
A ghost of shreds and patches. I'll call thee Penn.
Oh answer me; let me not burst in ignorance; but tell
How many fish you've caught—and where's the Otter?"

"The Otter is coming on with the fish," replied the ghost, in a sepulchral voice. "We've got about two hundred. In the mean time, hasten supper. I've had a narrow escape from drowning, and am now perishing with hunger."

At that moment Conway appeared with his load of fish, which were hailed with acclamations.

"Disciple of Izaak Walton!" said X., embracing the dripping body of Mr. Penn, and squeezing him like a sponge in his grateful ecstasy, "may you live forever. Glorious Otter! what a fry we'll have!" And Mr. X. forthwith repaired to the fallen hemlock, and furnished himself with the largest chip he could find, to serve as a plate for the anticipated supper.

While this was cooking, Mr. Penn seated himself on the end of a log at the fire, and narrated his adventure. He and Conway had been some distance up the Blackwater, and had been very successful. Mr. Penn was seated on a rock in the middle of the stream, and so intent was he on the sport, that he did not notice either the rain or the rise of the water. (As has been before observed, Mr. Penn has a remarkable gift of abstracting himself from worldly surroundings.) When the water began to pour over the rock on which he was sitting, he jumped up, and, to his amazement, found himself hemmed in by the foaming torrent. He made a plunge to gain the nearest bank, lost his footing, and was washed up like a piece of drift among some rocks. Here he found himself on the wrong side. The appearance of the stream was terrific, but the terror of an unsheltered and sup-perless night was greater. Presently he saw Conway on the other side, making unintelligible signs to him. He rushed into the water up to his arm-pits, but it looked like suicide to go on, and he struggled back to the bank. Then a large tree drifted by and lodged against the rocks, forming a temporary bridge that reached nearly across. The thought of supper braced him to the desperate venture, and he leaped upon the log. With his weight, the end upon which he jumped broke loose, and swung rapidly round like a flying ferry, bringing him within reach of the laurels on the opposite side. Penn grasped the bushes and saved himself, while the tree, loosed from its moorings, hurried on toward the falls.

"This I consider a very respectable adventure," said Penn, hand-ing over his tin cup for his second pint of coffee, and deliberately separating the rich salmon flakes from the spinal column of a large trout—deliberately, we say, for Mr. Penn was then on his fourteenth fish.

But all things must come to an end sooner or later. The party were all gathered under the bark roof, some smoking, others conversing in a more quiet and serious tone than had been usual among them. X. M. C. finally spoke out.

"Friends and fellow-woodmen," said he, "our sojourn in the wilderness is about to end. We have promised to be at Towers' on the 16th. To fulfill this promise, we must start homeward tomorrow morning. Owing to the early departure of Mr. Jones, we still have an abundance of provision, and might, if we were so disposed, remain a week longer; but the council seem to have determined on going. Well, let it be so. We have not realized all our expectations on coming out. We have killed neither bear, panther, nor deer. We have not even varied our diet with catfish soup—(nodding to Penn)—but we have manfully carried out the proposed objects of our expedition as far as circumstances permitted. We have explored the wilderness, fished in the Black Fork of Cheat, seen the Falls of the Canaan, surfeited on trout, and braved the unpropitious elements unflinchingly. As for me, the impressions made by this sojourn will never be effaced —never, though I were to live as long as the great hemlock felled by the mighty Dindon."

The return to the settlements was unmarked by any incident worthy of record. Accustomed to the forest, hardened to the toil, the difficulties of the march passed as matters of course; and an occasional unsuccessful shot at a deer, or the discovery of a bear's trail, only elicited a brief comment or a laugh. On the second day they breakfasted at Conway's, dined at Towers', and, twenty-four hours after, the heroes of the expedition into Canaan had resumed the dress, and, to all appearance, the habits of ordinary life. Yet, by a shrewd observer of character, they might still be distinguished from the common herd. There was a certain gallant swagger when they walked abroad, a lighting-up of the face when they met each other, or when the subject of hunting and fishing was introduced; an elevation of ideas, a largeness of speech, an ill-concealed disdain of the petty affairs of life, such as law, medicine, or agriculture; and for a long time, whenever they were invited out, even the heavy-handed and profuse housekeepers of their neighborhood seemed to have suddenly become close and thrifty, or to have made some unaccountable mistake in their calculations.

In the town of M—— were several returned Californians who had made the overland trip, dug gold and starved on the Yuba and Feather Rivers, and returned to their homes by the Horn or the Isthmus, with nothing to show for their trouble but a stock of hard-earned experience, and the hope of being heroes and story-tellers for the rest of their days. Alas! they happened in an unlucky time. Whenever one of them, thinking he had an audience in a bar-room or at a street corner, would commence *infandum renovare dolorem,* he was invariably trumped with, "Yes, that reminds me of the Black-water;" and in five minutes' time the poor Californian would stand mute and abashed at supposing that he had ever been hungry in his life, or had ever seen any thing worth talking about.

The Chimneys and the Warm Springs

AND thus they beguiled the time in pleasant chat until some two hours after midday, when they found themselves within sight of the neat little village of Mount Solon. The inn to which they were directed—the only one in the village—was a very modest-looking establishment altogether, and was kept by an old palsied man, who appeared as if he might have known better days. Ascertaining here that the object of their curiosity was only about two miles distant, they left their baggage and an order for supper with the landlord, and drove on.

After jolting over a rocky, uneven road for a short time, they at length had the satisfaction of seeing the black tops of the Chimneys towering above the trees in the distance. At this point our travelers left their vehicle, and proceeded on foot, by a path leading through a barn-yard, to the base of the rocks, about two hundred yards from the main road.

This curious group of natural towers rises at the point of a limestone hill, which juts out like a promontory into an extensive alluvial bottom. There are seven of them, some seventy or eighty feet in height, their bases washed by a small stream, and their whole appearance reminding one of the ruined stronghold of some feudal baron surrounded by its neglected moat. To those whose fancies are more exclusively American, they look like the chimneys of a deserted iron foundry, and, altogether, the picture presented is in a high degree unique and interesting. From no point can all the towers be seen at one view. The northern one is the tallest, the most completely detached from the hill, and in all respects the most perfect. Its round, regular stratifications, gradually narrowing toward the top, show like successive galleries and cornices, such as are represented in the old pictures of the Tower of Babel. This structure is about eighty feet in height, and thirty in diameter near its base. It is tunneled below by a wide archway, through which is the most convenient approach to the bases of the other towers; and, from one point of view, this huge mass appears supported only upon two pillars.

The southern group, consisting of three towers, united for about half their height, is also perforated by a cavernous passage, narrow at each entrance, but opening to a chamber of some size in the centre. None of the Chimneys are completely detached from the hill; and the view from every quarter is intercepted by a heavy growth of timber, much to the annoyance of the artist.

Although these rocks are highly picturesque, curious, and not wanting in grandeur, our travelers, having lately seen objects of such surpassing interest, expressed their gratification here in moderate terms, and were soon seated under some opportune appletrees, discussing their lunch with a zeal and earnestness which neither custom nor daily repetition had in the smallest degree abated.

Not so Mr. Crayon. He spent his time walking curiously about, examining the towers and caverns at all points. Having made

PORTE CRAYON SKETCHING

several unsuccessful attempts to ascend the rocks, he at length succeeded in reaching the summit of one of the lowest, which is joined to the hill by a natural wall several feet in thickness, and reaching more than half way to the top of the tower. Thinking this no great feat, and perceiving that the ladies were too much engaged to look at him, he came down and betook himself to his sketch-book. Having taken his position at some distance out in the meadow, to get a better view of the southern group, he was in a short time surrounded by all the dogs on the plantation, bull, ring, and bobtail, who barked and clamored until they were tired, and then trotted off, surprised and disgusted at the imperturbability of the artist.

The sketches being completed, and the curiosity of all parties satisfied, our friends returned to their carriage. It was unanimously agreed that, although they had been much gratified by their visit, yet there was nothing about the Chimneys to excite enthusiasm—in short, they were wanting in the quality of sublimity. Porte went on further to observe that he preferred the homely name of "The Chimneys" to the more elegant appellation of "Cyclopean Towers;" for, although an admirer of the classics in the abstract, and understanding fully the propriety of the name as applied to this style of architecture, yet he had always felt averse to mixing associations drawn from the Old World with American scenery. The most striking characteristic of our scenery, when compared with the European, is its freshness, observable even in the appearance of the rocks, and the charm of the impression is always disturbed by any association with the old mythology. The family of the Cyclops was Sicilian, and was disposed of long before the discovery of America by Columbus in 1492. Let them kick and sprawl till Doomsday under their mountain tomb. We doubt if the introduction of distinguished foreigners is of much advantage in any way to us on this side of the water.

Miss Dora expressed a doubt whether there were ever any such persons as the Cylops; but Crayon assured her that he had seen the place where they were buried.

Arrived at the barn-yard, they found their horses still engaged in munching some remarkably fine oats, which had been served up in an old pig-trough. Crayon complimented his man on his thoughtful attention, and desired him to go and pay the farmer for the feed.

The coachman replied that, having a suspicion that the horses might get hungry, he had taken the precaution to bring a supply with them, which he had procured from Mr. Moler's barn at the Cave Hotel.

Not recollecting any charge for extra oats at that place, a suspicion began to insinuate itself into Mr. Crayon's mind.

"What? why, here's a bushel more in the carriage-box! You scoundrel! have you been stealing, and feeding my horses on surreptitious oats?"

"No, indeed, Mass' Porte, dese ain't dem kind; dese is de best oats I seen sence I left home."

And Mice went on to declare that the oats in question fairly belonged to the horses, as they had not eaten their full allowance while stabled at the Cave Hotel, and he had only taken what he thought they ought to have eaten. He moreover added, by way of strengthening his defense, that the horses relished these oats especially, and that Mr. Moler had such a pile of them in his barn that he would not have missed ten bushels, if any one had seen fit to take that quantity. Notwithstanding this clear explanation, Crayon would have given his coachman a severe reprimand, but they all got into an uncontrollable fit of laughter, and one should never attempt to moralize without a sober countenance.

Fanny, being the first to recover her gravity sufficiently, reminded Mice of his devout belief in a place of future punishment, expressed while in the cave. This belief he reaffirmed, but felt assured that he "wasn't gwine to be saunt dere becase he took good care of his hosses." Porte Crayon then mildly but firmly suggested that, whenever there should be need of a fresh supply of oats, he should be informed, and they should be acquired by purchase in the regular way, as our government *formerly* acquired territory. Mice acquiesced, of course, promising faithfully to attend to the matter; but looked, at the same time, as if he thought this arrangement involved a very unnecessary and absurd expenditure of money.

Our adventurers were on the road next morning before sunrise, while the fields were yet white with frost.

"This is an improvement, girls. How well you all look this morning! This is the glorious time for traveling. The horses move gayly, and puff clouds of smoke from their nostrils like two steam-engines. Now the sun begins to show his red disk above the hills, and gilds the mountain-tops rising to the westward of us."

Dora's eyes sparkled as she suddenly plucked Crayon's sleeve. "Hist! cousin, there's a pheasant!"

"Where? quick! point him out!" whispered Crayon, unslinging his yager.

"There! don't you see? On that old log among the pines."

Mice had stopped the carriage upon the first intimation of game, and was looking intently into the bushes. "Da he is! I sees him! big as a turkey-gobbler. Good Lord, Mass' Porte, shoot quick: he gwine to fly!"

"Be quiet, you blockhead! I see him now. A fine cock, with his neck stretched and his ruff up."

Bang went the rifle; whir—r, whir—r, whir—r went the pheasants in every direction from among the grape-trees, where a large company of them were breakfasting.

"Fotch him!" shouted Mice, tumbling out of the carriage, and rushing into the bushes. Presently he returned, his face illuminated with a triumphant grin, carrying the bird by the legs. "Bullet tuck him right through the neck; mizzible good brile he'll make; fat as butter."

The whole company were now on the alert. "There's a pheasant! No, it's a ground squirrel." "There's one in the grapetree!" Bang! down he tumbled, whirring and fluttering among the dead leaves. The girls clapped their hands, and were so full of the sport that the carriage could scarcely hold them; and when Porte Crayon missed a shot in his haste, they were quite outrageous upon him. He reinstated himself, however, by shooting two more birds shortly after. "We've now come to an open country, and there will be no more pheasants this morning," remarked Crayon.

The girls were quite vexed, and insisted on going back over the same road. "How blood will show itself, in spite of every thing!" cried the delighted Crayon. "All our family take to hunting as naturally as sparrowhawks."

The appearance of the Augusta Springs diverted the attention of our travelers from the subject in hand; and as it was a pleasant, rural-looking spot, they determined to tarry for half an hour to see what was to be seen. This place is twelve miles distant from Staunton, and is more frequented by visitors from the neighborhood than by those from a distance, its name abroad being overshadowed by its more celebrated rivals in the counties of Bath and Greenbrier. The water is a sulphur, and is said to possess some value as a remedial agent. The girls here purchased a spotted fawn's skin from an old lady, for the purpose of making Porte Crayon a bullet-pouch, to be presented as a testimonial of his skill in shooting pheasants.

About two miles from these springs our friends struck the Lewisburg road, which passes the mountain at Jennings's Gap without a perceptible grade. From this point the country becomes more wild and rugged in its features. Mountains rise on every side, forests of pine and hemlock border the way, and limpid streams pour over rocky beds, murmuring of deer and trout. Human habitations become fewer and farther between, ruder in their character, and frequently ornamented on the outside with trophies of the chase— deers' horns, raccoon and bear skins, and turkeys' wings. At this season, too, the road seemed to be deserted by travel. Occasionally, indeed, they met a lonely teamster, who, after exchanging with Mice their characteristic salute, a crack of the whip, passed on his snail-like journey toward Staunton.

The horses made good speed that day, although the meridian sun was hot and the road dusty. Cloverdale was reached at length and left behind. It was still far to the Bath Alum, and the sun was rapidly declining. The mountains rose grandly, deep blue, with sharp-drawn outline against the glowing west. Still the tired horses jogged on, fetlock-deep in dust. The pine forests grew taller and gloomier in the fading twilight. No sign of life or civilization yet. Then utter darkness closed her wing over all the land. Night is the time for evil-doers to be abroad. Night is the time when wild birds range for their prey. Night is the season for the busy teeming fancy to conjure up its thousand phantoms. The girls whispered timidly among themselves, and Crayon instinctively examined his arms to feel assured that all was right.

"Drive cautiously, now, Mice: it is useless to hurry; it can get no darker, and we must trust to the instinct of the horses."

Presently these came to a dead halt of their own accord, nor was a cautious admonition of the voice and whip sufficient to induce them to stir. "Dey sees somethin'," said Mice, who believed firmly that horses could see ghosts and other strange things invisible to mortal eyes. But the animals snorted and gently pawed the ground, thereby intimating to their masters that they were neither frightened nor fatigued, but had stopped from some other motive.

"I think I see something myself," quoth Porte Crayon; "a tall white thing standing on the left of the road."

"Lord bless us, master!" cried Mice; "what you think it is?"

"I think it is a sign-post," replied Porte. "Fanny, feel in my knapsack, under the sketch-book, and rolled up in a silk handkerchief you will find my tin match-box. Hand it to me."

Crayon got out, and having lighted a wisp of paper, found that he had not been deceived. There was a sign-post standing where the road forked, and by the light of his flickering torch he managed to read the direction to the Bath Alum, one mile distant. The horses, satisfied with this reconnaissance, started off briskly before Crayon had fairly regained his seat, or the coachman had given the warning crack of his whip. "D'ye hear, Mice? these horses must be well rubbed and curried before you go to bed to-night; to-morrow they shall rest."

Now they see the star of hospitality twinkling in the distance, suggestive of smoking suppers and comfortable beds. These promises were, in the present instance, destined to be fully realized. Soon the cheerful board, spread with biscuit, corn cakes, and hot venison steaks, rejoiced the souls of our benighted travelers, while crackling fires roared in the chimneys of the parlors and bed-rooms. "Ah!" said Porte Crayon, throwing himself upon a springy sofa with a sigh of unspeakable satisfaction, and a dreamy retrospect of numberless corn dodgers, hot and brown, floating in butter, and of four broad-cut, generous portions of venison steak—"ah me! As much as I contemn luxury and despise civilization, with its attendant fopperies and vices, I don't mind taking a good supper occasionally."

"Indeed," said Fanny, "I don't think you could take many such meals as you made to-night; the sixth time your plate went up for steak, both the waiter and manager got into a titter."

"My plate went up but four times," replied Crayon, dogmatically; "and the manager was laughing at my wit, and not my appetite."

"It went up six times, as I live."

"Young woman," said Crayon, with feigned asperity, "I did observe, but did not intend to comment on your performance at supper. Suffice it to say, if you had been in a region where fashion takes cognizance of what and how much young ladies eat, you would have lost caste forever. Indeed, if those peony-colored cheeks of themselves would not be an insuperable objection to your admission into any refined society."

"Good gracious!" cried all the girls at once, "you don't mean to say our cheeks are red?"

"Red!" quoth Crayon, contemptuously; "the word don't express it. A respectable damask rose would look pale beside them."

"This comes of traveling in the sun and wind with these foolish bonnets," cried Fanny, spitefully.

"It comes of exercise, fresh air, and good appetites; for, besides, you are getting as fat as partridges."

"It is no such thing," said Minnie, indignantly. "Porte, you're a horrid bear! Come, girls, let us retire and leave him."

"And as freckled as turkey eggs," continued Crayon.

"It is positively insulting. He has no consideration for our feelings."

Porte shouted after them as they flounced out of the room, insisting that he had not intended to offend, but had really supposed he was complimenting them.

After enjoying his sofa for a while, it occurred to him to commend his pheasants to the cook, as they might probably be opportune at breakfast. Nor did he omit to assure himself of the well-being of the horses; and, not long after, our hero found himself mentally comparing the merits of a hair mattress with those of the hemlock couch of the Canaan. As no conclusion has ever been reported, it is supposed he fell asleep before finally disposing of the subject.

The drizzling rain which fell during the whole of next day did not prevent our friends from enjoying their comfortable quarters, nor even from making sundry out-door excursions. The improvements at the Bath Alum are certainly superior, in point of taste and elegance, to those at any watering-place in the mountains of Virginia. At a distance of several hundred yards from the hotel, beneath a slatestone cliff, fifteen feet in height, are found the Alum Springs, which are nothing more than six little reservoirs so excavated as to catch the drippings from the projecting rock. These reservoirs contain the alum water in different degrees of strength; one of them is a strong chalybeate, and one a mixture of chalybeate and alum. These waters are but recently known as a remedial agent, and have suddenly obtained immense celebrity by their success in curing diseases hitherto reckoned incurable. Those who are desirous of more accurate and extended information on the subject are commended to Dr. Burke's excellent work on the Virginia Springs, or, what might be still more to the purpose, a visit to the Springs themselves. As for our travelers, having taken large doses of broiled pheasant that morning, they confined their experiments in alum water to a cautious sip from the glass handed by the polite manager, a comical wry face, and a forced compliment to its flavor—faugh!

In the afternoon the rain increased to a continued heavy shower; notwithstanding which, Crayon, accompanied by his valet, went hunting, and it was near dark before they returned, weary, wet, and hungry, with only three or four unlucky squirrels for their pains.

From this place to the Warm Springs, the distance of five miles is accomplished by traversing the Great Warm Spring Mountain, on an easy, well-constructed road. When our friends set out from the Alum the rain had ceased, and fair promises of a clear day were given. Masses of damp-looking clouds still hung about the tops of the mountains, as if unwilling yet to yield the day to Phœbus, who, for his part, poured his bright rays through at every opening, producing in endless variety those brilliant and startling effects of light and shade so much sought after by the scenic school of English painters. When about half way up the mountain, the girls, who had walked in advance, were seen suddenly to turn and fly with all speed toward the slow-toiling carriage.

"Oh heavens! let us in—let us in quick!"

"What now? What's the matter? Have you encountered some untimely snake or frost-bitten lizard?"

To Crayon's inquiry they vouchsafed no reply, but in breathless haste bundled into the vehicle, and, ere they had fairly disposed themselves in their seats, the question was answered from another quarter. Where the road swept in a bold curve around the base of a cliff, now advanced with slow and stately tread, in all the pomp of bovine majesty, the vanguard of one of those monstrous herds of cattle wending their way from the rich pastures of Monroe and Green-brier to the eastward. First came a stout negro, with stupid face and loutish step, leading an ox, whose sublime proportions and majestic port might have served as a disguise for Jove himself.

"Large rolls of fat about his shoulders clung,
And from his neck the double dewlap hung,"

THE DROVE

while his horns sprung from his curling forehead in tapering length, a full cloth-yard each one. What horns! What noble drinking-cups they would have made. One of them would hold enough to fuddle a Thracian. The negro remarked Crayon's admiring glances, and, as he touched his hat, the dull face lighted up with an expression: "Am not I one of the chosen—I, who serve so magnificent a beast? Night and morning I curry him, and walk all day in his presence. He and I are the observed and envied of all." " 'Pears to me," said Mice, "dat fool nigger is proud to be a leadin' of dat big beef."

Following this leader came a train of thirty or forty others, scarcely inferior in size or appearance; and when the carriage, winding slowly through this formidable-looking company, turned the angle of rock, the road was visible in its windings for a mile or more, alive with cattle and bristling with horns. The horses held on their way through the living mass as steadily as if unaware of their presence, although the mountain resounded far and near with the hoarse bellowing of the beeves, mingled with the oaths and whoops of the drivers. The girls, who at first looked doubtfully upon the array of monstrous horns, and the red, lowering eyes of the savage troop, soon regained their self-possession, and commented coolly on their size and keeping.

The celebrated view from the summit of the Warm Spring Mountain did not strike our travelers very forcibly, probably owing to the clouds which hid the distant mountain-tops rising to the eastward. The view of the Warm Springs and the valley seen directly below them was extremely pretty. This village, which is the county-seat of Bath, owes its existence and name to the famous fountain, and, in fact, consists of nothing more than the group of hotels, cottages, and out-houses about the Springs, and the ordinary county buildings, a court-house, jail, etc. The principal hotel has heretofore had a high reputation for excellence; and the bathing-houses, although somewhat primitive in their constructure, furnish a bath at a natural temperature of 98° Fahrenheit, the luxury of which must be experienced to be appreciated.

Our party remained at this place but a few hours, and hurried on to the Hot Springs, five miles distant, where they arrived about five o'clock on Saturday evening, the 22d of October. Although the hotel here was closed for the season, the proprietor gave them a hospitable welcome, and they soon found themselves installed in comfortable quarters.

This place, to the scientific traveler, is one of the most curious and interesting in the mountains. The Hot Springs, about twenty in number, issue from the base of a hill or spur of the Warm Spring Mountain, and range in temperature from 98° to 106°, but, owing to the proximity of fountains of cold water at 53°, baths of any inter- mediate temperature may be had. The bathing-houses are numerous and well arranged to suit the purposes of invalids. These waters are chiefly celebrated for their efficacy in rheumatism, dyspepsia, and affections of the liver, although they are resorted to by all classes of invalids. The proprietor is himself an eminent physician, and to the enlightened use of the waters under his direction is probably owing much of their success in the cure of disease.

The hotel and cottages here are pleasantly situated and comfortable, and the table most unexceptionable. Sunday was a delightful day, and our friends passed it pleasantly and quietly, wandering up and down hills, through meadows and forests, drinking in buoyant health with the pure atmosphere, and enjoying the mellow beauties of the autumn landscape. The evening fell in still and solemn grandeur.

"We will have a brilliant starlit night," quoth Crayon; "the air is soft and balmy. To-morrow I will make two or three fine sketches before we leave here."

"To-morrow," said Fanny, "I will produce my colors, and attempt this bit of purple landscape opening to the south."

"To-morrow," laughed Minnie May, "I will gather leaves of the maple and hickory, and weave chaplets of crimson and gold to crown our artists withal."

"And what shall I do to-morrow?" inquired Dora. "I'll point Porte Crayon's pencils for him, and hold Fanny's color-box while she paints, and help Minnie to weave her chaplets."

To-morrow, ay, to-morrow—oh, simple-hearted schemers! who can reckon what a night may bring forth? In a night the gourd of Jonah grew, and in a night it withered. In a night the host of the Assyrian was blasted. And while your young eyelids are fanned by the soothing wings of sleep, in the darkness and silence of a night, what mighty changes may be wrought upon the face of nature!

A Virginia Snow-Storm

"PORTE CRAYON, Porte Crayon, arise and look out of the window!"
Porte Crayon opened his sleepy eyes, and gave a great yawn. "Methinks I heard a voice, and the pattering of light feet about my door."
Our hero arose and hastily donned his vestments; there was no one
at the door. He then drew the curtain of the window.

> "With wild surprise,
> As if to marble struck, devoid of sense,
> A stupid moment motionless he stood."

Presently, recovering his faculties in some degree, he rubbed his eyes
and looked again. Our hero was well read in the philosophy of
the schools, and knew how little credit was due to any appearance
based solely upon the evidence of the senses. He pinched his ear and
plucked his beard. He rapped his skull with his knuckles. *"Cogito,
ergo sum,"* quoth he; "and yet this morning I am inclined to be a
disciple of Pyrrho.

> "If I be I, as I do hope I be,
> There are three little girls in the adjoining room, and they know me."

No wonder that the view from the window confused our hero's
faculties and chilled his soul to marble. Lawn and grove, field and
forest, meadow and mountain, were all covered deep with a white
panoply of snow, and all the air was misty with the thick-descending
flakes. Crayon hastily completed his toilet and sallied forth. The first
person he met was his coachman, hat in hand, and with a countenance
of dumb dismay. "How now, Mice, what news?" Mice pointed to
the front porch of the hotel, where the snow lay eight inches deep.
"Mass' Porte, dis is redicklus."

"Go look after your horses; see that carriage and harness are sound and trim; then call for further orders."

The ladies were already in the breakfast-room, huddling around the fire, with looks equally expressive of dismay, but by no means dumb.

"Oh, Cousin Porte, what shall we do?"   "What shall we do, brother?"   "What a dreadful thing! what can we do?"

Porte Crayon had that morning been more unnerved at the sight of the snow than he would be willing now to admit; but of all things to rouse the pride and energies of man, there is nothing like an appeal from one or more frightened beauties.

"What shall we do? Do?" quoth our hero, giving his mustache a gallant twirl, *"Imprimis,* let us breakfast." The cock-eyed servant, with a polite bow, intimated that the meal alluded to awaited their orders. Hot coffee, muffins, and beef-steak are well calculated to inspire vigorous and stout-hearted counsels. Their position and prospects were discussed during the progress of the meal. While waiting for the butter to melt on his fourth muffin, Porte Crayon prefaced a harangue with a thump on the table, so energetic that it made the china dance, and he felt under the necessity of apologizing for his violence before going on with his speech.

"We will push on to the White Sulphur, if we are frozen to mummies. It is written in the programme, and we must accomplish it, or perish in the attempt."

Here Dora intimated that she entertained a peculiar dislike to the idea of perishing in the snow.

"True enough, child; you shall not perish; I'll engage to carry you through without the slightest risk, and even without any considerable discomfort. I never was the man," said he, with a valiant look—(here he stopped to point his discourse with a mouthful of muffin and a swig of coffee)—"I never was the man to be bullied by the weather. I am ready to beard old Hiems himself, though backed by his flunkies, blustering Boreas and Jack Frost both together."

Crayon's swaggering manner, conjointly with the beef-steak, inspired all about him. The girls went bravely to work preparing for the sortie. All the extra shawls and worsted comforters were put in requisition, and Crayon's supply of yarn socks were distributed round to serve as overshoes.

Mice brought up the carriage in complete order, the curtains all down, and the bottom covered knee-deep with fresh hay. All arrangements being now complete, not forgetting a bag plethoric with lunch, Crayon gallantly took the girls in his arms and carried them one by one to the carriage, safe and dry-shod. Then depositing his rifle in a dry place, and brushing the snow from his feet he took his seat beside the driver. The apron-cloth was drawn up over their legs, and with a brisk chirrup and a crack of the whip they started into the storm.

No spiteful spitting from a passing cloud was this; no accidental dredging from the snow-box; no light squadron of skirmishers adventuring far in advance of the imperial army of winter. Here was the Snow King himself, with all his host, marshaled in

"Battle's magnificently stern array,"

precipitating his columns upon the baggage-burdened retreat of Autumn. The 24th of October! Who ever heard of such a thing? It was a surprise, a base violation of compact, ungenerous, unlike a king, thus to take Nature all unwarned and unprepared. The forests, still encumbered with their tawdry apparel, were yielding fast on every side. The younger and lither trees bent their loaded crowns to the earth before the conqueror. The tall pine, whose evergreen top bore up the snow like a broad white canopy, would suddenly rip loose from the earth, and fall like some smitten giant. The stout oak, that had braved a hundred winters, stood, for a time, proud and defiant. "The Old Guard never yields!" Vain boast. A sudden crash proclaimed the triumph of his remorseless enemy, and, one by one, his fifty strong arms were riven, and fell helpless to the ground.

The horses bore themselves sturdily. The roan and sorrel were of good mettle. Their backs were white with snow; the snow balled in their hoofs and tripped them as they moved; but they never faltered. When they reached the toll-gate on Jackson's River, nine miles from their starting-place, the storm raged with unabated fury. The toll-gatherer begged them not to persist in the attempt to cross Morris's Hill. The road was blocked up so as to be impassable. A man had made the attempt that morning on horseback, and had returned. "We will try it. *En avant*."

"Good luck to you, stranger," shouted the gate-keeper, hurrying into the house.

As they slowly toiled up the mountain the scene opened in all its wildness. The North Wind, not then the blustering braggart, came down upon them in his might. The downy-cushioned earth and woods gave back no echo to the sound of his rushing wings, but with silent energy and hissing malignity he drove the drifting clouds before him; now blinding men and horses with the showering flakes; now revealing in a long, wintry vista the unbroken highway and snow-encumbered forest.

Sometimes the young growth was bowed from either side until the tops, interlocking in the centre, formed a snowy archway over the road. Then our adventurers would dash through, helter-skelter, and find themselves half buried in the avalanche from the shaken trees. Sometimes, through erring judgment, the rush would prove a failure, and they would be brought up standing, with their equipage so entangled in tree-tops and grape-vines that it was necessary to open the passage with their knives. Frequently trees were found lying across the way, as if forbidding their farther progress. Then Mice would descend, and, setting his ponderous strength against the obstacle, would roll it from the road, and pass on. When they encountered a tree too much for their strength, then, by deftly combining art with force, they would bend the limbs one by one, and hack them off with the hunting-knife until a passage was cleared.

When surrounded by difficulties, Porte Crayon is frequently in the habit of warming his courage by repeating heroic verses. On that occasion the noble lines of Scott, describing the battle of Flodden Field, were uppermost in his mind:

> "No thought was there of dastard flight,
> Linked in that serried phalanx tight,
> Groom fought like noble, squire like knight,
>   As fearlessly and well."

They are brave verses, although they seem to have no especial applicability to the subject.

In the warfare on Morris's Hill, the groom was the predominant character. In narrating the matter, Porte Crayon says: "I was no more to be compared with him on that field than the presumptuous frog to the doughty ox. To be sure I was not idle. I hacked and hewed with my knife to the best of my ability; I waded about in the snow and gave directions, shouted, sung, and made brave speeches; but Mice performed prodigies. Things that he took hold of seemed to lose their weight and tenacity. He would seize a moderate-sized pine-tree by the crown, and drag it out of the track as though it had been a bush. When the road for an eighth of a mile was so overhung with snow-bowed saplings and grape-vines that the possibility of penetrating them was doubtful, he would walk ahead, shaking, breaking, and tearing every thing before him, like an elephant in an Indian jungle, or a hippopotamus among the reeds of the Gariep.

"The events of that day," continues Crayon, "have covered the humble name of Little Mice with imperishable glory, nor shall a historian and limner be wanting to blazon his deeds to an admiring world. What a moment for the artist to seize him, as he issued from the bushes covered with snow, white as a polar bear, and trailing after him, by his unconscious legs, a hundred feet of grape-vine!"

The snow had by this time attained a depth of fourteen inches, and was still deepening and drifting furiously. While the storm grew mightier, human and equine energy had their limits. The horses panted and sobbed at every hard brush, and the snow-flakes no longer whitened their smoking hides. Wet, worn, and chilled, master and man sat drowsily in their seats, feeling the approach of that dangerous lethargy which steals over men too long exposed to cold.

"Mass' Porte, I wish we was at a tavern," exclaimed the subdued coachman.

Porte folded his arms across his breast, and, with a desperate look, took a rapid mental survey of their position. "It is now four o'clock; night will be upon us a little after five. Since we passed the toll-gate we have scarcely averaged a mile in an hour. The horses are failing; this over-done giant is losing his courage. We shall be benighted, and completely blocked up by the snow in this wild, inhospitable forest. Poor girls! it was my rashness and obstinacy that brought them into this perilous position. God knows what may happen. I dare not think of it. They have been silent within there for some time. I have had no desire to communicate with them. I must warn them against sleeping, however, and must be careful not to alarm their fears. No, not for the world; they would sink under it, if they even suspected their situation."

Crayon quickly lifted the corner of the front curtain, and peeped into the interior of the vehicle.

The first glance at his charge relieved him of any fears as to the state of their minds. They were not asleep, nor were they weeping; but Fanny had the lunch-sack on her lap, from which she had distributed sundry biscuits and slices of ham, and, at the exact moment of Crayon's observation, all three were so busy in dismembering a broiled chicken, that he dropped the curtain and regained his former position unperceived. One might have supposed that this exhibition of the *"mens æqua in arduis"* in a trio of women would have delighted our hero. On the contrary, he was highly indignant. He mentally accused them of lacking the wit to appreciate their danger, and of the most heartless indifference to his exposure and sufferings. Moreover, when he thought of the heroic labors of Mice and himself, and compared their present forlorn condition with that of the ungrateful girls, giggling over their lunch, he felt strongly inclined to break in upon the feast, and warn them of their approaching fate.

"Mass' Porte, please, Sir, ontie dis knot in my whip-lash; somehow my fingers won't work."

"Neither will mine," said Crayon, "and I can't limber them. My gloves are wet, and my pockets full of snow."

"Here, take these, Porte," and a dainty little hand appeared beneath the curtain, presenting a pair of fur-tipped gloves. He received them with a gruff acknowledgment, and then regarding the gift with a smile of indifference, muttered, "The inconsiderate child! I couldn't get three fingers into them." So saying, he thrust them carelessly into the left pocket of his vest. Crayon felt a genial warmth pervading his half congealed breast. It is difficult to believe that so trifling an addition to a man's clothing as those bits of fur and silk could produce so great a change; possibly their location in the vest pocket had something to do with it; but true it is, from that moment our hero felt neither cold nor despondency. Once more he sat erect, and his drooping eye again glanced defiance to the tempest.

"They shall not perish, positively," he growled, between his teeth. "Their entire *insouciance* doubtless proceeds from a firm reliance on my promise that no harm should befall them, and they believe in my ability to fulfill it as confidently as if I were ruler of the storm. How beautifully feminine the trait, and how abject the soul that would not fire with the assumed responsibility!" Crayon's bosom so glowed with these generous emotions, that all the snow melted off the breast of his coat, and he broke forth into voluntary song. What particular song he sung is not recorded. Doubtless it was a good one, for the curtain was drawn up, and voices from the interior of the carriage swelled the jolly chorus.

"Amid the storm they sang"

so blithe a carol, so hearty and so brave withal, that Boreas, in sheer disgust and impotence, gave up the war.

They had passed Morris's Hill, and the road lay before them plain and unencumbered, except by the depth of snow. The country, too, appeared more open, and the coachman's ardent wish to see a tavern seemed likely to be gratified speedily. Night overtook them, however, still toiling onward at a snail's pace. The driver dozed in his seat, abandoning the vehicle entirely to the discretion and instinct of the horses, and the silence was only disturbed by the creaking of the carriage and the monotonous crunching of the snow beneath the wheels. The effervescence of enthusiasm was past, and overwrought nature claimed her dues. Undisturbed by doubt or apprehension, our travelers sank unresistingly into pleasant reveries, and these, as if by a common instinct, turned toward their distant home. These siren thoughts insensibly glided into dreams. Their journey was accomplished; they had returned to their kindred; the welcome was over; the pantry ransacked to add to the profusion of the groaning board; "the fire fair blazing and the vestment warm" were prepared for them. Caressing friends sat listening with complacent admiration to their narratives of hair-breadth 'scapes and natural wonders. They recalled the Fort Mountains, the Cave, the Chimneys; they remembered the day they crossed Morris's Hill in a snow-storm. A terrible day it was, and stoutly they bore themselves through it all. . . . . .

At length the horses stopped, and the sorrel gave a loud snort, to which the roan replied with a triumphant whinny. Porte Crayon started from his sleep so suddenly that he flattened his cap against the top of the carriage. Before them, at a distance of no more than a

couple of hundred yards, he saw a number of lights and heard a confusion of loud voices. "Wake up, you lout! Here's a tavern at last!"
he shouted, shaking and pommeling his man with all his might. In
a state of complete bewilderment, Mice stretched his benumbed limbs,
and mechanically resumed the governorship of the carriage.

"Girls! girls! wake up. We've arrived at last."

"At home? Are we at home?" said Dora, eagerly.

"No, child; but, most fortunately for us, at a tavern."

"Oh, cousin, are we still in the storm?" said Minnie. "I have
had such a pleasant dream."

Before our travelers had fairly recovered their consciousness, their
vehicle had threaded its way among a number of road wagons, and
was drawn up in front of a country tavern—a long, low wooden
building, with a rude porch running the whole length of the front.
The girls were daintily transferred to the house, and the horses immediately driven off to the stables.

"May I be spavined," said a wagoner to the group that witnessed
the disembarkation, "if there baint an old feller with a beard as white
as Noah's when he came out of the ark!"

"Cuss my hide," said a drover, "if I know what started a flock
of wimmin to take the road sich a day as this."

The supper, at which the tidy hostess presided, was such as her
honest spouse had promised, and consisted of fried middling and
flapjacks, with six varieties of fruit preserved in the same fermented
molasses. But, like Baucis and Philemon of old,

> "The kindly hosts their entertainment grace
> With hearty welcome and with open face;
> In all they did you might discern with ease
> A willing mind and a desire to please."

During the meal the man was at his wit's end to know how he
should lodge his newly-arrived guests; but, on consultation with
his wife, it was agreed that their own room, which was in a cottage
standing in the yard, and a little way removed from the main building, should be arranged for the young ladies; the dame, with her
brood, retreating into the loft, and the man agreeing to take his
chance among the wagoners. Crayon desired nothing better for himself, and, taking leave of the girls, went in search of his lieutenant,

that he might have some assurance of the welfare of the horses. At the end of an hour he found him seated beside the kitchen fire, and there received the following artless report of his proceedings: The stables were even more crowded than the house. Not a stall was to be found, nor even a shed to shelter our faithful pair. The roan and sorrel looked wistfully into the crowded sheds, and saluted the possessors with many gracious and friendly whinnies. These salutations were civilly answered from within, but no movement was made to offer a place to the newcomers. Mice begged and diplomatized in vain; he received nothing but curses and threats from the wagoners. When these, one by one, had looked after their horses, and retired to the more attractive precincts of the bar-room, he cast his eyes upon the hostler, a negro lad, who had been kicked and cuffed enough that day to prepare him for any thing that might be proposed. Mice desired his good offices to assist him in getting his horses under shelter, at the same time greasing his palm with a quarter. The boy insisted that every place was "chock full," and then added, in a tone that might have passed for suggestive, "Dassent move any of 'em, no, indeed—eh! eh!"

"Whose hosses is dese?" asked Mice.

"Dem's Mr. Longbow's, biggest devil of 'em all."

"Here's a big, wide stall, only one hoss in!"

"Eh! eh! him kicks like forty jackasses."

Mice inquired still further, and finally ascertained that a couple of horses, occupying a very cozy place, belonged to an individual who was dead drunk over in the loft of the tavern. Without more ado he untied their halters, and kicking them out into the yard, introduced his suffering friends into the vacated places. The boy made a show of protesting, and threatened Mice with the awful consequences of his temerity. "De Lord knows," he sagely observed in reply, "a man what's dead drunk aint a-gwine to hurt any body." And, besides, he promised himself to get up before daylight, and replace the unlucky animals whose misfortune it was to have a master that got drunk. The roan and sorrel doubtless had a comfortable night, if, indeed, the general belief is correct that horses have no consciences.

That portion of the company which more particularly calls for the interest and solicitude of every gallant and humane traveler being disposed of for the present in the most satisfactory manner, if any one is desirous of knowing what further adventures befell our friends during their sojourn at this inn or elsewhere, he is referred to the next chapter of this veritable history.

A Virginia Hostelry

OUR hero, having cast about the premises, and seeing little chance of obtaining quarters elsewhere, with some reluctance betook himself to the bar-room. Here, around a glowing fire, sat ten or a dozen teamsters and drovers, whose looks and demeanor seemed entirely in accordance with the atmosphere of the room, which reeked with fumes of tobacco and corn whisky. As Crayon entered, a strapping, insolent-looking fellow, six feet three in his boots, and somewhat in liquor, welcomed him with a horse-laugh.

TIM LONGBOW

"Well! may I be stalded in a mud-hole if here ain't the fellow himself, with a beard as black as a Mexican Greaser's. Jist now I thought it was white. Stranger, step up and drink something."

Crayon was not altogether pleased with the prospect of the night before him, and might also have been nettled by the free and not over-polished commentaries on his personal appearance. He had, too, been contending all day with the conqueror of Napoleon, and it is not strange that he should have been disposed to look slightingly upon the anger of any mere mortal. He replied curtly by desiring the speaker to hold his peace.

"Why," said the giant, scornfully, "you appear to be an airy gentleman. Now may I never crack another whip if you sha'n't drink or fight before we part."

And, so saying, he rose and advanced several paces. Crayon, with the alertness of a rattlesnake, whipped out his hunting-knife, and standing on the defensive, so far as regarded his person, assaulted the wagoner with a volley of epithets, better understood and appreciated by the frequenters of Virginia bar-rooms than by the world at large.

"Tim Longbow! Tim Longbow!" cried the inn-keeper, rushing from the bar, and seizing the astonished teamster by the arms, "behave yourself in my house."

"Leave me go," cried Tim, laying hold of a chair; "I'll knock that frog-sticker out of his hand in no time."

Others of the company now laid hands on Tim, who, perceiving that his antagonist stood his ground, suffered himself to be held and reasoned with.

"You spoke oncivil to the stranger, you did," said the host; "and he's got ladies with him."

"That's a fact," replied Tim; "but it hain't oncivil to ask a man to drink."

"No, in gineral, not; but perhaps the stranger don't want to drink."

"Well, ain't the rule 'drink or fight' every whar'?"

"Jist so; it's the rule among your kind," argued the shrewd inn-keeper; "but you've no right to put your law in force on strangers in this here free country."

This argument touched Tim's weak point, which was an inordinate love of liberty, both of speech and action. "May be so," said he, doubtfully; "but I don't like to be stumped, nor yit to be called a squirrel-picker, by no set-up swell whomsomdever."

Crayon, by this time, ashamed of having "drawn among these heartless hinds," and perceiving that affairs were likely to take a humorous turn, put up his whittle, and, while he still firmly declined the spirits, offered to compromise the matter on a glass of water. This offer settled the point of honor; and Longbow observed that, seeing he was satisfied the gentleman wa'n't too proud to drink, he was free to drink water or any other truck he pleased; as for himself, he ginerally preferred old Monongahela.

The difficulty being thus amicably arranged, they all shook hands, and reseated themselves around the fire.

"Now, Mr. Longbow," said the landlord, with a sly wink at Crayon, "go on with that story you were telling a while ago about your trip to California."

Tim cast a doubtful glance at the new-comer. "Well, stranger, I reckon you've been to California yourself?" On being assured in the negative, Tim resumed his air of assurance and a somewhat tangled narrative, which had been interrupted by Crayon's entrance.

"As I was a-saying, we was a-sailing from San Francisco in a ship, and we was blew off a long ways out of our course, maybe about two months' sail; and as I was a-saying, we got out of provisions, and had nothing to eat for six weeks."

"Six weeks!" exclaimed one of the listeners.

"Six weeks," reiterated Tim, looking hard at the audacious author of the interruption. "We all got as thin as wagon-whips, and we might have starved if we hadn't had the luck to catch a whale."

"You must have found it rather coarse eating," suggested Crayon. Tim looked a little confused. "So it was; rather coarse and bony."

"But the roe you doubtless found very delicate?" observed Crayon.

"That it was," exclaimed Tim, "and a plenty of it. We packed forty-seven barrels with it, and, when briled and eaten with ship-biscuit, it was a treat to a hungry man. So, after a time, we got to Panama, and thar', thar' was no boats nor any way to git across, and the fellers was all gittin the ager and the yaller fever, and, for fear I should be tuck down myself, I tied my things in a wallet and swum across."

"How far was it?" inquired the landlord, with a humorous twinkle in his eye.

"Well, it mought have been about fifteen mile, more or less; but there was shallow places now and then, where I waded a piece and rested myself."

"How did you get across?" asked a fellow who was leaning against the chimney-jamb.

"I swum across, mister," responded Tim, fiercely. "Are you a-misdoubting of a gentleman's word? I'll leave it to the stranger if it hain't so."

The stranger agreed that it was all very probable.

"Then," pursued Tim, "I walked a-foot up to New-Orleans, and boated up and down for a while, and then I tuck a notion to come back to this or'nary country agin. Not to say nothin' agin the country neither, but the people are such ignorant ramuses, that if a feller happens to tell something that he's seen a little out of the way, they're a-winkin' and a-snickerin' at one another as if it were a lie." Here Tim cast a contemptuous and significant glance around the circle, and laying his weighty hand upon Crayon's shoulder, went on: "People that has traveled mostly knows a thing or two. Now I'll bet a hoss this gentleman has traveled some." Crayon admitted that he had traveled. "Well, now, what was the strangest country you ever was in, and what was the singularest thing you ever see?"

Crayon pondered for a moment, as if to consider the question, and then remarked that the strangest country he ever saw was the Arctic Zone, and the most surprising thing was the North Pole.

"Lord!" exclaimed Tim, "have you been thar'? It's pretty fur north, hain't it? belongs to these United States, does it?"

"It is the very tip end of the world north," replied Crayon; "and, although it does not belong to the States yet, they are getting up some filibustering parties to get hold of it as soon as possible, for the purpose of extending to its benighted inhabitants the blessings of American freedom during the winter—lights and firewood included."

"That's what I go in for," shouted Tim. "Hurrah for liberty! I'll wagon licker and provisions for 'em for nothing."

"That unhappy country has long suffered under a despotism worse than Lynch law. They have no better clothes than what they can manage to cheat the seals out of, with nothing better to eat than fish oil, such as you grease your gears with, and would consider tanners' dubbin' a prime delicacy." (Here followed a unanimous groan of commiseration.) "Besides inflicting these miseries on his own subjects, the insatiable tyrant Hiems—"

"Himes! Himes!" ejaculated Tim; "was he the Yankee feller that went in partnership with Miller about ten years ago to prophesy the eend of the world? Well, to be sure, the eend of the world wouldn't come down this way, so he went up thar' and got elected governor of it. These Yankees do beat all. I know'd one of them wonst—"

"Hold your disrespectful jaw," said the landlord, "and let the stranger talk."

Crayon went on to tell how this potentate, unmindful of our enormous navy and the wrath of country editors, insulted our flag, seized and destroyed our fishing vessels, and imprisoned for life our citizens both native and naturalized. This conduct was pronounced to be "a cussed or'nary shame." Then followed a minute description of the governor-general's palace of ice; his domestic arrangements; his superb sleigh, robed with white bearskins, and drawn by a team of reindeer; of his herds of sea-cows, and the manner in which they were milked, besides a catalogue of other wonders. What with a little natural history, and a fancy enlivened by recollections of the snow-storm, he so far outstripped the genius of the bar-room Munchausen that this worthy sat abashed and confounded; and at length, taking the shapeless, weather beaten felt from his frowzy pate, and handing it over to our hero, he sighed, "Here, stranger, I gin in; take my hat." Tim's overthrow was hailed with a shout of laughter, in which he joined with the best grace he could.

He evidently perceived, however, that he had dwindled in public estimation, and seemed puzzling his head to find some means of reinstating himself. Presently he visited his overcoat pocket, and drew forth a greasy, well-thumbed pack of cards, observing that, as thar' were no beds, they might as well amuse themselves somehow. A murmur of dissent went round the circle, which Longbow disregarded, while he gave the pack several scientific flips, and cast a significant look at the stranger. Crayon declined the challenge thus conveyed; but, being solicitous that the *entente cordiale* which now existed should not be disturbed, and to the end that his motives might not be misunderstood, he told the teamster to hand him the pack, and he would show him something which he probably had never seen before. The request was cheerfully complied with, and Crayon went on to exhibit a number of jugglers' tricks, to the great astonishment and admiration of the company. These successful performances elevated our hero to such a pitch in the public favor, that it was unanimously resolved they should order a pitcher of "hot-pot," and get drunk in honor of the occasion, whether he joined them or not.

While the savory stew was brewing, Tim went for his fiddle, and, to the practiced eye, there were unmistakable evidences of an approaching spree.

Crayon withdrew himself into a corner convenient for purposes of observation. The fiddler struck up "The Chickasaw Nation," which, with a variety of similar airs, he played with great unction. The pitcher circulated rapidly, and the party was momentarily increased by the addition of sleepers from the adjoining rooms, who had been wakened by the uproar.

As Mr. Longbow was about laying aside his instrument to rosin his throat with an additional pint of hot-pot, it occurred to him that he had been wanting in an act of courtesy usual on these occasions. Although something of a swell, a bully, and a liar, Tim was still a Virginian. Vanquished as he had been on certain points upon which he prided himself, he had too enlarged a soul to exhibit or even entertain any ill-will toward the victor. With a glass of hot-pot in one hand and the fiddle in the other, he advanced toward Crayon, and proffered the instrument, with this civil inquiry, "Perhaps, stranger, you can choke the goose yourself?" Considering the circumstances, the act was chivalric and worthy of Tim's birth-place.

One of our hero's early misfortunes was that he had been sent to college. Being naturally of an erratic and wayward disposition, he forsook the beaten track of learning, discarded the printed programme for the Sophomore year, and diligently perfected himself in the mysteries of "old sledge" and the fiddle. At the end of the year his Euclid and Græca Majora smelt as fresh as on the day they left the book-store, while he had sawed through innumerable strings of cat-gut, and thumbed to pieces pack after pack of Crehore's cards, with a perseverance which some persons might say was worthy of a better cause. The perusal of Chesterfield's Letters, and further acquaintance with the world, had long ago induced him to lay aside an accomplishment which, to say the least, is of doubtful utility to a gentleman; but it must be acknowledged, privately, he never laid eyes on a fiddle that his fingers did not itch to get hold of it. There was nothing in the surroundings there to remind him of Chesterfield, and, yielding to a natural impulse, he took the instrument, and sticking it under his chin, flourished off that brilliant extravaganza, "The Devil's Dream," in such effective style that the whole house, and especially Tim Longbow, were perfectly electrified. The excited herd stood for several moments mute and listening, then made a rush, *en masse,* upon the person of the fiddler. Before he could resist or protest, he found himself taking an Olympic promenade on the shoulders of the enthusiastic crowd.

Whether Crayon felt more like a Grecian hero or a rowdy, as he rode round and round the dusty bar-room, we have never been able to ascertain. His countenance, serene and Sphinx-like, betrayed none of the emotions of his soul, while he continued to flourish his fiddlestick with a furious zeal that would have done credit to the great Volker of the *Niebelungen Lied.* At the end of about half an hour he managed to make his escape into another part of the house, and finding there a sleeping-place, lately deserted by some fellow, he rolled himself in the blanket, and, pillowing his head on a saddle, slept soundly till morning.

Having sometimes attempted to rally Crayon on the subject of this involuntary ride, it is manifest that he does not care about alluding to it, and generally parries it with some good-humored jest.

On one occasion he changed the conversation by observing that, in some late researches which he had made, he had discovered that the fish upon which Arion is said to have ridden was not a dolphin, as commonly supposed, but a bull porpoise; and from the arguments, pictorial as well as verbal, he advanced in support of this theory, we are inclined to believe it correct.

At half past six next morning the thermometer stood at 20°; but, maugre the cold and their recent fatigue, our travelers were stirring at that early hour, *en route* for Callahan's, where they determined to breakfast, as they had ascertained it was only a few miles distant. In the light of an unclouded morning the terror of the snowstorm had vanished, and the whole country resembled a grand panoramic painting, the work of some wild, imaginative artist rather than cold reality. Field and forest were still clothed in their feathery white panoply, while rock, tree, and lowly shrub, hanging with icicles, glittered like fancy glass-work, and icy cataracts hung from the hill sides, rigid and motionless as the sparry concretions of a cave. But when the tardy sun began to illuminate the picture with his glancing rays, Crayon turned and thus addressed the inmates of the carriage:

"Look, girls! look, and enjoy it while you may. It is but an evanescent scene, but one might live for a hundred years and never look on such a sight again. Welcome the day of storm and travail! welcome the night of cold and darkness! that, like beneficent twin genii, have wrought this scene of more than earthly splendor."

"I sees de tavern," quoth Mice, "and smoke a-pourin' out of de kitchen chimbely."

" 'Tis well," sighed Crayon; "the wants of the body must not be forgotten."

Fresh, rosy, and sharp-set, our travelers stepped upon the platform at Callahan's, and in the shortest possible time thereafter were seated at a breakfast-table, which was indeed a pleasant picture in its way.

At this point in the story the editor of these papers laid down his pen, and gravely remonstrated with the narrator on the frequent recurrence of these extravagant and detailed accounts of breakfasts, dinners, and suppers. "It clogs the narrative," quoth he; "it detracts from the dignity of the subject, and gives a commonplace air to the adventures."

Porte Crayon responded with heat: "I despise your squeamish, transcendental, metaphysical dyspectic who can't eat. I have no respect for sentimentality or sick people. There must be something radically wrong either in the *morale* or *physique* of a person who does not enjoy a good meal, and whose mouth don't water at a good description. Is Walter Scott deficient in interest? and are not his best books juicy with sirloins and venison pasties? Does the eating scene between Cœur de Lion and Friar Tuck clog the narrative? Where will you find a more refreshing picture than that of the rustic repast served to the itinerant deities by old Baucis and Philemon?

Is Homer wanting in dignity? Are not his feasts of gods and heroes, his boilings of mighty chines and barbecuing of fat oxen the very essence, or, more properly, the sauce of his world-famous epic? Ah!" continued Porte, in a softened tone, "none but a mountain wanderer knows how fondly memory will cling to these daily recurring incidents of travel. All your beatification about scenery, sunrises, *et cetera,* serves very well to fill up space between my drawings, and the scraps of Latin and French that you get out of school-books to bamboozle the public into a belief that you are learned; but, depend upon it, nothing enriches a narrative like those touches of nature that would make a horse neigh with delight if he could only read."

Reflecting, probably, that in his zeal he might have been rather personal in his remarks, Crayon paused for a moment, and then, giving us a furtive wink, observed, "By the way, P——, I think there's the cold carcass of a wild turkey in the pantry; let us go down and lunch."

"Agreed."

And so the dispute ended, and the description of the breakfast at Callahan's was passed over.

As they intended to go on to the White Sulphur forthwith, the

THE STUDENT

horses were ordered immediately after breakfast, but, not appearing in due time, Crayon walked back to the stable to ascertain the cause of the delay. Hearing a voice as of some one soliloquizing, he looked through a crevice in the logs, and there, to his surprise, saw Mice seated on a heap of straw in a vacant stall. He seemed deeply immersed in the study of some difficult problem at cards, and, from time to time, dealt out hands to himself and an imaginary antagonist, and then would turn a trump, talking all the while to himself.

"Mist it dat time. Well, try agin. Ugh! ugh! Queen! Ha! dat won't do: cuss de luck! I wish I dast ask Mass' Porte to larn me how to thumb a jack dat way he does; it beats all!"

Porte slipped back to the house quietly, and sent a servant to require Mice's immediate attendance with the carriage, which soon made its appearance; and the party put themselves *en route* for the White Sulphur Springs.

The Natural Bridge

FROM Lexington our travelers pursued their journey for ten or twelve miles over an indifferent plank road, and about midday had the pleasure of lunching on cakes and beer with the old woman who keeps the toll-gate. At this point they left the main thoroughfare and turned their horses' heads eastward, toward the Natural Bridge.

A drive of five or six miles brought them to the end of their day's journey; and with baskets, shawls, and other accessories, they were soon in full possession of the old-fashioned sitting-room at the Bridge Hotel. Porte Crayon sat at one of the windows, to all appearance oblivious of the present, and humming that delectable air of Bellini's, *"Vi ravviso, O! luoghi ameni."* Had he been less abstracted and more considerate, he must have observed the fluttering, restless demeanor of his more youthful companions, for cold indeed must be that fancy, and impassive that soul, that can approach this far-famed wonder without emotion.

"Cousin, is the bridge near at hand?"

Porte started up, apologizing for his forgetfulness, and intimated to the ladies that if they would walk with him a short distance, they might have a distant glimpse of the bridge without delay. Starting from the tavern door, they followed the public road by a gentle ascent for sixty or eighty paces, when they came to a gate. Here Crayon entered, and, taking Minnie by the arm, he pushed aside the branches of an arbor vitæ, and led her forward several paces, until they reached a sort of rocky barrier.

"Look down, cousin!"

She shrieked, and would have fallen but for the support of her companion, who hastily withdrew her from the spot, and seated her, all pale and trembling, under the shade of an evergreen.

"What's the matter? What is it?" inquired the others, with alarmed eagerness.

"Oh, Porte, how could you do it! The bridge! the bridge! we're on the bridge! It was terrible!"

On hearing this, Fanny and Dora looked wildly about, as if seeking some place of refuge, and finally fled through the gate by which they had entered, and only halted when they had gained the middle of the highway.

"Come back, you silly creatures!"

"No, no, not for the world! we would not go on it again."

"Don't you know that you are on it now?"

Dora would have taken to her heels again, but Fanny stopped her. "Don't mind Porte's quizzing," said she. "Don't you see we are in the public road, and not on any bridge?"

Porte succeeded in capturing the runaways, and holding them securely before he gave the information, explained to them that they then stood over the centre of the arch, and yet so entirely hidden was the chasm which it spanned, by the natural parapets of rocks and trees, that he had himself seen persons pass over without being aware of it. Then, by dint of fair promises, he induced his captives to return to the point of view.

"No tricks, brother; no surprises!"

" 'Pon honor, none; I was too much frightened at the result of my last to try another."

He then led the ladies, one at a time, to the parapet, where on their hands and knees they ventured to look over the brink into that awful chasm which few have nerve sufficient to view from an upright position. Fanny attempted it, holding to her brother's arm, but found she could endure it only for a moment, when her dizzy brain and trembling knees warned her to desist. Crayon looked long and earnestly into the abyss, bounded by dark impending cliffs of jagged limestone, festooned with rich wreaths of arbor vitæ, the most beautiful of all the tribe of evergreens.

"Girls, come here; observe that decayed cedar stump projecting from a crevice in the rock, over the centre of the chasm there, two

THE HEROINE

hundred and twenty feet in depth by the line." It was cut or sawed off even with the top of the bridge, and presented a flat surface about twelve inches in diameter, and distant two feet or more from the parapet. "Once upon a time, so I was told, a young lady, a Miss ——, stepped out and stood with both feet on that stump. Her female friend who was with her fainted outright, while the heroine waved her scarf, and blew kisses to the beaux who stood aghast behind the parapet. When I was twenty years younger, I had the hardihood, or rather the folly, to place one foot upon that same stump, and remain in that position for some moments. I had a great mind to try it with both feet, but was restrained by the philosophic reflection that, after all, I was emulating a woman, and could only surpass her by breaking my neck, which I had no mind to do at that time, to say nothing of the probability of the whole story being a lie."

Here Porte Crayon fell into a soliloquy. "The very recollection makes me shudder now. Are my nerves less firm than of yore? or is it merely want of usage? 'The native hue of resolution sicklied o'er with the pale cast of thought;' or, as plain people say, maybe I've got more sense now!"

Crayon took a stick and commenced poking the stump, which appeared to be entirely decayed. "It wouldn't bear stepping on now, at any rate," he muttered. "It is a mere shell."

"Brother, what are you meditating? Surely not to set foot on that stump?"

"No, child, nothing of the kind.

'Days of my youth, I mourn not your decay.'

Days of fevered blood and sickly fancies, of restless anticipation and disappointed hopes, of cankered blossoms and sour fruit, of warring with phantoms and worshiping of shadows. Wretched indeed must be his manhood who looks back with regret, and would recall the days of his youth. Probably few would sincerely wish to roll back the wheels of time, and the frequent expression of the sentiment is nothing more than one of the forms of cant with which the world is pleased to express its chronic discontent. For me, thrice blessed is the calm current of maturity; and one of the chiefest joys of manhood is the reflection that I am no longer a boy—that my bark has descended the headlong brawling torrent, bruised and battered indeed, but still afloat, to return no more."

Whether the foregoing are Mr. Crayon's standing sentiments, or whether they were the result of his peculiar position at the time, we can not positively say. But any man who is commander-in-chief of a good carriage and a pair of stout horses, the possessor of a sound stomach and a plump purse, and sole guardian to three uncommonly pretty and interesting girls, two of them cousins to boot, may be excused for speaking in praise of that particular time of life, and in disparagement of all others. Ah! old fox, which of those sweet cousins was it that, some days back, possibly in Lexington, leaned softly on thine arm, and said "she detested boys?" and wherefore, since that day, hast thou combed thy beard so broad, descanted so complacently and poetically on the superiority of a full-blown intellect, and been at such pains to pluck two coarse gray hairs from each of thine eyebrows?

It appearing that there still remained several hours of daylight, our friends determined to visit the bridge below, where they were assured they might enjoy the grandeur of the scene unmixed with terror.

Following their leader down a rapidly descending path which wound around the abrupt point of a hill, they presently entered a grove of noble evergreens, and on emerging from this all stood still with one accord. In front and below them was the yawning gorge, rugged and wild, clothed as it were in sombre shadows, through which the light glanced from the cascades of Cedar Creek with faint and trembling sheen. Above, with its outline of tree and rock cutting sharp against the blue sky, rose the eternal arch; so massive, yet so light it springs, uniting its tremendous buttresses high in mid air, while beneath its stern shadow the eye can mark, in fair perspective, rocks, trees, hill-tops, and distant sailing clouds. There are few objects in nature which so entirely fill the soul as this bridge in its unique and simple grandeur. In consideration of the perfection of its adaptation to circumstances, the simplicity of its design, the sublimity of its proportions, the spectator experiences a fullness of satisfaction which familiarity only serves to increase; and while that sentiment of awe inseparable from the first impression may be weakened or disappear altogether, wonder and admiration grow with time.

Continuing their descent, our friends reached the banks of the stream, and passed beneath the arch, pausing at every step to feast their eyes upon the varying aspects in which the scene was presented. Crossing Cedar Creek under the bridge, they gained a point above on the stream, from whence the view is equally fine with that first obtained from the descending path on the opposite side. This picture exhibits the turn of the arch to greater advantage. Then the flanking row of embattled cliffs, their sides wreathed with dark foliage, and their bases washed by the stream, forms a noble addition to the scene.

The average height of these cliffs is about two hundred and fifty feet, the height of the bridge about two hundred and twenty. The span of the arch is ninety-three feet, its average width eighty, and its thickness in the centre fifty-five feet. It does not cross the chasm precisely at right angles, but in an oblique direction, like what engineers call a skew bridge. While the cliffs are perpendicular, and in some places overhanging, the abutments under the arch approach until their bases are not more than fifty feet apart. At ordinary times the stream does not occupy more than half this space, although from its traces and water-marks it frequently sweeps through in an unbroken volume, extending from rock to rock. The top of the bridge is covered with a clay soil to the depth of several feet, which nourishes a considerable growth of trees, generally of the evergreen species. These, with masses of rock, serve to form natural parapets along the

THE NATURAL BRIDGE

sides, as if for greater security, and entirely obscure the view of the chasm from the passer. It is now further protected by lines of board fencing, placed there by the owner of the property. Although this precaution is rather distasteful to a lover of the picturesque. yet it detracts but little from the general view, every thing being on so grand a scale that they are scarcely observed.

As our friends became familiarized with the objects around them, conversation began to resume its sway, and Crayon, as cicerone of the party, began to recall the traditionary anecdotes and minor wonders with which every place of this sort abounds. He pointed out the route by which a man is said to have climbed up the cliffs, and not the bridge, as is commonly supposed. He also robbed the story of its superhuman attributes by expressing his belief that any cool-headed man accustomed to climbing—a sailor, for instance—could do the same thing easily. He had even attempted it himself; but on attaining an elevation of thirty or forty feet, he began to perceive how things looked "to a man up a tree," and concluded to descend. He then pointed out the spread eagle which is pictured on the under side of the arch, scratching the eyes out of the British Lion, all of which the ladies were patriotic enough to see plainly; although Dora, who had lately been reading history, puzzled Crayon by asking whether he thought the picture was there before the Revolution. He got out of the difficulty by saying that if it was there prior to the separation, it must have been prophetic; but as it was formed by the growth of moss, it might have come out since the wars. Indeed, by looking a while steadily, and allowing a little latitude to the fancy, one may see a great many things that hitherto have not been re-marked. For example, in the eagle's other claw there appears to be a scroll upon which is mapped a number of the golden provinces of a neighboring republic, while she appears to be endeavoring to swallow a long, irregularly-shaped object that resembles an island.

"Your eagle," quoth Fanny, "seems to be something of a cormo-rant."

Porte went on to point out the spot where Washington is said to have written the initials of his name, although he confessed he had never been able to make them out. After considering the spot attentively, Fanny declared she did not believe that any mortal could have reached it without a ladder, and Dora said that, while she knew from her history that Washington was a great general and statesman, she never heard that he could climb better than other people. Minnie observed that, for her part, she had always felt averse to hearing such stories about Washington, or to believing he had ever done any thing so childish. It seemed rather a derogation from the dignity of his character, who had written his name so high upon

"The steep where Fame's proud temple shines afar."

As they were grouped around the hostel fire that night, Crayon intimated to the ladies that he might be persuaded to relate an adventure which befell him in the neighborhood during his first visit to the bridge. As the proposition met with cordial approbation, he commenced as follows:

"In the fall of 1834 I made a pedestrian tour—to which you have sometimes heard me allude—in company with my friend, Jack Rawlins. Our route was nearly the same which we have followed, and on our arrival here we were entertained in the room which we now occupy. I remember every thing as if it had been but yesterday. The house was temporarily in charge of a couple of youths not much older than their guests, and who, for the sake of convenience, I shall call Bob and Tom Johnson, although, in truth, I do not recollect their real names. But you must bear in mind that the names are the only fictions made use of in the narrative. While we were studying the bridge, I heard, with emulous breast, of the feats of General Washington, Miss ——, and the nameless man who climbed the cliff, and was burning to write my name somewhere, whether in the Temple of Fame or the Booth of Folly it mattered little, for at that age I ranked the heroine of the stump and the successful cliff-climber with the founder of universities and the leader of armies.

"One night the elder of our entertainers happened to speak of a wonderful cavern that was in the neighborhood. He described it as a great opening like a well, near the top of a hill several miles distant. It had never been explored, nor even fathomed, and was an object of mingled curiosity and terror to all who knew of it, and many were the stories and traditions connected with its fame. It was said that, during the Revolutionary war, chests of money had been thrown into it to secure them from Tarleton's thieving dragoons, and the owners, having been slain in battle, had, of course, never returned to claim the treasures. Men and cattle that disappeared from the country were all accredited to this mysterious hole, and murderers were suspected of throwing the bodies of their victims therein for better concealment, although Bob frankly acknowledged that since his day there had been no one murdered thereabout that he knew of. He went on to say that on many a Sunday he had amused himself, with some of the bolder spirits of the neighborhood, in throwing rocks and logs into its yawning mouth, and listening with awe to the hollow crash and booming reverberations that followed. 'No one has ever dared to descend,' said he; 'and, indeed, I should be sorry to see any one undertake it.' My feelings during this narrative resembled those of St. George when he found the dragon's nest. Here was a dragon indeed worthy of my daring. 'Bah!' said I, affecting care-lessness—for I was bursting with anxiety lest some one might go down into the hole before I could get to it in the morning—'Pshaw! I will descend and explore this wonderful place, if you will only point it out to me to-morrow morning.' The young man looked at me with an expression of mingled terror and incredulity. Jack Rawlins began to protest, when Tom laughingly remarked that he need not be uneasy; he'd warrant that I'd go no farther than the mouth. 'There, you've settled the matter,' cried Jack, in despair; 'he'd go now, if it was the mouth of the bottomless pit.'

"Bob took an early opportunity to call me aside, and with a countenance playing between eagerness and doubt, asked if I seriously intended to do what I had said. I assured him of my determination. 'Well, stranger, if perhaps you should find those chests of money—' Here he paused warily. 'Oh, we'll divide, of course,' said I, 'we four.' 'Certainly,' he replied, with delight; 'that's no more than fair. We will show you the way and assist in letting you down; but we must keep dark about it, for the place belongs to a stingy old fellow, who would go crazy if he heard of our enterprise, and would claim every thing we might happen to find.' Although I set but little store upon the imagined treasures, I was ready enough to amuse myself with the golden hopes of my host or to bedevil any stingy old fellow at a venture, and it was arranged in full council that we should start after an early breakfast next morning.

"Whether I slept well or ill, or what was the character of my dreams that night, I do not remember; but I do recollect that in the cool of the morning, during the secret preparation of ropes and lights, some awkward misgivings begin to sneak into the castle of my determination. But I was fully committed, and my native pride, assisted by the stimulus of a rapid walk of several miles, brought me to the scene of action in such high condition that I surveyed the black mouth of the awful pit without a tremor.

"'Young man,' said Bob Johnson, significantly, 'I reckon you'll not venture?' I stiffened up, and to this implied doubt made scornful answer, 'Do you think, sir, that I would walk all this distance, with a pack of ropes and candles, merely to look down into a hole in the ground? Get your ropes ready.'

"The bed-cords were unrolled, and a short stout stick, like a well-digger's horse, tied to the end of one of them. A couple of sound fence-rails were then procured and cautiously laid across the centre of the opening, which was eight or ten feet in diameter. In the mean time I had taken off my coat, tied a handkerchief about my waist, when Jack Rawlins suggested that although we had taken the precaution to measure the depth of the cavern, we had forgotten to try whether it contained bad air. This suggestion was immediately acted upon. The lantern with a lighted candle was attached to the end of a cord and lowered until it touched the bottom, from whence it was drawn up after a few minutes, still burning. The experiment was reckoned satisfactory. Jack Rawlins shook hands with me and said, 'Well, Porte, I've done my best to prevent you going on this fool's errand; all I can do now is to wish you good luck.' I was getting impatient, and chid my lagging assistants, who seemed loth to begin; but at length every thing was arranged. I bestrode the stick and gave the coil of rope to the two Johnsons; another rope I knotted around my waist, put it in charge of Rawlins, and then, with lantern in hand, slid to the opening. Steadying myself with one hand on the rock and the other on the rail, I swung off, crying, 'Now keep cool, boys, and lower away!'

"Down I went steadily enough for a time, griping the cords with one hand, the lantern with the other, and pushing myself clear of the black, slimy rocks with my feet and elbows. For the first thirty or forty feet the opening was walled around like a well, but presently I swung clear of every thing; the cords, which were new, began to untwist, and I whizzed round like a teetotum. 'Lower away, boys!'

I shouted, for I had become so dizzy that I could neither see nor hear. After a time I stopped with a bump. 'The rope's run out!' cried a voice so high and faint that it sounded like the note of a wild goose. 'All's well! I have arrived safe.'

"As I recovered from my dizziness, I disengaged myself from the ropes and looked about me. I was seated upon the apex of a pyramid of mossy rocks and decayed logs, which rose in the centre of a black cavern of unknown dimensions. I seemed to be walled around with thick darkness, and the opening through which I had descended shone above me like a moon in an inky firmament. Taking the candle, I descended from my resting place and proceeded to explore my newly-discovered empire. The feeble rays of my tallow dip revealed nothing more than an irregular floor of moist clay and walls of limestone rock, covered here and there with a few dull, dirty incrustations. After groping about two thirds of the way around this circular hall, I found an arched opening about the size of an ordinary doorway. Into this passage I penetrated with difficulty for twenty or thirty yards, when my heels flew from under me, and I slid, I can not tell how far, down into what seemed, by the sense of touch, to be a bed of soft mud. It is needless to say I lost my candle in the fall, and was left in utter darkness. Here was a predicament for a hero. Above, below, on every side, I felt nothing but slimy mud. I feared to move, lest I might sink into some deeper quagmire.

"I was not so much alarmed at first, but, as my body began to chill, my heart sunk with the temperature of my blood. I began to calculate the chances of escape. 'If I am not forthcoming in due time, will Jack Rawlins come to my assistance? will any one come? Portentous question. Is not this cavern the bugbear of the country, and will my disappearance serve to allay that terror?' Oh, powers of mud, the heroic spirit was subdued within me—no! not all subdued; the idea occurred to me that possibly a cry for help might reach the ears of my companions and hasten my relief. But pride forbade; I resolved to die first.

"Anon I began to fancy that I could see the walls of my prison and the passage through which I had fallen, and soon the doubt brightened into reality. My eyes, becoming accustomed to the darkness, had begun to take in the feeble light that was reflected from the main cavern. Cautiously I crawled up the slippery ascent, and in a few minutes re-entered the hall, which appeared so light that I could see over its whole extent without the aid of a candle. I scraped myself as well as I could, and then looked about for the chests of gold and dead men's bones. My search was unsuccessful, and I concluded they must be concealed under the pyramid of rubbish which had been thrown down the opening, and for aught I know they may be there at this day. I took no very accurate observation as to the size of the cavern, but guessed it was about one hundred feet in diameter, the same as its depth, which we ascertained by measuring the ropes.

"I called to my friends above that I wished to ascend, and received the prompt reply that all was ready. Mounting my wooden horse, I carelessly drew the other cord around my body without even tying it, and ordered them to hoist away. No sooner was I clear of the bottom than the spinning motion recommenced, and continued with such rapidity that I presently lost all cognizance of things around me. A sharp bump on the head advised me of my arrival at the ledge, and I eagerly grasped at the rock, but the projection shelled off and crashed into the gulf below. 'Pull, boys, pull!' I was drawn up several feet; then there was a pause, and I was lowered again out of reach of the rock, and the dangerous whirling was renewed. Dizzy as I was, I divined the cause of the difficulty. My friends were working at the two ropes on opposite sides of the pit, and the new cords had become twisted together until they could no longer separate them, and I consequently remained dangling in the air. Nor was this all. In their fright and confusion the Johnsons threw down their rope, and seemed ready to take to their heels. Rawlins, however, planted himself against a rock, and with straining sinews held on until he perceived the stone against which he was propped slowly moving from its position. It lay upon the declivity near the mouth of the cave, and if it had rolled must inevitably have gone down the opening. Just at that moment they heard my order to put the ropes together and all pull on the same side. Such was their want of presence of mind that this simple idea had not occurred to them before. The Johnsons seized the cord, ran to the other side, and the trio pulled with renewed vigor. With such energy was I now dragged up, that my knees, elbows, and shoulders were bruised and lacerated by the sharp rocks, and when I was within twenty feet of the top the stick upon which I rode slipped from under me, and I held on by my hands alone. Upon that grip hung life or death. I knew it. The blood started from my finger ends, but my nerves were firm. Presently I found myself landed in the upper regions, and, before I relaxed my grasp, or my half-phrensied comrades considered me safe, I was dragged a hundred feet from the mouth of the cavern. For several minutes all were silent, and sat pale and exhausted, panting like overdone hounds. The first greeting I received was from Bob Johnson. 'You blasted fool,' cried he, 'I've a mind to club you within an inch of your life. I never was so scared.' Tom swore he would not pull another man up from that hole for all the gold in Rockbridge.

"As for me, I sat for some time in a state of profound physical and mental apathy, the usual result of excitement and violent exertion. When at length I rose to start homeward, I found that I moved with difficulty, and could not put on my coat without assistance. Although I managed to walk back to the hotel, it was several days before I could use my hands as usual. At supper I was ravenous, and the desperate efforts I made to handle my knife and fork were ludicrous enough.

"And thus ends the story of that perilous adventure."

"And," exclaimed Fanny, "I never heard of any thing so absurd. I don't wonder the young man threatened to club you. I was myself ready to boil over with indignation at your obstinacy in going down.'

"Ah! Fanny, you women don't understand these things. A certain amount of glorification is necessary to boys as well as nations. Boys must slay their dragons, and nations have their wars. If their hands and heads ache for it, so much the better; they are both likely to be more rational, at least for some time afterward."

"And did you never think of it afterward, cousin, and shudder at the dangers you escaped?" asked Minnie.

"Yes, indeed, and for many a night after I had evil dreams; sometimes fancying I was a spider swinging by a single invisible thread, and at others a mud-turtle, lying on my back and smothering in my native element."

"And what had your friends, the Johnsons, to say about the money?"

"They scarcely referred to the subject afterward. Their curiosity was satisfied, and they seemed sufficiently pleased with the termination of the affair.

"Now, Dora," said Porte Crayon, pinching the sleeper's dimpled cheek, "what comments have you to make on my story?"

"Gracious!" exclaimed she, with a start, "I must have been asleep."

"You dropped off about the time I was floundering in the mud at the bottom of the cave. Thank you, Cousin Dimple, for your attention and sympathy with my dangers and afflictions."

"Ah! Porte, excuse me; I couldn't help it. But how did you get out of that dreadful place? I must have gone off in a dream, for I thought you had found a great many chests of gold and jewelry, and beautiful shawls, and that you had presented each of us with charming sets of pearls, diamonds, and mosaic—bracelets, ear-rings, and all—and such splendid Turkish shawls, and silks of such lovely colors."

"With such a dream as that, sweet cousin, you were better entertained than in listening to me. Good-night, girls."

As they retired, Fanny struck up, rather appropriately,

"Go thou and dream o'er that joy in thy slumber."

Next day our friends revisited each point of view above and below the bridge with increased gratification, while Crayon employed himself in the attempt to portray its most striking features upon tinted paper. This, he avers, can not be accomplished by mortal hand; for while he acknowledges he has seen several sketches that rendered the general outline and even minute details with great accuracy, he never saw one that conveyed, even in a remote degree, any idea of the majestic grandeur of the original. One of the most satisfactory views is obtained from a hill side about half a mile below the bridge. From this point the perfection of the arch is more remarkable; and there is a fine view of the hill, which, a short distance to the right of its apex, is cleft to its base by this singular chasm.

The most rational hypothesis which has been advanced in regard to the formation of this wonderful structure is that this hill was formerly perforated by one of the limestone caverns common in this region, and that by the combined action of water and force of some earthquake the superincumbent masses have fallen in, leaving the chasm open to the day, except where the arch now stands.

Another view well worth attention is that from the cliffs in the tavern yard. These upper views are perhaps more impressive than any other, as combining more of the terrible with the sublime.

It was doubtless from this quarter that Mice got his impressions, when, in reply to some questions, he told Miss Fanny "it was de quarest place he had seed yit," and he supposed "it mought have been built by the devil."

As the Piersons, man and wife, are the most kindly and obliging of hosts, the table delightfully served, and, according to the coachman's account, the oats are unexceptionable, it may be well to leave our travelers to their repose for a season.

The Great Valley

THERE is perhaps no fairer land beneath the sun than that section of Virginia called the Great Valley. Bounded by the North Mountain on the northwest, and the Blue Ridge on the southeast, it extends across the state from the Potomac to the southern line, nearly two hundred and fifty miles in length, and varying from twenty to forty in breadth. Through its northern portion the Shenandoah pursues its regular and orderly course along the base of the Ridge, while, farther south, the Upper James, the Staunton, and New Rivers wind in tortuous channels across the Valley, cutting sheer through the mountain barriers east and west, and flowing in opposite directions toward their respective receivers.

Leaving to the geographer and political economist the task of setting forth the agricultural and mineral resources of this happy region, its healthful and invigorating atmosphere, its abundance, even to superfluity, in all the good things that make it a desirable residence for man, we turn, with the instincts of painter and poet, from advantages more strictly utilitarian, to rejoice in the matchless gift of beauty with which Heaven has endowed this "delicious land"—not the evanescent bloom of flowering savannas, nor the wild but chilling grandeur of Alpine rocks and snows. This is a picture—soft and luxuriant, yet enduring as the everlasting hills—of rolling plains and rich woodlands, watered by crystal streams, enriched with rare and curious gems wrought by the plastic hand of Nature, as if in wanton sport, sparkling waterfalls, fairy caverns, the unique and wonderous Bridge, all superbly set in an azure frame of mountains, beautiful always, and sometimes rising to sublimity.

The first authentic account we have of the discovery of this Valley is from an expedition which crossed the Ridge in 1710, planned and commanded by Alexander Spotswood, then governor of the colony of Virginia. In noticing this event, Burke, the historian, says: "An opinion had long prevailed that these mountains presented an ever-lasting barrier to the ambition of the whites. Their great height, their prodigious extent, their rugged and horrid appearance, sug-gested to the imagination undefined images of terror. The wolf, the bear, the panther, and the Indian were the tenants of these forlorn and inaccessible precipices."

To one familiar with mountain scenery these sounding phrases seem like gross exaggeration when applied to the wooded and gentle slopes of the Blue Ridge, which seldom rise beyond a thousand or twelve hundred feet above its base. But every thing in the world is estimated by comparison, and the good people from the lower country, in the early times, doubtless viewed this modest ridge with mingled awe and wonder.

It may also afford some entertainment to the western Virginian to receive the following interesting piece of information from a book, pleasantly entitled "Modern History; or, the present State of all Nations," printed at Dublin in 1793: "There are no mountains in Virginia, unless we take in the Apalachian Mountains, which separate it from Florida." This, too, in a volume published twenty-nine years after Spottswood's expedition, and several years after actual settlements had been made in the Valley.

As early as 1732, adventurous emigrants from New York, New Jersey, and Pennsylvania had made their way to the newly-explored region; and during the reign of James the Second the Valley settle-ments received considerable accessions from the north of Ireland.

Thus the Scotch-Irish and German elements form the basis of the Valley population, and the manners and characteristics of the people, although modified by the connection and intermixture with the lower country, still very much resemble those of the Middle States.

In following our travelers on their interesting tour, we have traversed consecutively the counties of Berkeley, Frederick, Warren, Shenandoah, Rockingham, and Augusta. Thence passing the North Mountain boundary at Jennings's Gap, we have visited Bath, Alleghany, and Greenbrier, in the Alleghany region, and, returning to the Valley by Clifton Forge, have passed through Rockbridge and Botetourt. In this last-mentioned county we again overtake the carriage, toiling slowly up the western slope of the Blue Ridge.

The company, as usual, were on foot, and we find Porte Crayon in conversation with some emigrants who had halted by the road side to cook their midday meal. Addressing himself to the man of the party with jocular familiarity, he desired to know if people were getting too thick to thrive below the Ridge, or if he had fallen out with the Governor, that he was going to leave the Old Commonwealth. The emigrant replied civilly that, although there might be room for a few more in his county, yet, while there, he had only been a renter and not a proprietor. Having realized a few hundred dollars by his labor, he had invested it in purchasing a homestead where lands were cheaper if not better than in his old neighborhood. He, moreover, informed Crayon that he by no means meditated giving up his allegiance to his native state, but was going to settle in Nicholas County, which he described as a Land of Promise—pleasant, fertile, and abounding in fish and game.

Philosophy reasons, Prudence frowns, but Instinct governs after all. "A rolling stone gathers no moss," says the wise grandam, giving her spinning-wheel a whirl. "A bird in the hand is worth two in the bush," observes grandpap, drawing his purse-strings close, and tying them in a hard knot. But who ever saw a stone that would not roll if it had an opportunity, or a youngster who would not cut up his little fish for bait to catch a big one withal?

"My friend, may you prosper in your new home," said Crayon, with animation. "Indeed, I am half envious of your fortune, especially the hunting and fishing, for I would rather live in that country in a log hut than dwell in marble halls; I mean more particularly during the summer and fall."

"To be sure," rejoined the emigrant, "you might find the winter kind o' lonesome out thar'."

"I am glad to hear, however, that you are not going to leave Virginia, for," continued Crayon, "I don't like the idea of building up new states in the Far West when the old ones are scarcely half finished. Why are men hurrying away to the shores of the Pacific to seek for homes, while there exist extensive and fertile districts within our own borders, as pure and intact in their virginity as the vales of the Rocky Mountains or the banks of the Columbia? I believe the true secret of this restlessness is, that the dreamers are always in hopes of finding some *El Dorado* where they may live and get rich without work."

"The stranger is right," interrupted the sallow matron, who had overheard the conversation, and who seemed particularly struck by the last observation. "I always was set agin the Fur West, for I've been told it's a mighty hard country on wimmen and hosses, and easy on men and dogs; and I told *him,* thar, that I wouldn't agree to leave the state on no account."

Crayon did not fail to compliment madam on this manifestation of her spirit and good sense, and remarked, further, that women in general were more sincere in their patriotism than men, and if it were not for the care of the children, that kept them at home, they would, in all probability make better soldiers. "I could tell you a story about one Sally Jones, in our part of the country, somewhat to the point. If all our Virginia girls were of the same stamp, these vacant districts would soon be filled up, and the prosperity of the Old Commonwealth fixed on the most reliable and permanent basis."

A story illustrating so important a principle in political economy could not be passed over, and Crayon was requested to continue his discourse, which he did as follows:

"Nathan Jones, a small farmer in our vicinity, had a daughter, as pretty and buxom a lass as ever thumped buttermilk in a churn; and whether you saw her carrying eggs to market on the flea-bitten mare, or helping to stir apple-butter at a boiling frolic, or making a long reach at a quilting, or sitting demurely in the log meeting-house on a Sunday—in short, wherever you saw her, she always looked as pretty, if not prettier, than she had ever done before.

"Notwithstanding her attractions, it will scarcely be credited that Sally had reached the mature age of eighteen without an avowed suiter. Admirers, nay, lovers she had by the score; and whenever liquor was convenient, many a sober youth got drunk because of her, and many a sighing bachelor would willingly have given his riding-horse, or even his share in Dad's farm, for her. There was, indeed, no lack of will on their part; the difficulty was in mustering up courage to make the proposal. Mankind seemed, for once, to be impressed with a proper sense of its own unworthiness. Now, far be it from any one to infer from this that Sally was prudish or unapproachable. On the contrary, she was as good-humored, as comely, and disposed to be as loving as she was lovable. Poor Sally! It is a great misfortune for a girl to be too handsome—almost as great as to be too ugly. There she was, sociable and warm-hearted as a pigeon, amiable as a turtle-dove, looking soft encouragement, as plainly as maiden modesty permitted, to her bashful company of admirers, who dawdled about her, twiddling their thumbs, biting the bark off their riding-switches, and playing a number of other sheepish tricks, but saying never a word to the purpose.

> " 'Either he fears his fate too much,
>   Or his desert is small,
> Who dares not put it to the touch,
>   And win or lose it all.'

"Sally was entering on her nineteenth year, when she was one day heard to observe that men were the meanest, slowest, cowardliest, or'nariest creatures—in short, good for nothing but to lie under an apple-tree with their mouths open, and wait until the apples dropped into them.

"This observation was circulated from mouth to mouth, and, like the riddle of the Sphinx, was deeply pondered by Sally's lovers. If any of them had wit enough to solve its meaning, certainly no one had pluck enough to prove the answer.

"Not of this poor-spirited crowd was Sam Bates, a stalwart youth, who stood, in winter, six feet two inches in his stockings (in summer he didn't wear any). Sam was not handsome in the ordinary sense of the term. He was freckled, had a big mouth, and carroty hair. His feet—but no matter; he usually bought number fourteen and a half boots, because they fitted him better than sevens or eights. Sam was a wagon-maker by profession, owned a flourishing shop and several hundred acres of unimproved land, which secured to him the reputation of independence. For the rest, he was a roystering blade, a good rider, a crack shot with the rifle, and an accomplished fiddler. Bold to the confines of impudence, he was a favorite of the fair; with a heart as big as his foot, and a fist like a sledge-hammer, he was the acknowledged cock of the walk, and *preux chevalier* of the pine-hill country.

"Mr. Bates met Sally Jones for the first time at a quilting, and in sixty seconds after sight he had determined to court her. He sat beside her as she stitched, and even had the audacity to squeeze her hand under the quilt. Truth is mighty, and must be told. Although Sally did resent the impertinence by a stick with her needle, she was not half so indignant as she ought to have been. I dare not say she was pleased, but perhaps I should not be far from the truth if I did. It is undeniable that, the more gentle and modest a woman is, the more she admires courage and boldness in the other sex. Sally blushed every time her eyes met those of her new beau, and that was as often as she looked up. As for Sam, the longer he gazed the deeper he sunk in the mire of love, and by the end of the evening his heart and his confidence were both completely overwhelmed. As he undertook to see Sally home, he felt a numbness in his joints that was entirely new to him, and when he tried to make known his sentiments, as he had previously determined, he found his heart was so swelled up that it closed his throat, and he couldn't utter a word.

" 'What a darned cussed sneak I was!' groaned Sam, as he turned that night on his sleepless pillow. 'What's come over me that I can't speak my mind to a pretty gal without a-chokin'? O Lord! but she is too pretty to live on this airth. Well, I'm a-goin' to church with her to-morrow, and if I don't fix matters afore I git back, drat me.'

"It is probable Sam Bates had never hearkened to the story of 'Rasselas, Prince of Abyssinia,' or he would have been less credulous while thus listening to the whispers of fancy, and less ready to take it for granted that the deficiencies of the day would be supplied by the morrow. To-morrow came, and in due time Mr. Bates, tricked off in a bran-new twelve-dollar suit of Jews' clothes, was on his way to meeting beside the beautiful Sally. His horse, bedecked with a new fair leather bridle and a new saddle with brass stirrups, looked as gay as his master. As they rode up to the meeting-house door, Sam could not forbear casting a triumphant glance at the crowd of Sally's adorers that stood around, filled with mortification and envy at his successful audacity. Sally's face was roseate with pleasure and bashfulness.

" 'Stop a minute, now, Miss Sally; I'll jist git down and lift ye off.'

"Sam essayed to dismount, but in so doing found that both feet were hopelessly fast in the stirrups. His face swelled and reddened like a turkey gobbler's. In vain he twisted and kicked; the crowd was expectant; Sally was waiting. 'Gosh darn the steerup!' exclaimed Sam, endeavoring to break the leathers with his desperate kicks. At this unwonted exclamation, Sally looked up and saw her beau's predicament. The by-standers began to snicker. Sally was grieved and indignant. Bouncing out of her saddle, in a twinkling she handed her entrapped escort a stone. 'Here, Sammy, chunk your foot out with this!'

"Oh, Sally Jones! into what an error did your kind heart betray you, to offer this untimely civility in the presence of the assembled county—admirers, rivals, and all!

"Sam took the stone and struck a frantic blow at the pertinacious stirrup, but, missing his aim, it fell with crashing force upon a soft corn that had come from wearing tight boots. 'Whoa, darn ye!' cried he, losing all control of himself, and threatening to beat his horse's brains out with the stone.

" 'Don't strike the critter, Sammy,' said old Jones; 'you'll gin him the poll evil; but jist let me ongirth the saddle, and we'll git you loose in no time.'

"In short, the saddle was unbuckled, and Sam dismounted with his feet still fast in the stirrups, looking like a criminal in foothopples. With some labor he pulled off his boots, squeezed them out of the stirrups, and pulled them on again. The tender Sally stood by, all the while manifesting the kindest concern; and when he was finally extricated, she took his arm and walked him into church. But this unlucky adventure was too much for Sam; he sneaked out of meeting during the first prayer, pulled off his boots, and rode home in his stockings.

"From that time Sam Bates disappeared from society. Literally and metaphorically, he shut up shop and hung up his fiddle. He did not take to liquor, like a fool, but took to his axe, and cleared I don't know how many acres of rugged, heavy-timbered land, thereby increasing the value of his tract to the amount of several hundred dollars.

"Sally indirectly sent him divers civil messages, intimating that she took no account of that little accident at the meeting-house, and at length ventured on a direct present of a pair of gray yarn stockings, knit with her own hands. But, while every effort to win him back to the world was unsuccessful, the yarn stockings were a great comfort in his self-imposed exile. Sam wore them continually, not on his feet, as some matter-of-fact booby might suppose, but in his bosom; and often, during the intervals of his work in the lonely clearing, would he draw them out and ponder on them until a big tear gathered in his eye. 'Oh, Sally Jones! Sally Jones! if I had only had the spunk to have courted ye Saturday night, instead of waiting till Sunday morning, things might have been different!' and then he would pick up his axe, and whack it into the next tree with the energy of despair.

"At length the whole country was electrified by the announcement that 'Farmer Jones had concluded to sell out and go West.' On the day appointed for the sale there could not have been less than a hundred horses tethered in his barn-yard. Sam Bates was there, looking as uneasy as a pig in a strange cornfield.

"Sally might have been a little thinner than usual, just enough to heighten rather than diminish her charms. It was generally known that she was averse to moving West; in fact, she took no pains to conceal her sentiments on the subject, and her pretty eyes were evidently red with recent weeping. She looked mournfully around at each familiar object. The old homestead, with its chunked and daubed walls; the cherry-trees under which she had played in childhood; the flowers she had planted; and then to see the dear old furniture auctioned off—the churn, the apple-butter pot, the venerable quilting-frame, the occasion of so many social gatherings. But harder than all was it when her own white cow was put up—her pet that, when a calf, she had saved from the butcher—it was too much, and the tears trickled afresh down Sally's blooming cheeks.

" 'Ten dollars! ten dollars for the cow!'

" 'Fifty dollars!' shouted Bates.

" 'Why, Sammy,' whispered a prudent neighbor, 'she hain't worth twenty, at the outside.'

" 'I'll gin fifty for her,' replied Sam, doggedly.

"Now, when Sally heard of this piece of gallantry, she must needs thank the purchaser for the compliment, and commend Sukey to his especial kindness. Then she extended her plump hand, when Sam seized with such a devouring grip that the little maiden could scarcely suppress a scream. She did suppress it, however, that she might hear whether he had any thing further to say, but she was disappointed. He turned away dumb, swallowing, as it were, great hunks of grief as big as dumplings. When every thing was sold off and dinner was over, the company disposed itself about the yard in groups, reclining on the grass, or seated on benches and dismantled furniture. The conversation naturally turned on the events of the day and the prospects of the Jones family, and it was unanimously voted a cussed pity that so fine a girl as Sally should be permitted to leave the country so evidently against her will.

" 'Hain't none of you sneaking whelps the sperit to stop her?' asked the white-headed miller, addressing a group of young bachelors lying near. The louts snickered, turned over, whispered to each other, but no one showed any disposition to try the experiment.

"The sun was declining in the west. Some of those who lived at a distance were already gone to harness up their horses. To-morrow the belle of Cacapon Valley would be on her way to Missouri. Just then Sally rushed from the house, with a face all excitement, a step all determination. Arrived in the middle of the yard, she mounted the reversed apple-butter kettle: 'I don't want to go West, I don't—I don't want to leave Old Virginny; and I won't leave, if there's a man among ye that has spunk enough to ask me to stay.'

"But where is Southern chivalry? withered beneath the sneers of cold-blooded malignity? choked by the maxims of dollar-jingling prudence? distanced on the circular race-course of progress? bankrupt through the tricks of counterfeiting politicians? Deluded querist, no! Like a strong and generous lion it sleeps—sleeps so soundly that even apes may grimace and chatter insults in its face, and pull hairs from its tail with impunity; but give it a good hard poke, and you will hear a roar that will make the coward tremble and the brave prudent.

"Hearken to the sequel of Sally Jones:

"Scarcely had she finished her patriotic address when there was a general rush. The less active were trampled over like puffed goat-skins at a bacchanalian festival: 'Miss Sally, I axes you;' 'Miss Sally, I spoke first;' 'I bespeaks her for my son Bill,' squeaked an octogenarian, struggling forward to seize her arm. To hide her confusion, Sally covered her face with her apron, when she felt a strong arm thrown round her, and heard a stentorian voice shout, 'She's mine, by gauley!'

"Sam Bates cleared a swath as if he had been in a grain-field, bore his unresisting prize into the house, and slammed the door on the cheering crowd.

"The wedding came off that night, and on the following morning Sam rode home, driving his white cow before and carrying his wife behind him."

Porte Crayon took his leave and hastened up the road. He overtook his companions just as they were crossing a brook that came brawling down through a gorge in the mountains.

As they tarried on the bank, Minnie remarked that the brook reminded her of Passage Creek, in the Fort Mountains.

"Truly it does," said Crayon; "and the resemblance recalls a pretty allusion which you made at the time we crossed it to Undines, water-spirits, or some such animals, which I thought very poetic, and worthy of being versified."

"Ah! cousin, do by all means write me some verses; you know I adore poetry. The piece shall be set to music, and Fanny will sing it."

"I never heard that Cousin Porte could write poetry," said Dora, innocently.

Porte, who had hitherto made a show of resistance, appeared to be piqued by this remark, and, seating himself upon a rock, he drew forth pencil and paper with an expression that seemed to say, I'll show you, Miss, in a few minutes, whether I can write verses or not. Crayon whittled his pencil with a thoughtful and abstracted air. "This scene," said he, "does very much resemble the other in its general features, but the season is far advanced, and nature wears a drearier aspect. Yet the fresh beauty which she has lost still blooms in your cheeks, my fair companions. Seat yourselves near me, therefore, that in your loveliness I may find inspiration for an impromptu."

The girls laughingly did as they were commanded, while Porte Crayon alternately pinched his eyebrows and scribbled. Presently, with an air of great unconcern, he handed the results to Cousin Minnie, who read first to herself, and then, with some hesitation, aloud, the following verses:

THE WATER-SPRITE.

Bright flashing, soft dimpling, the streamlet is flowing;
A maiden trips over, with vermeil cheek glowing;
In mirror of silver, once furtively glancing,
She marks a sweet shadow 'mid cool wavelets dancing.

'Twas a voice—is she dreaming?—that rose from the water,
Articulate murmuring, "Come with me, fair daughter,
I'll lead thee to shades where the forest discloses
Its green arching bowers, enwreathed with wild roses.

"When erst thou hast laved in my bosom, pure gushing,
Immortal, unfading, in fresh beauty blushing,
Young sister, forever we'll joyously wander,
Free through the mirk woodland, the shady boughs under."

Heed not, list'ning maiden, the Water-sprite's song,
For false her weird accents and murmuring tongue;
No mortal heart throbs in her shivering breast,
Ever sparkling and foaming, she never knows rest.

From summer clouds lowering the big rain descendeth,
The hemlock's spire towering the red levin rendeth,
All turbid and foul in wild fury she hasteth,
Rose, wreath, and green bower in madness she wasteth.

When stern winter cometh, with tyrannous hand
His icy chain bindeth both water and land;
The wanderer hastes over, no spirit-voice woos him;
White, white lies the snow-shroud on her frozen bosom.

Then rest thee, loved maiden, where true hearts beat warm,
And strong arms may guard thee through danger and storm;
Where unchanging affection may sweeten thy tears,
And love that can brighten the winter of years.

The verses were highly commended, and Dora expressed herself greatly astonished that any one who could write such poetry had not written books of it, and become famous, like Milton and Lord Byron, or at least have published some in the newspapers.

Crayon made a deprecatory and scornful gesture. "Trash!" said he; "mere trash; jingling nonsense. Versification is at best but a meretricious art, giving undue value to vapid thoughts and sentiments, serving to obscure and weaken sense that would be better expressed in prose."

"Why, cousin," exclaimed Minnie, "are these your real sentiments, or is it merely a way of underrating your own performance? Hear what Shakspeare says of poets:

> " 'The poet's eye in a fine frenzy rolling,
> Doth glance from heaven to earth, from earth to heaven,
> And as imagination bodies forth
> The forms of things unknown, the poet's pen
> Turns them to shapes, and gives to airy nothing
> A local habitation and a name.' "

"Upon my word," said Dora, "one would think that Shakspeare had seen Cousin Porte writing verses."

"Well, well," said our hero, shrugging his shoulders with an air of resignation, "when one has condescended to a business only fit for scribbling women—"

"Scribbling women!" repeated Fanny; "why, brother, you ought to be ashamed to talk so, when you have been at least a month writing this impromptu."

"Truly, Miss, how came you to know what I have been studying for a month past? Is my skull so transparent, or have you more shrewdness than I have been accustomed to allow your sex?"

"Indeed, Porte, it required no great shrewdness to make the discovery, for about three weeks ago I found this bit of paper in the bottom of the carriage."

Our hero examined the scrap to convince himself of its authenticity, which he acknowledged by immediately tearing it up. Observing, however, that Minnie had secured his verses in that charming receptacle where a lady hides whatever she thinks too precious to be trusted in her pockets or work-basket, and consoled that they had thus reached their destination, he bore the laugh with reasonable fortitude.

Repeating a harmless line from Martial, *"Risu inepto res ineptior nulla est,"* our author turned his back on the pests, and, starting up the road at a rapid pace, was soon out of sight.

It was near sunset before the carriage overtook him. He was then standing, with folded arms, absorbed in the contemplation of a view which was presented for the first time through a vista in the forest. To the right of the road, and at an immense distance below, appeared a champaign country, stretching away in endless perspective, the line of whose horizon was lost in mist. In front rose a lofty conical peak, whose sharp, forked apex was yet gilded by the rays of the declining sun, while its base was enveloped in misty shadows.

As Crayon ascended the carriage, he informed the ladies that they saw to the right a portion of the map of Old Virginia, and before them stood the South Peak of the Otter, one of the twin kings of the Blue Ridge, crowned with his diadem of granite—a diadem so grand, and so curiously wrought withal, that it remains equally the admiration and the puzzle of artists and philosophers. His brother, the Round Top, was then hidden by a spur of the Ridge, but would be visible shortly. The Peak loomed in the gathering twilight, and our travelers gazed in silence on his unique form and gloomy brow—a silence that was not broken until, winding down the notch between the two mountains, they halted at the gate of the Otter Peaks Hotel.

This celebrated hotel might readily have been mistaken by the inexperienced traveler for a negro cabin, for it was nothing more than a log hut, showing a single door and window in front. Yet, to the more knowing, its central and commanding position, amid the group of outbuildings of proportionate size and finish, proved it unmistakably the dwelling of a landed proprietor—what the negroes call sometimes, by excess of courtesy, the "Great House." Crayon's ringing halloo was answered by the appearance of a full pack of dogs and negroes, whose barking and vociferation were equally unintelligible. The travelers disembarked at a venture, and were met at the door by a smiling motherly woman, who ushered them into the great parlor, reception-room, and chamber of the hotel. The bare log walls, and cold, yawning fire-place, were made dimly manifest by the rays of a single tallow dip; but the united labors of the landlady, her little son and daughter, four negro children, and a grown servant-woman, soon remedied all deficiencies.

An enormous fire roared and crackled in the spacious chimney, the rafters glowed with a cheerful, ruddy light, and a genial warmth pervaded the apartment, which soon restored our chilled and disappointed adventurers to their accustomed good-humor. The supper, which was excellent beyond all expectation, furnished Porte Crayon an occasion to lecture on "the deceitfulness of appearances in this sublunary sphere," and also to narrate a pleasant anecdote concerning a supper that his friend Jack Rawlins and himself had eaten in this house, while they were on that famous pedestrian tour, so often alluded to heretofore. According to his statement, Jack had eaten twenty-two good-sized biscuit, duly relished with bear-steak, broiled ham, preserves, and buttermilk. Porte credited himself with sixteen biscuit only. Fanny, who understood something of domestic arithmetic, immediately did a sum in multiplication, based upon the supposition that twelve gentlemen had stepped in to supper at the Hall.

"Two hundred and sixty-four biscuit!" exclaimed she. "Porte, I don't believe a word of it."

Dame Wilkinson, who had just entered, was appealed to by Crayon to verify his story.

"Madam, do you recollect ever having seen me before?"

The hostess adjusted her cap and twisted her apron, but was finally forced to acknowledge her memory at fault.

Porte then went on to give the date and details of the transaction, when a ray of remembrance lighted the good woman's perplexed countenance.

"Well, indeed, sir, I do remember them boys. They come here a-foot, and did eat enormous. Of that, sir, I tuck no account, for I like to see folks eat hearty, especially young ones; but when they come to pay their bill, they said it was a shame to charge only three fourpenny bits for such a supper, and wanted to make me take double."

"And you refused. My good woman, I was one of those boys."

"God bless you, sir! is it possible? Why, your chin was then as smooth as mine, and I should have expected to have seen you looking fatter, or maybe something stouter than you are."

"A very natural supposition," replied Mr. Crayon, with a sigh; "but these things are controlled by destiny; I must have been born under a lean star."

Mrs. Wilkinson had come in to know if her guests desired to ascend the Peak in time to see the sun rise, that she might arrange her housekeeping accordingly. The idea was favorably received by the party, and it was unanimously determined to carry it out. The coachman was instructed to arouse Mr. Crayon at the proper hour; and then, by the landlady's advice, they all went to bed.

What time the glittering belts of Orion hung high in the heavens, and dim, twinkling stars in the alborescent east gave token of approaching day, Porte Crayon started from his downy couch, aroused by a sharp tap at the window. "Mass' Porte! Mass' Porte! day is breakin'—roosters been a-crowin' dis hour!"

"Begone, you untimely varlet! How dare you disturb my dreams? Go help Apollo to get out his horses yourself—I'm no stable-boy." And Mice's retreating footsteps were heard crunching in the hard frost as he returned to his quarters, not displeased with the result of his mission. Porte Crayon closed his eyes again, and tried to woo back a charming dream that had been interrupted by the unwelcome summons. What luck he met with in the endeavor we are unable to say.

Our friends were consoled for the loss of the sunrise view by a comfortable breakfast between eight and nine o'clock. In answer to their apologies for changing their plans, the hostess informed them that she had rather calculated on their not going, as most of her visitors did the same thing, especially in cold weather.

The Peaks of Otter are in Bedford County, on the southeastern front of the Blue Ridge, and about sixteen miles distant from the Natural Bridge. Their height above the level country at their base is estimated at four thousand two hundred and sixty feet, and more than five thousand feet above the ocean tides. They have heretofore been considered the highest points in Virginia, but by recent measurements the Iron Mountains appear to overtop them. The North Peak, called the Round Top, has the largest base, and is said to be the highest, but the difference is not appreciable by the eye. From a distance, its summit presents an outline like a Cupid's bow.

The South Peak is considered the greater curiosity, and receives almost exclusively the attention of visitors. Its shape is that of a regular cone, terminating in a sharp point or points formed by three irregular pyramids of granite boulders. The largest of these heaps is about sixty feet in height, and upon its apex stands an egg-shaped rock about ten feet in diameter. It seems so insecurely placed that it would require apparently but little force to send it thundering down the side of the mountain. It has, nevertheless, resisted the efforts of more than one mischievous party.

The remarkable regularity of this peak in all its aspects would give the impression that it owed its formation to volcanic action, but there is nothing more than its shape to sustain the idea.

The hotel is situated in the notch formed by the junction of the peaks, about midway between their bases and summits, and travelers starting from this point have to ascend not more than two thousand or twenty-five hundred feet. To persons unaccustomed to such exercise this is no trifling undertaking, and horses are frequently in requisition to perform a part of the journey. Our friends, however, fresh from the Alleghanies, and vigorous from four weeks' previous travel, scorned all extraneous assistance, and started from the hotel on foot.

As the fallen leaves had entirely obliterated the path, a negro boy was detailed to lead the way. Porte Crayon followed next, with his rifle slung, and knapsack stuffed with shawls and comforts, to protect the ladies from the keen air of the summit. The girls straggled after in Indian file, with flying bonnets, each holding a light, springy staff to steady her in climbing. Mice, armed with a borrowed shot-gun, brought up the rear. For a mile they tugged along with great resolution, pausing at intervals to rest on the sofas of rock and fallen timber so temptingly cushioned with moss. At length they arrived at a small plateau where the horse-path terminates, and as there seemed no further necessity for a guide, the boy was here dismissed.

The ascent from this point is much more difficult. The path becomes steeper and more rugged, a sort of irregular stairway of rocks, that often shakes beneath the traveler's tread, and affords at best but an uncertain footing.

"Now, girls, is the time to show your training. Forward! forward!" shouted Crayon, as he bent his breast to the steep ascent.

> " 'Non sotto l'ombra in piaggia molle
> Tra fonti e fior, tra Ninfe e tra Sirene,
> Ma in cima all' erto e faticoso colle
> Della virtù, reposto e il nostro bene.'

" 'The spirit is willing, but the flesh is weak.' Poor things! how they struggle!" said Porte, looking back at his wards, who, with disheveled hair and purple cheeks, staggered up the difficult pathway.

"Ah!" cried Minnie,

> " 'Who can tell how hard it is to climb?' "

and she sunk exhausted and palpitating upon a rock.

"Come, child, your hand; the road to the Temple of Fame is nothing to this. In fact, the temple does not stand on an eminence, as the simple-hearted poets of the olden time imagined, but down in a hollow, and people nowadays reach it by traveling down hill. Mice, help the hindmost."

What with the assistance of the men and frequent rests, they at length reached the summit. Here, between the granite pinnacles, they found a little level, carpeted with dried grass, and protected from the wind by the rocks and stunted thickets. The shawls were immediately produced, and the ladies nestled in a sunny corner, while Crayon and his man kindled a brisk fire of dried sticks.

A brief repose served to recruit the energies of our fair travelers. A rude ladder assisted them in the ascent of the largest pinnacle, which looks eastward; and then (first carefully assuring themselves of their footing) they turned their eyes upon the glorious panorama that lay unfolded beneath them. The sensations produced by this first look would be difficult to describe. The isolation from earth is seemingly as complete as if you were sailing in a balloon—as if the rocks upon which you stood were floating in the air. For a few moments "the blue above and the blue below" is all that is appreciable by the eye, until the lenses are adjusted properly to take cognizance of the details of the landscape.

Looking east, a vast plain rises like an ocean, its surface delicately pictured with alternating field and woodland, threaded with silver streams, and dotted with villages and farm-houses. Sweeping from north to south, dividing the country with the regularity of an artificial rampart, its monotonous length broken at intervals by conical peaks and rounded knobs, the endless line of the Blue Ridge is visible, until in either direction it fades out in the distance. Westward, rising from the valley, are discovered the unique forms of the House Mountains; and beyond them, ridge peeps over ridge, growing dimmer and dimmer, until you can not distinguish between the light clouds of the horizon and the pale outline of the Alleghanies. On your left hand, in sublime proximity, the Round Top "lifts his awful form" like an uncouth giant, insolently thrusting his shaggy pate into the etherial company of the clouds.

While our friends reveled in this illimitable feast, for a time silence reigned supreme, until Porte Crayon, who had been sitting apart upon the apex of the egg, slid down from his perch and approached the group of ladies.

"Girls, there must be something in our altitude calculated to produce a corresponding loftiness of sentiment. I am in a state of exaltation—overflowing with patriotism. I don't allude to the marketable staple produced by the combined stimulus of cornwhisky and lust of office, but the more common instinct of loyalty to kindred and country, vivified, perhaps, and intensified by this bracing air and magnificent prospect. I feel as if I should like to be Governor of Virginia; not for the sake of gain—no, I scorn emolument—but simply for the glorification; to be enabled to do something great for the Old Commonwealth—to make her a great speech. For instance:

"Looking down from this lofty height over the length and breadth of the land, what enlarged and comprehensive views do I not take of her physical features and capacities. My intellectual vision penetrates the mists which dim the material horizon. I can see the whole state, like a map unrolled, from the Big Sandy to Cape Charles, from the Dismal Swamp to the Pan Handle—that pragmatical bit of territory that sticks up so stiff and straight, like the tail of a plucky animal, Virginian to the very tip."

"Porte, can we see Berkeley from here?" inquired Dora.

"Certainly, child; look northward there, and you may even see the chimneys of the old Hall peering above the locust-trees."

"To be sure, cousin, I can see it now; better, I think, with my eyes shut than open."

"Your silly interruption has put me out. I had a great deal more to say that possibly might have been important to the State, for you must know that in Virginia speeches are of more account than food and raiment. It is all lost, however, and I will conclude in the words of the most egotistical of bards:

> " 'Could I embody and unbosom now
> That which is most within me; could I wreak
> My thoughts upon expression, and thus throw
> Soul, heart, mind, passions, feelings strong and weak,
> All that I would have sought, and all I seek,
> Bear, know, feel, and yet breathe into one word,
> And that one word were lightning, I would speak.
> But as it is, I live and die unheard,
> With a most voiceless thought, sheathing it as a sword.' "

"I'm glad you've done it," said Dora.

"I should not have commenced, perhaps. The effect of eloquence depends too much on adventitious circumstances. In this rarefied atmosphere the most sonorous voice seems weak and piping."

Fanny suggested that this fact appeared like an intimation from Nature that these sublime solitudes were fitter for reflection than noise.

"I never could bear speeches any where," rejoined Dora.

"Very naturally, Miss Dimple. Your sex prefers addresses."

Having relieved his surcharged feelings to some extent by these straggling remarks, Mr. Crayon gave the ladies a peremptory invitation to get up on the egg. It was accepted without hesitation, although in fear and trembling. Mice, according to his own account, made "a lather" of himself, by means of which they were enabled to ascend with comparative ease and safety.

On the rock they formed a group at once picturesque and characteristic. Every eye kindled as it swept the boundless horizon, and, by a common impulse, Crayon took off his cap, and the girls spread scarf and kerchief to the breeze, waving an enthusiastic salute to the

THE GREAT VALLEY

fair and generous land.—Dead indeed must be his soul, who, standing upon the peak, could not feel full justification for such enthusiasm.

Cautiously descending from the airy pinnacle, our friends made their way back to their gipsy encampment. As they tarried here, the comfortable warmth of the fire by degrees led back their wandering thoughts to the common path of life. Fancy, that, like the eagle spreading her wings from her eyrie in the rocks, had soared away among the clouds, now began circling gently downward—down, down, downward still—until suddenly, with pinions collapsed, she swooped upon a fat turkey—supposed, of course, to be roasted.

> "Then down their road they took
> Through those dilapidated crags, that oft
> Moved underneath their feet."

Although the descent has its peculiar difficulties, it is accomplished in a much shorter time than the ascent. Our travelers reached their place of sojourn in the vale about 2 o'clock P.M., where they found dinner had been waiting some time, and the turkey overdone.

The descent from the hotel to the foot of the Peaks affords a number of striking views, well worthy of record by pen and pencil.

As they rolled rapidly over the road toward Liberty, the signs of a milder climate became momentarily more evident. The appearance of open, cultivated fields, of elegant residences surrounded by shrubbery, and, notwithstanding the lateness of the season, cottages embowered in fragrant roses and showy chrysanthemums, threw the girls into quite an excitement of pleasure, and for a time entirely diverted their thoughts from what they had left behind. But Porte Crayon, heedless or half scornful of these softer beauties, still cast his longing, lingering looks behind, where a blue mist was gathering over the twin peaks, that stood like giant sentinels at the gates of the mountain land.

"*Au revoir, Messieurs!*" and with this implied consolation he turned away. "A traveler's business is with the present, not the past. Our sketching henceforward will be more of life and character than of inanimate nature. Even while I speak, behold a victim!"

On the Road

LIBERTY, the county town of Bedford, is a pleasant, and, to all appearance, a thriving little town. The travelers passed the night at a very comfortable hotel kept by Leftwitch, and were introduced to the daughter of their host, a bright-eyed maiden of thirteen years, who had lately performed the feat of riding to the top of the South Peak on horseback.

"Of the next day's journey from Liberty to Lynchburg," Mr. Crayon jocosely remarks, "we will have more to say than we could have wished." The weather was delightful. An Indian summer haze threw a softening veil over the landscape, and the Peaks, still in full view, loomed up grandly against the western sky.

Of the road which they traveled that day Mr. C. declines undertaking any description; "for," said he, "to use an expression of the orator Isocrates, if I were to stick to the truth I couldn't tell the half, and if I were to lie I couldn't exceed the reality of its unspeakable abominations."

In passing through the town of New London, Mr. C. remonstrated with the toll-gatherer, but to no purpose. About five miles and a half from Lynchburg our adventurers were descending a hill. The hill was very steep—so steep that the driver was obliged to zigzag his horses to check the impetus of the carriage. The road at that point was of good old conservative corduroy—corded with stout saplings of various diameters, a species of rail-road much used in the Old Dominion. They had descended many such hills before, and as they neared the bottom, Mice, according to custom, let his horses out. Down they rattled at full speed. The corduroy terminated in a mud-hole—so did the carriage. With a terrific crash, the fore-axle broke sheer in two, the wheels rolled off to either side, and the dashboard plowed the mud. Porte Crayon, in a state of bewilderment, found himself astride of the roan, without knowing precisely how he got there, while Mice's bullet-head struck the unlucky sorrel such a blow on the rump that he squatted like a rabbit.

RAIL-ROAD ACCIDENT

Crayon, with that admirable presence of mind which characterizes him, immediately dismounted, and lost no time in rescuing his rifle from the wreck. Ascertaining to his satisfaction that it was not hurt, he gallantly rushed to the assistance of the ladies. He found them in the fore part of the carriage, mixed up in a sort of *olla podrida* composed of shawls, baskets, bonnets, cold meat, geological specimens, apples, a variety of shrubbery more or less dried, biscuits and butter, skins and feathers, trophies of the chase, and other ingredients not remembered.

"Are you all alive?" inquired he, anxiously.

Three voices replied in a rather doubtful affirmative. The door was with some difficulty forced open, and the living were delivered from their entanglement without further damage—a work that required no little delicacy and judgment.

"Oh, my bonnet!" cried Fanny, as she limped to the road side; "it looks like a crow's nest!"

"Just look at mine!" screamed Dora; "some one's foot has been jammed through the crown."

"Cousin Minnie, what are you looking for in all that rubblish? Have you lost your breast-pin?"

"I've lost something," quoth she, blushing. Presently she snatched up a bit of folded paper, and adroitly slipping it into her bosom, remarked, "Well, no matter—it is of no importance whatever."

Mice, in the mean time, had recovered his upright posture, and by dint of rubbing and scratching had righted his senses, which had been knocked topsy-turvy by the collision. The horses stood quietly in their tracks, evincing not the slightest sympathy in the perplexity of their fellow-travelers—seeming to say, "Good people, take your time to it; this is your business, not ours."

How different was the feeling of the kindly driver, who stood stroking and patting the sorrel's hips!

"Mass' Porte, I'se glad to see him standin' up dis way, 'case I thought at fust he's back was broke."

The women were left to exercise their ingenuity in repairing their damaged apparel, while a private consultation was held between the commander of the expedition and his lieutenant on the present state of the war. It was unanimously agreed that Mr. Crayon and the ladies should stroll on until they found some vehicle to take them into Lynchburg, thinking there could be no difficulty in finding one in the vicinity of so important and populous a town. Mice magnanimously undertook to remain on the ground until he could engage a passing teamster to assist him in transporting the wreck.

Porte mustered his company and started forthwith.

For a short time they got along very well; but the sun shone hot, the road was dusty, and before they had accomplished a mile the girls began to complain of exhaustion. In fact, they had scarcely recovered from the fatigue the previous day.

They sat down upon a bank beside the highway to wait until some vehicle should come in sight, but during the next half hour they saw no living thing. At length an old negro hobbled by with a staff and cloak, whose very gait seemed to mock their patience. By advancing a dime, Mr. Crayon obtained the important information that his name was "Uncle Peter," and nothing farther.

Disheartened by so unfavorable a prospect, Crayon encouraged his wards to make another effort, holding forth vague promises of relief

in some form or other that he could not exactly particularize himself.
Once their hopes were excited by the appearance of a vehicle in the
distance, but, on a nearer approach, the ladies determined not to take
advantage of the opportunity offered, because the animals did not
match.

NOT A MATCH

Porte Crayon's inquiries at two or three farm-houses were likewise unsuccessful. There seemed no chance for any other mode of
conveyance than that which they had rightfully inherited from Adam
and Eve. What a pity that a mode so healthful, independent, graceful,
and beautifying, should have fallen into such general disrepute! With
clouded countenances they accomplished another mile, when the
cousins declared they were about to faint, and Fanny said, decidedly,
that she would not walk another step.

It is universally conceded that romancers and historians are privi-
leged to draw their characters entirely from fancy, and may so arrange
incidents as to exhibit their heroes and heroines as models of perfection. Unfortunately, the editor of these papers enjoys no such license.
The wings of his fancy have been clipped by stubborn fact, and conscience has hedged his way on either side with thorns. If persevering
good-humor at length becomes wearisome, and the high-mettled steel
of chivalry requires occasional repose, charge it up in the general account against human nature, and not to your humble and faithful
narrator.

As the young ladies sunk down one after another by the road-side, murmurs ripened into reproaches. Their gallant escort was blamed with all the inconveniences under which they were suffering—the heat, the dust, the distance to Lynchburg, and, above all, their fatigue.

"Hadn't he forced them to climb the Peak the day before?"

"Instead of taking you up in the carriage," suggested he.

"Then, would any one who had the sense of a—"

"A woman," interrupted Crayon.

"Or the least consideration, have started on such a journey in a carriage with a cracked axle?"

"That has carried us some four hundred miles over hill and dale, rock and river," replied he, mildly.

"Why, then, did you bring us over this nasty, hilly, muddy, dusty road?"

"To get you to Lynchburg."

"Was there no other way to Lynchburg?"

"My children," replied the philosopher, with admirable calmness, "cultivate patience, and don't entirely take leave of your feeble wits; and," cried he, with increasing fervor, "didn't you have an opportunity of riding just now, which you refused with one voice? Am I responsible for every thing, your whims included? You may go to grass!"

Whatever reply this abrupt conclusion might have elicited was arrested by an extraordinary screeching that seemed to issue from a wood hard by. Presently a wagon hove in sight, whose ungreased axles made the distressing outcry. The *attelage* was likewise out of the common line. The yoke at the wheels consisted of a great ox and a diminutive donkey, with a single horse in the lead. The driver, a deformed negro boy, was very good imitation of the baboon that rides the pony in a menagerie.

"By blood!" exclaimed Crayon, knitting his brows, "here's a conveyance, and you shall ride, whether you will or not. Halloo, boy! stop your team! I want to engage you to carry these ladies to town."

"Dey is gone, Sir," answered the baboon, respectfully touching his hat.

Our hero looked round, and, to his astonishment, saw the ladies already more than two hundred yards distant, footing it rapidly down the road. Such was their speed that it cost him some effort to overtake them.

"Cousin Porte," said Minnie May, in a deprecating tone, "we have concluded to walk to Lynchburg. The distance is so small that it will be scarcely worth while to engage any conveyance."

Mr. Crayon affectionately desired the young ladies not to walk so rapidly, observing that they would the sooner exhaust themselves by undue haste. As it was, there was no occasion to be in a hurry, the town being only three miles distant. He then kindly offered an arm to each of his cousins, requesting them to lean as heavily as possible upon the support; at the same time he nodded to Fanny, regretting that he had not a third arm to offer, but promising her a turn presently. Fanny smilingly acknowledged the civility, and said that, since the breeze had sprung up and cooled the air, she did not feel the slightest fatigue.

"Cousin Porte," said Minnie, in gentle accents, "we were very foolish to reproach you as we did."

"No more, sweet cousin. I pray you do not recall my unphilosophic and ungallant behavior, which I would fain dismiss from my own memory, as I hope it may be from yours, forever."

Peace having been thus re-established, Miss Dora ventured to inquire "why the people of this region, instead of using horses, harnessed such ridiculous menageries to their wagons."

Crayon, who never liked to acknowledge himself at a loss, informed her that "it was done to encourage a spirit of emulation in the different races of quadrupeds, and thereby to get more work out of them."

A number of handsome suburban residences indicated the proximity of a considerable town, and our friends at length paused upon the brow of the bluff on the declivity of which Lynchburg is built. As they stood here enjoying the view, they perceived a huge column of dust approaching, out of which proceeded a confusion of sounds, snorting, creaking, trampling, shouting, cracking, and rumbling. As the cloud whirled by, a shadowy group was dimly visible, a carriage mounted on the running-gear of a wagon, and drawn by four horses.

A huge figure occupied the front seat, and "the driving was like the driving of Jehu, the son of Nimshi." In the foaming leaders Crayon thought he recognized their much-enduring friends the roan and sorrel, and in the human figure the gigantic outline of the indomitable Mice.

The pedestrians, all dusted and travel-worn, slipped quietly down a by-street, hoping to gain the Norvall House without observation, but the burly squire was in ahead of them. His odd-looking, hybrid vehicle was of itself sufficient to excite attention, but his gasconading account of the accident aroused the whole neighborhood. When our friends timidly glanced up the main street, they had the satisfaction of seeing all the managers, clerks, waiters, and chambermaids of the hotel out to receive them, and the sidewalk lined with spectators. In the midst stood Mice, covered with dust and perspiration, looking as magnificent as Murat after a successful cavalry charge. The ladies clung closer to Crayon's arms, and drew their dusty veils over their faces. The valet took off his cap, and, addressing himself to the head manager, said, in a low voice, but with marked emphasis,

"Them's them, Sir!"

On the morning of the 6th of November, our travelers again found themselves and carriage in condition to take the road. Their route lay northward through the county of Amherst, and at noon they dined at the Court House. Now we do not wish it understood literally that they took their refreshment in the halls of justice. In Virginia, the village or collection of houses in which the seat of justice of each county is located is called the Court House. Sometimes you find nothing more than a tavern, a store, and a smithy. Besides the county buildings, Amherst Court House contains about a dozen houses, and probably has not yet attained the dignity of a corporate town. The soil of this, in common with many other of the *piedmont* counties, is of a bright red in many places, generally fertile, but poorly cultivated. The world down here seems to have been asleep for many years, and an air of loneliness pervades the whole region. As the roads were heavy, and the chances of finding entertainment but few, the driver stopped at an early hour in front of a house of rather unpromising exterior. Porte Crayon, who has a facility of making himself at home every where, went to the kitchen with a bunch of squirrels, the spoil of his German rifle. He returned in high spirits.

"Girls, we will be well fed here; we are fortunate. I have just seen the cook: not a mere black woman that does the cooking, but one bearing a patent stamped by the broad seal of Nature; the type of a class whose skill is not of books or training, but a gift both rich and rare; who flourishes her spit as Amphitrite does her trident (or her husband's, which is all the same); whose ladle is as a royal sceptre in her hands; who has grown sleek and fat on the steam of her own genius; whose children have the first dip in all gravies, the exclusive right to all livers and gizzards, not to mention breasts of fried chickens; who brazens her mistress, boxes her scullions, and scalds the dogs (I'll warrant there is not a dog on the place with a full suit of hair on him). I was awed to that degree by the severity of her deportment when I presented the squirrels, that my orders dwindled into a humble request, and, throwing half a dollar on the table, as I retreated I felt my coat-tails, to ascertain whether she had not pinned a dishrag to them. In short, she is a perfect she-Czar, and may I never butter another corn-cake if I don't have her portrait to-morrow."

The supper fully justified Crayon's prognosis; and the sleep of our travelers, like that of the laboring man, "was sweet, whether they ate little or much."

In the morning our hero felt lightsome, and rose before the sun. Not finding his shoes at the chamber door, he went down stairs in his stockings to seek them, and in a hall between the house and kitchen he found the boot-black.

"Uncle! I am looking for my shoes."

"Massa wears shoes?" replied the old man, scanning our hero's person with an inquiring look. "Well, well, boots hain't no distinction now. Take a chair, young master; I'll find 'em and polish 'em up in no time. Weddin' party stopped here last night—brung me an uncommon pile of work."

Billy Devilbug was a specimen of his race that merited more than a casual glance. Time had made strong marks upon his face,

A CONSERVATIVE PHILOSOPHER

but good temper and full feeding had kept out the petty wrinkles
which indicate decrepitude. His broad forehead, fringed with grizzled
wool, imparted an air of dignity to his countenance; his one eye

beamed with honesty; while his quiet, deferential manner inspired the respect it tendered.

Porte Crayon's shoes were finished and delivered, yet he still lingered.

"Master," quoth Billy, "when I was young there was gentlemen then. They wore fa' top-boots them days; to see a fa' top-boot was to see a gentleman. Nowadays, sence these store-boots come in, under the new constitution, there hain't no distinctions; every thing is mixed up; every thing w'ars boots now, and sich boots! Look here, master!" cried Billy, thrusting his fist into a boot-leg, and fixing his one eye upon it with ineffable scorn, "what sort of a thing is that, master? Is that a boot? Yes, indeed, that's what they call a boot these times. Ke-chuck, ke-chuck, ke-chuck! I'se afear'd to rub 'em hard, for fear to rub the sole off 'em. Them's like gentlemen nowadays!"

Porte Crayon recognized in his swarthy friend a brother philosopher and high conservative, and, as he turned to depart, a considerable gratuity chinked in Billy's hand.

"Young master," said the boot-black, rising, and touching his forehead respectfully, "I'll be bound your father wore fa' top-boots, anyhow."

The University and Monticello

As the moon, with red and stupid phiz, stared from behind the ragged mountains of Albemarle, her rays faintly illuminated a scene that might have served for the opening incident of a romance: A wrecked carriage; a pair of patient, drooping horses standing near; a group of human figures, male and female, that in the dim light appeared to be all of one color. But who could fail to recognize the Herculean contour of Little Mice, or the philosophic shrug that accompanied the following characteristic remark:

" 'Misfortunes never come alone!' Curse the luck and the man that mended the axle!"

"What we gwine to do now, master?"

"I hear dogs barking at no great distance ahead; there must be a house at hand. We will first provide a shelter for the helpless beings under our care—the women and horses—then turn our attention to the vehicle and baggage."

Fortunately for our friend, Squire Oliver's soul was greater than his house; and through his hospitable care they were comfortably fed, lodged, and sped on their way next morning. Their equipage was accommodated precisely as it had been after the accident near Lynchburg; and, notwithstanding its somewhat cumbrous appearance, they made their way to Charlottesville, thirteen miles distant, with comparative ease and rapidity.

The girls, who never were able to attain that stoical contempt for appearances so frequently enlarged upon by their philosophic companion, could not but congratulate themselves that they passed the University during lecture hours, and, in consequence, escaped the observation of some five hundred quizzing students.

THE STUDENT

After dinner they set off on foot to visit the University, which is about one mile distant from the town of Charlottesville. On the way Crayon indulged in some sage observations on the subject of giggling; general propriety of deportment, especially among strangers—more especially if the strangers happened to be young persons—students, for example. Not, indeed, that he intended these remarks to be understood as suggestions upon this occasion; hoped the ladies would not think so for a moment; too much confidence, etc. But seeing students always reminded him of dignity, "As Cæsar's triumph shorn of Pompey's bust," etc.

Having at length arrived at the College, they felt at a loss for a chaperon. Dora intimated that her cousin, Ned Twiggs, was then at the University—that he was an amiable, well-mannered youth—but she felt a delicacy in interrupting his studies, as she had understood from his letters home that he was in the habit of studying nineteen hours a day. Fanny thought it was a great shame only to allow himself five hours for sleep and recreation, and that his health must give way under it. Crayon heard these remarks with a contemptuous shrug, and went directly to the proctor's office to ascertain the number of Ned's room.

Now that young gentleman did look as if he hadn't slept his wholesome allowance for some time; but Crayon took pains to insinuate afterward that young men at colleges sometimes lost their rest from other causes than mere devotion to their legitimate studies. Ned was vastly delighted to see his fair relatives, and undertook the office of chaperon with an alacrity and good-humor that fully justified Dora's good opinion of his manners.

"Indeed," says Crayon, "it gives me great pleasure to say that, although the vivacity of these blooded colts at our Virginia colleges frequently leads them into all sorts of deviltries and excesses, they have almost invariably the manners of gentlemen."

The University was established by an act of Assembly dated January 25, 1819, upon the site of the Central College of Albemarle. It was planned, built, and organized under the immediate supervision of Mr. Jefferson.

The students' dormitories, professors' houses, and classrooms, are built upon three sides of a quadrangle, and are connected by a continuous colonnade. Outside of these, at some distance, are second lines of dormitories and offices, the space between the ranges being occupied by well-cultivated gardens. The whole has a very pleasing and pretty effect, but the buildings are too low, and the architecture wants finish.

Although this institution was an especial pet of its distinguished founder, and bequeathed by him to the fostering care of our venerable Commonwealth, it was not eminently successful in its early years. Latterly, however, it seems to be taking the position that it should have attained long ago, and its present catalogue shows over five hundred students.

The ladies were so much delighted with every thing they saw, and had so much to say about the students, that Crayon began to grow morose and cynical.

"Women," said he, "always make the most fuss about matters of which they know the least. They are prodigious admirers of learning, or, more strictly speaking, the name of learning; for any owlish fellow who gets a reputation for profundity, or malapert who has written verses for a magazine, is, in their estimation, a Newton or a Milton. While they pretend to be in love with scholarship, they are sworn foes of every means of acquiring it. So jealous and exacting of the time and attention of their unlucky admirers, that an interesting book is as bad as a rival beauty; the solution of an abstruse problem is equivalent to a quarrel; the study of a science amounts to prolonged absence and consequent oblivion. As for themselves, they will read nothing but novels, and listen to nothing but nonsense. Improving conversation is ever drowned in untimely giggling, and a useful lecture is looked upon as an inadmissible bore."

"I think," interrupted Fanny, "that lectures may be bores without even the pretense of being useful."

"If I had Cousin Porte's talents," said Minnie, "I would write a novel to demonstrate the impropriety of novel reading, and deliver a public lecture on the frivolity of frivolousness."

Dora yawned, and, with an air of unaffected simplicity, avowed that, for her part, she thought more of the scholars than she did of scholarship.

"To be sure," said Minnie, with enthusiasm, "we do not so much admire the laborious, pains-taking student, the mere bookworm; but the brilliant, dashing genius, whose productions seem the results of intuition rather than of labor, whose eloquence is unstudied, whose verses are impromptu—"

Minnie stopped suddenly, and turned away her suffused cheek under the pretense of arranging her sewing. Crayon bit his lip, and began whistling like a fifer, when, fortunately, the servant ushered in Mr. Twiggs and several of his friends.

While the Freshmen are paying their compliments to the ladies, we can not forbear indulging in a few moral reflections.

While every body's mouth and every body's book are filled with laudations of Nature, her skill in adapting her gifts to the necessities of every age and clime, the unerring truth of her teachings, the infallibility of her intuitions, the eternal fitness of things, why has not some bold philosopher overthrown this host of slang, and battered this castle of paper walls with the artillery of every-day facts and experiences? Why do babies cry after the moon? Why does all the world want what it can't get? Why have boys of sixteen or thereabout such an inordinate desire for beards? And why, when the gift would be most acceptable, does the hard-hearted dame insult them with a sprinkling of peach fuzz instead? And why, when years have matured the hirsute harvest, does the desire for it disappear, and the man become involved in expenditure of time and money to get rid of that appendage which, as a youth, he would have gloried in?

During the journey our hero's beard had grown broad and long, until he resembled a *sapeur* of the French Guard. In looking on the downy lips of the students, a most unphilosophic sense of superiority took possession of him. He was annoyed, at the same time, to perceive the interest which the ladies appeared to take in their beardless conversation.

Crayon assumed a magisterial air. "Ned, my boy, how are you getting on with the classics?"

Ned replied, modestly, that he had passed his last examination very creditably.

"Are you of opinion that Dido was really in love with the pious Æneas?"

"Virgil says so," replied Ned.

"But does not Virgil frequently say, *'Dido et Dux,'* and, worse than all, *'Dux Trojanorum'* (which species was probably larger than our fowl—a sort of aquatic Shanghai), and how do you reconcile this with his previous statement?"

TO SHAVE OR DYE, THAT IS THE QUESTION

"If she *eat* ducks," said Dora, "she certainly couldn't have been much in love."

"Certainly not. Dido was a humbug."

"Cousin Crayon," said Ned, beginning to show a little pluck, "who was first found guilty of a breach of the peace?"

"According to Holy Writ," said Porte, "it must have been *the first Cain.*"

"Not so," said Ned; "for before his time, and even before the creation, it is said *'Nihil fit.'*"

"So he did, indeed," said Crayon.

Although the girls did not entirely understand this sally, they laughed all the more, while Crayon looked quite vexed.

"Very well, younster, very well; you'll get along. With twenty years of study and patience you may become a ripe scholar, and grow a beard like mine, probably. For the present, Ned, let me counsel you to cream your face and submit it to the cat; and for the rest, be content with the distinctions that appertain to your age and con-

SHAVING

dition. *'Pro Ingenuo adolescenti, sedula scholasticæ disciplinæ observantia, et in literis profectu egregio.'*"

Now, before the girls, this was rather too bad. Crayon must have forgotten that he had once been a boy. Ned turned very red, bit his lip, and then writing a verse on the back of a card, handed it to Crayon, and asked him to translate it.

"Qui pascit barbam, si crescit mente, Platoni,
Hirce, parem nitido te tua barba fecit."

"Devil take the puppy!" thought our hero. But the ladies didn't understand Latin; so he complimented Ned on his scholarship, and put the joke in his pocket, taking good care not to allude to the subject afterward.

As their own carriage was still at the shop undergoing repairs, our friends hired a hack to visit Monticello, once the seat of Mr. Jefferson. On their way up the mountain they turned aside, a little way from the road, to visit the tomb of the departed sage and statesman. The gate of the inclosure was off its hinges, and the wall itself crumbling to ruin. The grave was formerly marked by a simple granite obelisk, eight or nine feet high, in one face of which was sunk a slab of white marble, containing the following inscription:

HERE LIES BURIED THOMAS JEFFERSON,
AUTHOR OF THE DECLARATION OF AMERICAN INDEPENDENCE;
OF THE STATUTE OF VIRGINIA FOR RELIGIOUS FREEDOM,
AND FATHER OF THE UNIVERSITY OF VIRGINIA.

The marble slab has disappeared entirely, and of the obelisk there remains but a shapeless heap of granite. A good-sized flint stone, which had evidently served very often for a hammer, lay beside the remains of the monument.

"Is this broken, nameless stone all that marks the grave of Jefferson?" inquired Minnie.

"It seems," said Fanny, "as if some Vandal enemy had visited the place. Such sacrilege and wanton destruction is a disgrace to civilization."

"It must have been the British," said Dora. "You know how they were censured and abused for breaking the Naval Monument at Washington."

"Be more particular in your chronology, Dora. The last war with England terminated in 1815, and Jefferson died in 1826."

"Sure enough; I forgot that. But how can any one tell when he died, when the tomb is broken to pieces? It is very disgraceful."

"Women always jump at conclusions," replied Crayon. "The modes of showing respect to the dead are altogether conventional, and are different in different countries. Among some barbarous and semi-civilized people it is customary for every passer to cast a stone upon the grave of departed greatness, and the monument thus raised grows in magnitude and respect from year to year and from age to age. In this country, justly proud of its enlightenment, it is, on the contrary, customary for visitors to carry away a portion of any monument or memorial that may have become hallowed by association with an illustrious name. While the unpretending name which private affection has carved upon the mortuary slab may remain undisturbed until the dead and his posterity are forgotten, the monuments of the great are cracked up and scattered abroad to enrich innumerable curiosity cabinets throughout the land. It must be a source of gratification to the admirers of Mr. Jefferson to observe these unmistakable evidences of popular respect for his memory."

The exterior of the house at Monticello is striking, although time and the elements are playing sad havoc with the perishable materials of which it is built. Unless speedily repaired, brick, stucco, and woodwork will soon tumble into absolute ruin. The interior is better preserved, and the two principal rooms have some pretensions to elegance. For the rest, it is difficult to conceive of an interior plan more ridiculous and ill-contrived. The stairways are so narrow and steep that they would scarcely be admissible as passages to a kitchen loft. It is not uncommon to find great men ambitious of little things entirely out of their line, and we suppose the statesman, here as at the University, meddled a good deal with the builders. The view

ORIGINAL DRAWINGS BY PORTE CRAYON

(Courtesy D. H. Strother)

I

"Wirt. Oct: 1854. Moray Randolph's. Hardy Co. Va." (in Porte Crayon's handwriting). Pencil, ink, and wash drawing.

II

(Above) Carriage and horses used by Porte Crayon and the girls on their trip through western Virginia. The sketch was the basis for "En Route" in *Virginia Illustrated* (see p. i). Pencil. (Below, left) "Betsey. April 11th 1856." Porte Crayon revised this slightly and included it as "Betsy Sweat" in *North Carolina Illustrated* (see p. 168). Pencil, ink, and wash. (Below, right) Sketch used by Crayon in "The Drove" in *Virginia Illustrated* (see p. 46). Pencil.

III

(Above) "Siesta at Carr's." (Below) Porte Crayon "Sketching the Falls of the Blackwater. Sunday July 2nd 1854." He did not use this self-portrait in *Virginia Illustrated*. Pencil, ink, and wash.

IV

"The Crown of Otter. Botetourt Co. Virginia. Sketch Commenced Nov: 1852 [pencilled over as 1853]—Completed Sept: 21st 1872." Pencil and ink.

V

"Officers Training. Berkeley Springs, April 27th 1859." (Above, left) "The Adjutant." (Above, right) "Trying the colt." (Below, left) "Eyes Right." (Below, right) "The horse." Ink and wash sketch.

VI

"Hut on the Winston farm. June, 1851." This pencil, ink, and wash drawing became the basis for "Thornhill's Cabin" in *Virginia Illustrated* (see p. 9).

VII

A sketch on the reverse of this ink and wash drawing is dated December 5, 1856.

VIII

(Above) Sketch used in "Not a Match" in *Virginia Illustrated* (see p. 108). Pencil, ink, and wash. (Below) "Drummond. The Lake of the Dismal Swamp. March 19th 1856. D. H. Strother." Used in "Lake Drummond," *The Dismal Swamp* (see p. 137). Pencil, ink, and wash.

West. Oct: 1854
Mary Randolph
Henry Co
Va

I

II

Siesta — at Carr's

Sketching — the Falls
of the
Blackwater.
Sunday — July 2nd 1854

III

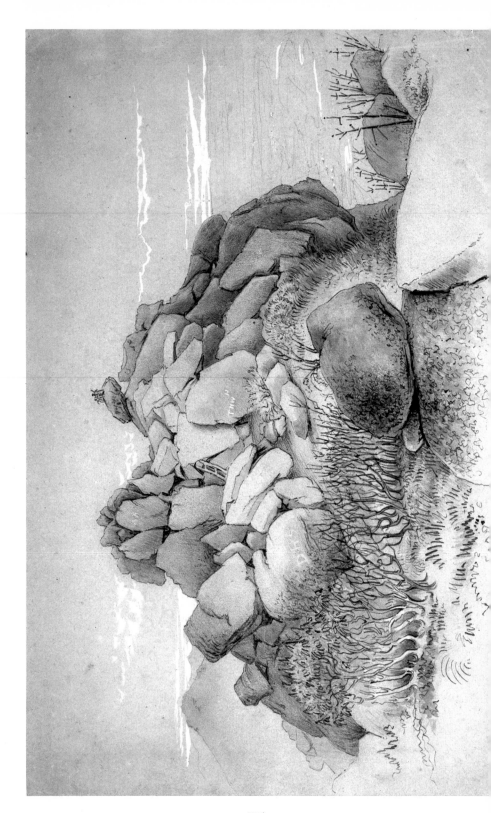

IV

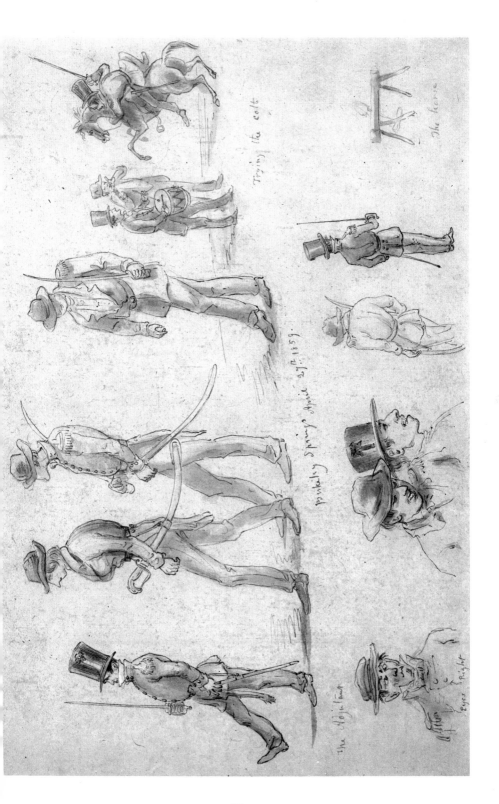

Trying the colt

The harem

Berkeley Springs April 27. 1859

The Mojo Taur

Lyes Taylor

VI

VII

The Lake of the Dismal Swamp
March 19th 1856

VIII

from the plateau, for beauty, variety, and extent, can scarcely be surpassed; and what, after all, are the considerations of convenience, expense, or technical criticism, to one who can appreciate the glorious
surroundings of this classic dwelling?

Monticello is situated upon the apex of a mountain, five hundred
feet above the Rivanna River, which flows at the base. It is three
miles distant from the town of Charlottesville, which, with the Uni·
versity, is in full view from the house.

As they were descending the mountain, our travelers heard a
sharp crash, and the carriage sank on one side until it was suddenly
brought up against a gravel-bank.

"What's the matter?" asked one of the girls, with a yawn.

"Oh, nothing!" replied Porte, quietly accommondating his person
to the change of level; "a wheel is smashed, I believe."

The driver made his appearance at the window in a state of great
perturbation, but was soon calmed by the impassive manner of the
travelers.

"Detach your horses, Uncle, ride to town, and bring us another
carriage. You need not hurry about it, but try to bring us one that
will last to the hotel."

"Did you say onhitch 'em, master?"

"Yes! yes! onhitch 'em."

"Dat I will do dat," replied the obsequious negro.

Presently his horses' feet were heard clattering down the road,
and soon the sound died away in the distance. The ladies drew
their shawls around them, and, one after another, dropped to sleep.
Wakeful on his post, like a chivalrous sentinel, Porte Crayon looked
on the sleeping beauties, proud of his responsibility, and filled with
knight-errant imaginings. Half an hour after, when the ruddy moon
peeped in at the carriage window, she found sentinel and all asleep,
and so Uncle Pompey found them when he returned with his new
carriage.

After leaving Charlottesville, our travelers floundered on through
the mud of Orange and Culpepper, which part of the journey the
philosopher characterized as "dead slow," and wondered that counties
that contained so many handsome country residences, and had fur-

nished so many great names to history, could tolerate such thorough-fares.—Not unfrequently the overdone horses would come to a halt in the centre of the highway, and the ladies would be disembarked by means of a bridge or rails, constructed from the door of the carriage to the shore. Then Mice would, by dint of coaxing, whipping, and putting his own shoulder to the wheel, get his horses out of that difficulty, shortly to fall into another of like character.

One day, as they journeyed, Mice tied the reins to his leg, and drawing up his carpet bag, with some hesitation pulled out a bundle about the size and shape of a man's head.

"What!" exclaimed Porte, with surprise. "Have you turned naturalist too? What are you going to do with that hornet's nest?"

"Dis ain't no hornets' ness, Mass' Porte; dem's bank-notes; and please, Sir, I want you to count 'em for me."

On examination of the bundle, it proved to be a wad of one-dollar notes, a circulating medium then in tolerable repute in South-western Virginia, furnished, for the most part, by the Washington City bankers: a medium much more convenient than gold and silver (Old Bullion to the contrary notwithstanding), as it may be manu-factured to any extent without the trouble of washing and mining in outlandish and inhospitable regions. When he saw of what material this ball was composed, Crayon's countenance fell, and vague suspi-cions of bank robberies crossed his mind.

"Where, in the name of Fortune, did this come from? Did you find it, or have you robbed a country store? Confess instantly."

"No, indeed, Mass' Porte," replied Mice, with honest fervor, "I never stealed money in all my life—I didn't. Fact is, Massa, I larnt de way to thumb a Jack, what you showed dem wagoners, and so I skun dem nigger waiters at Lynchburg and Charlottesville outen dat money honestly, Mass' Porte—honestly. Dat money and dese two watches."

Here Mice produced a brace of copper watches, which might have figured at a New York mock-auction.

"Honor and honesty, like every thing else, seem to be purely conventional."

"Dat's a fac, Mass' Porte. Dem's my sentiments."

In the mean time Crayon counted the money, and ascertained that what he had taken for one or two thousand amounted to less than one hundred dollars. He returned the coachman his ill-gotten gains, and lectured him soundly on the general impropriety of his conduct. Mice acquiesced easily in every thing, and promised amendment for the future, especially as the Popish idea of restitution was not suggested. He muttered, at the same time, that he "didn't see the use of gittin' larnin' if he wasn't 'lowed to use it."

THE DISMAL SWAMP

The Dismal Swamp

"Away to the Dismal Swamp he speeds;
His path was rugged and sore,
Through tangled juniper, beds of reeds,
And many a fen where the serpent feeds,
And man never trod before."

MAN, like the inferior animals, has his instincts, less imperious and less reliable, but oftener controlling his godlike reason than most are willing to admit. Possibly we might get along better if these promptings were more frequently regarded. Let philosophers work out the problem; we haven't time at present. But who has not felt the restlessness that precedes the approach of spring, long before the face of nature has manifested any of its indications? that yearning for the open air, while yet the north wind nips ears and noses? that itching to sow and plant, before the frozen earth can receive the seed? that longing for greens, before there are any sprouts? The sap begins to rise in the trees, and the blood courses warmer in the veins, suggesting dreams of blossoms and balmy breezes. What though the snow lies deep and the wind howls—spring is coming!

On the 2d of February, 1856, the sun rose bright, and the crusted snow seemed at last to be yielding to his genial rays. Books had become a bore, and I sallied forth to see my friend Porte Crayon. I found him at a table busily engaged in pointing his pencils, while his knapsack lay upon the floor surrounded by a number of articles which indicated preparation for a journey.

"Good-morning, P——. You see I am getting ready for a trip. I am tired of hearing sleigh-bells and below zero."

"Then you must meditate a journey toward the tropics?"

"Southward, ho! To meet the coming spring, to cull the earliest flowers, and eat green peas in Charleston; to steal upon Old Rip Van Winkle, and sketch him while he sleeps. In short, to gratify an irresistible yearning for movement. I feel the spring in my veins,

'Awakening long buried memories of youth and love.' "

"How long buried?" asked Crayon, reddening. "How old do you imagine I am? P——, you are impertinent."

"I beg pardon. Do you take the ladies with you this time?"

"I think not," replied Crayon, sighing audibly. "Their companionship would indeed be agreeable, vastly agreeable; but to travel advantageously, the eyes and thoughts of the traveler should be disengaged, and his movements untrammeled. He should, indeed, be all eyes and ears. With sweet faces always so near, the enchantment of the more distant landscape is often disregarded, and the merry laugh, while it beguiles the tedium of the journey, cheats the ear of much useful information."

"True," said I; "and besides their exorbitant claims on one's time and attention, it is a confounded tiresome business lugging them along in a narrative, if perchance we should conclude to write an account of your travels in these Southern climes. They talk so much, and so little to the point, that every subject gets complicated, and one can never finish."

"In addition to these difficulties, circumstances render it impossible for them to accompany me at this time, even if I wished it."

"What circumstances? if I may be permitted to inquire."

"Why, in short, they don't like the proposed route. Having no information of the country beyond what they get from the geography, they think there is nothing to be seen but swamps and turpentine, and, in consequence, have peremptorily declined my invitation."

"If the conversation had commenced at this point, it might have been shorter."

"I don't know," replied Crayon. "One must always have good reasons for yielding to necessity, and I have taken the opportunity to state mine beforehand."

At this point Uncle Jim entered with a hod of coal.

"Uncle, what do you think of the weather? Are we going to have a break-up?"

"Not yit, master, not yit," said Jim, depositing the hod on the hearth; "and if Mass' Porte da is a-gwine to travel, I 'vises him to put it off good six weeks yit; for what I am a-gwine to tell you ain't no lie, but a fac—sign never fails. Mass' Porte knows a ground hog, eh?"

"Certainly I do. Here's a picture of one."

"Dat's him all over. Well now, masters, on dis day, 2d of Feb'way, ground hog comes out he hole to look about, see how times is, ef so be den he can't see his shadow, day dark and clowdy, de creeter runs round and takes his pleasure, for den he knows spring is comin' sure enough, but if so be dat he sees his shadows like to-day, de creeter goes back and stays six weeks, kase he knows it gwine to be hard weather."

"Why, Uncle Jim, how does he know it?"

"Dunno, mass'r, dunno; dese beast creeters knows things better dan larned men; how dey knows um, Lord above only knows; but if you takes my 'vice, Mass' Porte, you'll stay in de house dese six weeks comin'. Mind what I tells you; dat's a fac."

Porte Crayon looked blank, and cursed the ground hog roundly. "Many a one," said he, "have I seen, while watching for deer, as, all unconscious of my proximity, he would come out of his hole and play around. I spared their lives because I considered them harmless creatures; and now, in return, the devilish beasts have broken up my trip, or at least deferred it for six weeks."

The weather that followed fully justified Uncle Jim's prognosis; and as I frequently thereafter saw our hero sleighing around with one or another of his quondam fellow-travelers, I presume the delay did not go so hard with him.

On Sunday, the 9th of March, Crayon informed me that he was tired waiting for the blasted ground hog, and had determined to start next morning at all hazards. During the night the snow fell to the depth of eight inches, and on Monday morning, at eight o'clock, the thermometer stood at zero. Notwithstanding this unpromising condition of things, my persevering friend was at the cars in due time, fully equipped for the journey. At the warning scream of the steam-whistle we parted, with a promise on his part to keep us fully informed in regard to his movements and adventures.

The following rambling notes we have selected from the letters we have since received; and that they may lose none of the freshness of out-door sketches, we have preserved, as nearly as possible, the form and phraseology of the originals. Of how our hero danced at a ball in the Federal City—of how he tarried in Richmond, and supped at Ballard's Exchange with the assembled wisdom of the Old Commonwealth; and how the assembled wisdom drank Champagne until it grew wiser and wiser—of the ancient borough of Norfolk, famous for its chivalry and hospitality, and, latterly, more famous for its unspeakable misfortunes, we shall not at present speak, for our hero had not yet unpacked his sketch-book, and without his sketches Porte Crayon scarcely rises above the commonplace. Our narrative opens at Suffolk, Virginia.

March 18th. In Norfolk I was advised to enter the Swamp from Suffolk, as the distance from that place to Lake Drummond, by the Land Company's canal, is considerably less than by the route from Norfolk. I consequently took the cars on the Seaboard and Roanoke Railroad, and reached here about half-past eight this morning. Suffolk, the county seat of Nansemond, is one of the oldest towns in the State. It is situated on the Nansemond river, and contains twelve or thirteen hundred inhabitants, and except the loss of its commercial importance, it stands pretty much where it did before the Revolutionary war. I expected to have found a very old, decayed, desolate looking village, such as may be seen elsewhere in Virginia, but was agreeably disappointed. With few exceptions the houses are of wood, painted white, each standing by itself and surrounded with shrubbery, flowers, and trees. Its single street, about three quarters of a mile in length, is shaded on either side by fine rows of trees, while the dwellings, without any pretensions to architectural elegance, have a neat, rural air, quite captivating to one wearied of towns and cities. On stepping from the cars I was accosted by an amiable looking mulatto boy, who took my knapsack out of my hand and warmly recommended the Central Hotel to my favorable consideration. The Central was an old fashioned wooden building, which had evidently at one time been a private residence and tastefully improved. Two gigantic box-trees stood within a paled inclosure, one on either side of the principal entrance, while the old Virginia outside chimneys were covered to the tops with ivy. To be sure the Venetians had lost half their slats, and some of them hung awry, while the white and green paint had become dingy and faded; but I must confess I was rather taken with the air of decayed respectability which the establishment

wore from this circumstance. I scarcely know why I have taken the
pains to describe this old house so minutely, as it has no historic associations that I know of, nor is it to be the theatre of any tragedy,
love plot, or ghostly apparition. But M'Guire is one of the most
obliging of hosts, and I spent two weeks there very pleasantly eating
fish and oysters. Moreover, its appearance pleased my fancy, and is
characteristic of the Southern country. Through the kind offices of
some friends I completed my arrangements to vist the Swamp on the
following morning. A basket of provisions, a roll of blankets, and
a buffalo robe for bedding, were put upon mine host's buggy wagon,
and about ten o'clock A.M., on the 19th, we mounted in person and
drove off to the canal, two miles distant. Here I found a large covered
barge and two stout negroes at my service. My baggage was quickly
transferred from the buggy to the boat. Each negro had a covered
tin bucket containing his day's provision, but on ascertaining that I
contemplated staying several days, a large iron kettle and a couple of
skillets or, as they are here called, spiders, were put into the barge.
The boatmen each took hold of a long pole, and by the help of a
peg and a withe rigged it horizontally, one to the bow and the other to
the stern of the boat, so that the ends projected over the tow-path.
They then bore their breasts upon the poles, and, with one foot
advanced, stood motionless, with eyes fixed upon me as if waiting a
signal. "Forward!" The barge went rippling through the water.
I waved adieu to my friends at the bridge, and without more ceremony
took my stand upon the bow of the boat, from whence my straining
eyes strove to follow an excited fancy onward to the shores of the
dusky lake.

The lake of the Dismal Swamp has haunted my imagination from
my earliest recollection, owing, probably, to the fact that the exquisite
ballad of Moore's was my lullaby in infancy, and even now, when in
sad and dreamy mood, that old wailing melody invariably recurs to
me as it was sung over my cradle, soothing the real with the wilder
sorrow of the poet's fancy.

Before I was aware of it I was in the Swamp. Lofty trees threw
their arching limbs over the canal, clothed to their tops with a gauze-
like drapery of tangled vines; walls of matted reeds closed up the view
on either side, while thickets of myrtle, green briar, bay, and juniper,

hung over the black, narrow canal, until the boat could scarcely find a passage between. The sky was obscured with leaden colored clouds, and all nature was silent, monotonous, deathlike. The surface of the canal was glassy smooth, and reflected the towering trees, the festooned vines, and pendant moss, with the clearness of a mirror. Before and behind the perspective lines ran to a point. The low whispering ripple

THE BARGE

of the water, and the sullen tramp, tramp, tramp, of the bargemen, did not disturb the stillness, but made it seem all the more dreary, like the ticking of an old clock in a deserted house at midnight. I was alone, utterly alone. My men were voiceless as the mutes of an Eastern despot. With the eternal tramp, tramp, tramp, they might have been ghouls, or cunningly-devised machines, set in motion by some malignant sorcerer, to bear me away living into a region of stag-

nation and death. Occasional glimpses through the thick undergrowth showed on either side extensive pools of black, slimy water,
from which rose the broad-based cypress, and grouped around those
strange contorted roots, called knees, gnarled and knotted like stalag-
mites in a cave. There, upon a decayed log, lay coiled a dead snake,
dragged untimely from his winter retreat by a hungry otter. As
we passed, I heard a rushing of wings above us, and saw a lazy, loathsome buzzard, scared from his perch and sailing away above the tree
tops. The tow-path now was nothing more than a line of juniper
logs, laid along the bank among the grass and reeds. The overarching
gums had given place to a thick grove of pointed juniper trunks,
deadened by a recent fire. This region bore some resemblance to the
crowded docks of a maritime town. The horizontally projecting limbs
were the booms and yards, while the hanging vines served as cordage.
Then the gums and cypresses reappeared, the same beds of reeds,
evergreens, and briars, in endless perspective. We were entering on
the fourth hour.

Monotony is wearisome, dreary, solemn, terrible. Tramp, tramp,
tramp. It sounded like the dread footstep of the Commander in
Don Giovanni. Tramp, tramp, tramp, like the beating pinions of
Sleep and Death, as they bore away the body of Sarpedon.

Tramp, tramp, tramp. I tried to sing, and my voice woke the
hollow, sullen echoes for the first time. What could I sing but the
old mournful lullaby, that rose to my lips unbidden:

> "They made her a grave too cold and damp
>   For a soul so warm and true;
>   She has gone to the Lake of the Dismal Swamp,
>   Where all night long, by a fire-fly lamp,
>   She paddles her white canoe.

> "Her fire-fly lamp I soon shall see,
>   Her paddle I soon shall hear;
>   Long, long, and loving our lives shall be,
>   I'll hide the maid in a cypress-tree,
>   When the footstep of Death is near.

> "Away to the Dismal Swamp he speeds;
>   His path was rugged and sore,
>   Through tangled juniper, beds of reeds,
>   And many a fen where the serpent feeds,
>   And man never trod before.

"And when on the ground he sunk to sleep—
    If slumber his eyelids knew—
He lay where the deadly vine doth weep
Its venomous tear, and nightly steep
    The flesh with blistering dew.

"And near him the she-wolf stirred the brake,
    The coppersnake breathed in his ear;
'Till starting, he cries, from his dreams awake,
'Oh! when shall I see the dusky lake,
    And the white canoe of my dear?'

"He saw the lake, and a meteor bright
    Quick over its surface played;
'Oh, welcome,' he cried, 'my dear one's light!'
And the dim shores echoed for many a night
    The name of the death-cold maid.

"He hollowed a boat of the birchen bark,
    Which carried him off from the shore;
Far, far, he followed the meteor spark,
The winds were high and the clouds were dark,
    And the boat returned no more.

"But oft from the Indian hunter's camp
    This maid and her lover so true,
Are seen, at the hour of midnight damp,
To cross the lake by a fire-fly lamp,
    And paddle their white canoe."

The bargemen seemed to bend to the poles more vigorously. I was glad to hear them pant, for it sounded like life. With a louder note I again broke forth,

"Oh! when shall I see the dusky lake?"

The perspective lines were run out at last. We turned a reedy point, and a broad sheet of water lay before us. Ely Reed threw up his hand and cried, "The lake!" Jim Pierce yelled, "The lake! the lake!" "The lake!" I shouted, and then quickly relapsed into silence.

The barge was made fast to the shore, hard by the entrance of the canal. I signed to the men to land the baggage, and then, by creeping through the reeds and leaping from tussock to tussock, I got off far enough to be out of sight, and out of the sound of their voices, and seated myself upon a cypress root. There it was—the dream

LAKE DRUMMOND

of my childhood fulfilled. It was neither new nor strange. I had seen it a thousand times in my waking and sleeping dreams, as I saw it then; the broad expanse of dusky water with its dim circling shores, the same dark leaden waves rolling over its surface and losing themselves silently among the reeds and rushes. Then those gigantic skeletons of cypress that rose so grandly in the foreground, their wild, contorted limbs waving with weepers of funereal moss, that hung down even to the water. It was complete at all points, a picture of desolation—Desolation. He that is happy, whose love is true, whose debts are paid, whose children blooming, may find strange pleasure in thus fancifully wooing this awful phantom; but when inexorable fate has laid its icy grasp upon the heartstrings, then a man puts this by impatiently, and beckons joy to come—even folly and frivolity are welcomer guests to him.

I have seen the lake, and a life long yearning has been gratified. I have seen the lake, and the romance of boyhood is undisturbed. I have seen the lake, and the recollection still enhances the mournful beauty of the old song.

There may be those who have seen it with different or indifferent

eyes—let them call me fanciful, but disturb not my dream. Just then a bald eagle hovered over my head. Our glorious national emblem reminded me of stealing; and stealing, of niggers; and these, very naturally, of dinner. When I returned, I found Jim Pierce cooking some ham and eggs under a shed which had evidently been recently occupied by some fisherman. Jim was a tall wiry black, with his hair plaited into numerous pig-tails—a mode of dressing the wool common among the blacks at the South. He has goggle eyes and an intelligent countenance, talks better than negroes usually do, and cooks remarkably well. Ely Reed is a turkey-egg mulatto, well-formed, but with an unprepossessing face

JIM PIERCE

—with nothing about him sufficiently striking to justify either a description or a sketch. I have pictured my men at this time because it was the first moment since we entered the Swamp that I had felt sufficiently disengaged to notice them. I made a hearty meal on the bacon and eggs, and after dinner took a nap upon a bed of dried reeds. Toward evening it cleared off, and I ordered out the barge for a row on the lake. The sunset was glorious, but the rowing with but

CAMP ON THE LAKE

two oarsmen was rather heavy work, and I soon returned. The men built a fresh fire at the camp, and stretched themselves to sleep on two bits of plank. As the twilight faded out a mist began to gather over the water, and presently the full moon rose.

These circumstances seemed like an invitation to indulge in a little more romance, and I sat myself down upon a tussock apart from the negroes, to watch the moon rolling up from behind a group of frantic-looking old cypresses. I thought I heard the faint sound of a paddle far over the lake. As I bent to listen the sound became more and more distinct. Strange thought! Is it only fancy, or can there be other wanderers in this solitude besides ourselves? The sound of a paddle had now become quite distinct, and was evidently nearing the point where I lay. By the light of the broad moon I could also see a white object moving rapidly toward me, which soon took the well-defined form of a boat. I felt strangely. Can the old ballad be true, then? and do the phantom lovers still haunt the lonely lake?

"Now all my flesh's hair upstood."

The white canoe shot up into the bay near our barge; paddled not by the death-cold maid, as I confidently expected, but by Joe Skeeters. Joe Skeeters holds the office of shingle-counter for the Dismal Swamp Land Company, and in addition is a thoroughbred swamper, and an occasional fisherman on the lake. The camp of which we had taken possession belonged to him, as did the nets which hung about it. Skeeters was not particularly prepossessing in his appearance, and maybe a little blunt in his manners at first, but when he came to be properly understood, he was a good fellow, and a very fair specimen of a Swamp gentleman. No French noble of the ancient régime could have done the honors of a palace more appropriately than Joe did the honors of Lake Drummond to the stranger.

He had with him a friend, or sort of lieutenant, who helped to paddle the new cypress canoe, to fish his gill nets, or cook, as he was wanted. The lieutenant landed two or three dozen speckled perch, while Skeeters and myself took a drink of bald-face together, which in these parts is the sacred pledge of hospitality, like the eating of salt among the Turks. "Jim Pierce," said the lieutenant, for they seemed to be well acquainted, "gim'me dad da spida' da." Jim handed over the utensil, when the fisherman proceeded to fry up some fat middling until the bottom of the skillet was fluent with grease. Into this he poured some hot water, and when it got hot he laid in the fish with some salt and several pods of red pepper. This mess was put to stew over a slow fire. In the mean time the lieutenant fried several of the larger perch with special care until they were very brown and crisp.

"Jim Pierce," said he again, "dad da spida' a bilin' da?"

"Yes, Sir," said Jim.

"Den liff it off den."

When the mess was ready Skeeters approached me, and, with a bow, presented a clean cypress shingle:

"Come, stranger, you must eat a pearch with us."

I had dined late, and commenced apologizing, but the lieutenant hospitably laid a large fish on my shingle:

"Come, stranga', you muss eat; I briled him puppus faw you."

There was no resisting such genuine politeness. I ate the fish, and found it so sweet that I tried a second; then Skeeters pressed me to take some of the soup. I held out my shingle without resistance this time, but Joe recommended that it should be served in a tin cup. It was quite a luxury in its way, and I made a very hearty supper. After the meal was finished we told stories of hunting and fishing adventures in the mountains and the swamps alternately.

The game is almost identically the same, and the mode of life not so dissimilar as one might suppose. In the Swamp are found bear, deer, otter, raccoons, possums, etc., pheasants, partridges, and wild ducks. The waters also abound in fine fresh-water fish, the most esteemed of which are the speckled perch. There are also a number of wild cattle that subsist upon the leaves and shoots of the reed. Their flesh is of a remarkably fine flavor, and their ferocity sometimes renders them extremely dangerous to the hunter. It is not to be supposed, however, that this vast wilderness is by any means a common hunting-ground. On the contrary, it is rarely entered except by the most resolute and experienced swampers, and the wild beasts remain for the most part undisturbed in their gloomy and inaccessible retreat. When conversation began to flag Skeeter's friend produced a dirty, well-thumbed pack of cards, and proposed a game of seven-up, mentioning, at the same time, that as he had no money we would not bet any thing.

With this innocent and moderately exciting amusement we passed the time until ten o'clock, when it was thought proper to look after the gill nets. I requested permission to accompany the lieutenant, and we paddled away out in the lake, which lay smooth as glass in the misty moonlight. It was a wild, weird scene, suggestive to the imagination of more than language can express; but it was recommended to sit steady in the canoe, and I soon became interested in the fishing. The sport was novel, but hardly more exciting than the game of all-fours, for most of the nets had nothing in them, and half a dozen perch, about the size of my hand, were the only reward of our labor. As we turned our prow landward I saw one of the nets shaken violently, and something flashing and struggling in the water. A few strokes of the paddle brought us alongside, and after an exciting fight, we succeeded in capturing a large black fish, who had unadvisedly fallen into our trap. The prize measured twenty-eight inches in length. On our return to camp we felt chilled, so hot toddy was served round, and we afterward withdrew to our sleeping apartment. This was a board shanty, some paces distant from the cooking camp, which was the residence of the fishermen during the sporting season. Here I found my buffalo robe and blankets spread upon the bed of honor—an old bedstead bottomed with some smooth planks. The rest of the party took the floor. It might look like effeminacy to sleep on clean smooth planks, but how could I refuse the delicate attention? I enjoyed a night of sweet repose, awaking two or three times to turn over and be again soothed to sleep by the snoring quartette performed by my companions.

The morning was frosty, brisk, and bright, and we were stirring betimes. The lake was entirely hidden by a thick coverlet of white mist, which lay upon its surface almost as palpable as if it had been a light cotton comforter, or mayhap an extensive worsted nube. This was presently rolled off by a lively northwestern breeze (that acted probably as maid of honor to the lake), and packed away for future use, we did not see where. Jim Pierce, meanwhile, had got us a capital breakfast; strong coffee, fish, ham and eggs, and for half an hour the shingles circulated freely.

I was not romantic this morning, and as the wind promised no sport at the fishery, I determined to turn my prow landward.

Once more in the canal, we were completely protected from the wind by the dense undergrowth, and, under a cloudless sky, the aspect of things was more cheerful. We also met a number of lighters, bound for the distant shores of the lake, to take in lumber, or carrying sand, to be used in the construction of a watergate, at the lake terminus of the canal. Although statistics are stupid, it may be well to relieve the tedium of our homeward journey by some less poetical and more practical account of the Swamp. It would be difficult to define accurately the limits of the great Dismal Swamp. On the Virginia side it occupies considerable portions of Nansemond and Princess Anne counties, and in North Carolina, portions of Gates, Pasquotank, Camden, and Currituck. Its area has been estimated at from six hundred to a thousand square miles. Lake Drummond lies on the Virginia side, and near the centre of the Swamp. It is a pond of eighteen or

HORSE CAMP

twenty miles in circuit, about seven across, measured from its most
distant points, and averaging twelve or fifteen feet in depth. The
water of the lake and of the Swamp generally is dark-colored, like
French brandy or strong coffee. It is fresh, healthful, pleasant to the
taste, and, it is said, will keep pure for an unlimited time. Hence it
is often used by vessels going on long voyages. The lake is twelve
miles distant from Suffolk, and twenty-two from Norfolk; its surface
is eleven or twelve feet above mid-tide, and there has been for a long
time a question of supplying the latter city with water from this
source. The practicability of so doing remains to be tested.

Some years ago a hotel was erected on the shore of the lake, for the
accommodation of pleasuring parties that frequently resort there during the months of May and June. A stranger was one day dining at
the house, and seeing before him a bottle containing a liquid which

he took to be brandy, he helped himself, and mixed from another bottle which seemed to contain water. The mixture was rather strong, and he added more water, and so kept on watering and drinking until he was entirely drunk and thoroughly perplexed.

"Landlord!" he stammered, "come here. This is darn'd queer brandy of yours. The more water I put in the stronger it gets."

Now the landlord had furnished white whisky, that it might be readily distinguished from the water, and the innocent stranger had taken Swamp water for brandy, and had persevered in weakening his drink with white whisky. The interior of the Swamp is said to be prefectly healthy, and free from those miasmatic diseases which prevail in the tide-water country generally. It was part of the scheme of the hotel speculator to make the lake a place of summer resort, where the people of the neighborhood might take refuge from the epidemics; but before the month of August, visitors, servants, and proprietors, had

CARTING SHINGLES

all cleared out and left the place in full possession of the mosquitoes and yellow-flies. These insects are said to be savage enough to worry the life out of a mule. The hotel was taken down.

The principal trees in the Swamp are the gum, white pine, cypress, and juniper. The juniper is an evergreen, like the cedar. The undergrowth is more varied, and during the summer months is surpassingly rich and luxuriant. The yellow jessamine, the laurel, the myrtle, and evergreen bay are the most striking. The reeds prevail every where. The land where the gum grows is reclaimable, and very fertile; elsewhere the soil seems to be a spongy, half-formed peat, into which one may thrust a stick for ten or twenty feet without finding solid bottom. In dry seasons, it sometimes takes fire, and burns to the depth of four or five feet below the ordinary surface level. Besides the animals and wild fowl previously mentioned, the Swamp abounds in all the reptiles and insects common to the surrounding country. A canal, passing through the Swamp, connects Norfolk harbor with the Pasquotank river in North Carolina. This canal passes within three or four miles of Lake Drummond, and is supplied by a feeder from the lake. Other improvements of a similar character, traversing portions of the Swamp and connecting the waters of Virginia with those of North Carolina, are now in progress. The Land Company's canal, the same by which I entered, connects the lake with the Nansemond river, near Suffolk. It is a narrow ditch, varying from seven to ten feet in width, and serves for the transportation of lumber from the interior of the Swamp.

This Land Company, to which I have so frequently referred, was organized by General Washington, after the termination of the Revolutionary War, and its original design was to reclaim and reduce the land to cultivation. This project failed, and has since been demonstrated to be impracticable, but the Company has realized almost fabulous proceeds from the timber—juniper, cypress, and white pine— that covers their grant. The Company owns a number of slaves, and hires others, who are employed in getting out the lumber in the shape of shingles, staves, etc. These hands are tasked, furnished with provisions at a fixed rate, and paid for all work exceeding the required amount. Thus an expert and industrious workman may gain a considerable sum for himself in the course of the year. The Swamp is said to be inhabited by a number of escaped slaves, who spend their lives, and even raise families, in its impenetrable fastnesses.

These people live by woodcraft, external depredation, and more frequently, it is probable, by working for the task shingle-makers at reduced wages. These employés often return greater quantities of work than could by any possibility have been produced by their own labor, and draw for two or three times the amount of provisions necessary for their own subsistence. But the provisions are furnished, the work paid for, and no questions are asked, so that the matter always remains involved in mystery.

But we have arrived at the Horse Camp, and the barge is hauled up a rude wharf, piled high with fresh-made shingles. From the landing a road, or causeway of logs, leads back into the Swamp. A hundred paces brings us to Horse Camp, the head-quarters of the shingle-makers in this district. A group of picturesque sheds afford accommodation for a number of men and mules.

CART-BOY

The occupants were absent at the time of my visit, and I had full opportunity to examine the premises. Although of the rudest character, there seemed to be every material for physical comfort in abundance. There was bacon, salt fish, meal, molasses, whisky, and sweet potatoes, besides plenty of fodder for the mules. While I was sketching, a distant rumbling advised me of the approach of the shingle-carts. These presently passed, seven in number, loaded high with shingles, and each attended by a boy on foot. When they discharged their cargoes at the landing, the boys mounted the carts and returned at a brisker pace. These youthful drivers were not particularly well dressed; but not appear to be ill-fed or overworked. Why this place is called Horse Camp I was not able to understand, as I was informed that a horse was never seen there—mules being the only animals proper for this particular service. Probably with that deference for high-blooded ancestry common in the Old Dominion, it is called after the progenitors of the present occupants.

These nimble-footed animals get over the rough and unsteady causeway quite rapidly, and, to all appearance, understand the negro lingo perfectly. They have no bridle-reins, but are managed entirely by words and gestures, mostly consisting of oaths and kicks. When his load was discharged, I saw one of them walk off the causeway into a puddle, to get a drink or cool his feet, perhaps. His conductor pranced and hallooed,

"Wha he done gwine now? Debbelish cuss—go on de road, da. I lam de har' off you wid a shingle! Hear me tell you get on de road? I beat your head wid a rail!"

This last threat decided the mule, and he quickly regained the causeway—clearly, to my mind, understanding the difference between being lammed with a shingle and pounded with a rail.

The desire to eat forbidden fruit and see forbidden sights is the natural inheritance of the human race. Now I had long nurtured a wish to see one of those sable outlaws who dwell in the fastnesses of the Swamp; who, from impatience of servitude, or to escape the consequences of crime, have fled from society, and taken up their abode among the wild beasts of the wilderness. I had been informed that they were often employed in getting out lumber by the Swamp hands, and although I had been told there would be danger in any attempt to gratify this fancy, I determined to visit the spot where the shingle-makers were at work, to see what I could. I had previously ventured to question my men on the subject, but they evaded the questions, and changed the conversation immediately. I therefore ordered them back to the boat to prepare dinner, and walked alone along the causeway. When I had gone a mile or more I heard the sounds of labor, and saw the smoke from a camp-fire. I here left the causeway, and made my way with the greatest difficulty through the tangled undergrowth. It is impossible to estimate distance under

OSMAN

these circumstances, but I crawled and struggled on until I was nearly exhausted. At length my attention was arrested by the crackling sound of other footsteps than my own. I paused, held my breath, and sunk quietly down among the reeds.

About thirty paces from me I saw a gigantic negro, with a tattered blanket wrapped about his shoulders, and a gun in his hand. His head was bare, and he had little other clothing than a pair of ragged breeches and boots. His hair and beard were tipped with gray, and his purely African features were cast in a mould betokening, in the highest degree, strength and energy. The expression of the face was of mingled fear and ferocity, and every movement betrayed a life of habitual caution and watchfulness. He reached forward his iron hand to clear away the briery screen that half concealed him while it interrupted his scrutinizing glance. Fortunately he did not discover me, but presently turned and disappeared. When the sound of his retreating footsteps died away, I drew a long free breath, and got back to the causeway with all haste. There I sat down to rest, and to make a hasty sketch of the remarkable figure I had just seen. On

COMING OUT

returning to the barge I found dinner waiting, and intentionally left my drawing where the men could see it. As Jim Pierce passed it he uttered an exclamation, and beckoned to Ely. I fancied I heard the word Osman.

"Do you know that, Jim?"

"No, Sir," said he, promptly; "dunno nothin' 'bout um."

The men continued to converse together in low whispers, and with looks expressive of astonishment. I began to get nervous. I had been rash in showing the picture—yet how, and why? Who was Osman? Was I the possessor of a dangerous secret? In the Swamp a man might easily be murdered and concealed where the buzzards couldn't find him. Ely Reed approached me, and doffing his hat, made a deferential bow. I expected a startling revelation.

"Master," said Ely, "will you draw my picter, and give it to me to take home?"

"What do you want with your picture, Ely?"

"To take home, Sir, to my wife and little daughter, to see if they'll know it."

There was nothing to be apprehended from Ely. "He that hath wife and children hath given hostages to fortune," or, as it were, bonds to society for his good behavior; consequently no bachelor ought to have a vote or be eligible to public office. I gratified Ely's request, and we started homeward.

From the effects of a hearty dinner, and a weariness of the perceptive faculties, I slept during the greater part of this portion of the journey. I was not aware that I missed any thing by so doing, except some whisky. But I asked no questions, and intend no insinuations.

At Bonneville's I left my barge, took leave of my men, shouldered my knapsack, and returned to Suffolk on foot.

The weather continued so cold and blustering, that I remained here two weeks, enjoying the hospitality of a society which combines most agreeably the simplicity of the country with the elegant refinement of city life.

It is not to be expected that so small a place affords a great variety of public amusements, but I was charmed to observe that which was most in vogue indicated an acquaintance with the writings and an appreciation of the tastes of the ancient philosophers.

The sages of antiquity were accustomed to recreate themselves with the game of the discus. The sages of Suffolk, not having discuses convenient, have substituted the Mexican dollar: in other respects the game is the same. The rising generation, emulous of the skill of their fathers, commence early practicing with cents, and burn with impatience to see the day when they shall enjoy the privilege of pitching genuine dollars like bearded men.

But in an age like this it is not to be supposed that the elegant arts even of ancient Greece should be imitated and not improved upon. The men of old seasoned their game with Attic salt and sage discourses, which must have been, at best, but dry stuff. The moderns, when they have finished their game, step in and take a drink.

But we must not leave this part of the country without an introduction to Uncle Alick, a reverend gentleman of color who resides on the border of the Swamp, two or three miles distant from town. Alick is a character, and a man of mark in his way, whose experiences in life have been varied, if we take his own account for granted. He has been a pretty extensive sinner in his time, and is now a zealous minister of the Gospel. In company with several friends, I called on him one Sunday evening. He was standing before the door of his cabin, and received us with the dignified politeness of the old school. He issued orders to *"our folks,"* like one habitually in authority, to bring out seats, and refreshments in the shape of sundry gourds of cool water, for the weather was warm. Having done the honors in a satisfactory manner, without more words he pulled out a greasy, dog-eared book, put on his spectacles, and commenced reading a sermon on the scriptural use of the exclamation Behold! Alick is small in stature, like St. Paul, and bandy-legged, like the rest of his race, with an intellectual expression of face, in common phraseology, "sharp as a steel-trap." He read with such fluency, and the book was so dirty withal, that I suspected him of knowing the sermon by heart. When he got through, we engaged him in conversation on a variety of topics. He was easily started, talked with great volubility, and, including gestures, his descriptions were very graphic. He told us of his conversion, which occurred while he was playing the fife at a militia training during the war of 1812; and then, of how he had seen a bear eat a pig in the Swamp. This latter picture was inimitable.

"Now, mass'r," said he, "all de sense I got I larned from white folks; colored folk ain't borned wid no sense naterally; 'ceps dey larns some from white folks dey never has any woth talkin' about."

The good man has had his troubles, which, I am informed, he has not always endured with the philosophy of Socrates or the patience of Job. One heavy grief has been the passage of the railroad through his sweet-potato patch, and his subsequent troubles with the Irish laborers engaged in the construction. In alluding to these matters he used some expressions savoring more of humanity than Christianity.

"But, Uncle," said one, "you know the Scriptures tell us 'to love our enemies, and pray for them that despitefully use us.'"

"Dat's a fac'; so it does, mass'r, so it does," said he, throwing himself in to an oratorical attitude. "But my 'pinions on dat subjec' is briefly dis: ef a man dat is a sinner has got ambition in him" (Uncle Alick means temper), "an' arterward he gits conwerted, dat ambition is still in him, 'spite of de Gospel. Den, ef he is wexed arter dat—dat is, ef he is owdaciously wexed—dat ambition will rise. Now, mass'r, when dem Irishmens tuck an' burnt up my fence-rails, day arter day, an' left de pigs root up de fruits of my labors, I calls dat a owdacious wexation, an' I feels very sinful 'gin dem Irishmens. I try to pray for 'em, but all de time I wish de debbil had 'em!"

Who is there that will cast the first stone at Uncle Alick?

NORTH CAROLINA ILLUSTRATED

The Fisheries

Yet more; the difference is as great between
The optics seeing, as the objects seen.
All manners take a tincture from our own,
Or come discolored, through our passions shown;
Or Fancy's beam enlarges, multiplies,
Contracts, inverts, and gives ten thousand dyes.

POPE.

ON a pleasant morning in the month of April we find our adventurous traveler, Porte Crayon, standing on the promenade deck of the steamer *Stag,* which is just backing out from the Blackwater Station, on the Sea-board and Roanoke Railroad.

On approaching this station, about twenty miles distant from the town of Suffolk, one looks in vain for the promised steamboat that is to convey him to Edenton. His search for the navigable river whose waters are to float the boat is equally fruitless; and not without many misgivings does he see the train go off, leaving him standing agape beside his baggage, in the midst of an apparently interminable cypress swamp.

Anon, a blowing and fizzing draws his attention to the swamp on the left. He starts, supposing it to be the noise of an enormous alligator, but is relieved on perceiving a white column of steam rising from the midst of the forest, and a black smoke-pipe peering above the dense undergrowth. At the same moment, a negro approaches and shoulders his baggage.

"Gwine aboard, Massa?"

The traveler cheerfully follows him down a narrow path, and presently is surprised to find himself aboard of a very promising steamboat. Then, for the first time, looking over her stern, he sees the Blackwater River, a narrow, black ditch, embanked with tangled bushes and cypress-knees, and overarched completely with trees clothed in vines and hanging moss. The stream being barely wide enough to float the boat, she is obliged to *crab* her way along for a considerable distance, her alternate sides butting the cypress-knees, and her wheel-houses raked by the overhanging boughs.

At length the river begins to grow wider, and, taking advantage of a sudden bend, the boat turns round and pursues her course headforemost. One of the passengers openly expressed his satisfaction at this change, for he said it always made him sick to ride backward.

As his fellow-travelers were not numerous, and showed no disposition to be talkative at this stage of the journey, our hero had ample opportunity to sit apart and amuse himself by indulging in such fancies as the scene suggested.

The tortuous stream lay motionless, like a dead serpent, under the dismal shadow of the never-ending forest. When the prow of the advancing boat disturbed its glassy surface, the waves heaved up as if they might have been uncouth, lazy reptiles, hastening to get out of her way, and flinging themselves over the skeleton-like cypress roots, disappeared, tumbling and wallowing among the reeds. Although the genius of Moore has given immortal pre-eminence to the Great Dismal that surrounds Lake Drummond, all the swamps bordering the southern tide-water present the same characteristics, becoming more striking, and, if possible, more dismal, as the traveler advances southward.

At the confluence of the Blackwater and Nottoway rivers we enter North Carolina. There is a stout rope stretched across the river here, which the passenger with the weak stomach took for the State line. On inquiring of the captain, however, he was informed that it was a rope ferry, of which he was presently satisfied by seeing a flat-boat pulled across.

William Byrd, of Westover, one of the commissioners who located this dividing line in 1727, says, "The borderers laid it to heart if their land was taken in Virginia; they chose much rather to belong to Carolina, where they pay no tribute to God or to Cæsar."

As the day advanced the thoroughfare gradually widened into a broad and noble river, the view became more extended and more animated, but could scarcely be characterized as interesting. However, the announcement that he had entered a new State aroused Porte Crayon from his reveries, and induced him to look about with more alertness. The bordering swamps were still the same, and there was no perceptible change in land or water. Buzzards sailed in lazy majesty athwart the blue sky, and mud-colored terrapins basked luxuriously upon convenient drift logs, motionless as stones, until the waves from the passing boat rolled them over and unceremoniously plumped them into the water. But this paradise seemed as yet untenanted by the human race.

Porte Crayon listlessly whittled his pencil—ah, there's a living

STEAMBOATING ON THE BLACKWATER

wight at last! a native Carolinian under his own beaming sun, lying in a canoe watching his fish-trap after the Southern fashion, while the sagacious eagle, with contemptuous audacity, settles down and carries off the prey.

To the inquiring mind there might be something suggestive in this picture. We, however, prefer to let every one draw his own inferences and make his own comments thereon. While our stanch little steamer paddles industriously on her way, we may be permitted to relieve the tedium of the journey by extracting some interesting historical notices of the early settlement of North Carolina.

In April, 1684, Sir Walter Raleigh sent out two ships, under Amidas and Barlow, on a voyage of discovery to the New World. In July the same year they landed on the coast of what is now North Carolina, thanked God, and took possession after the fashion of those days. They made explorations and had some intercourse with the natives by whom they were received with "Arcadian hospitality." On their return to England they gave such glowing accounts of the new country that the public imagination was fired, and a company of adventurers was easily formed to colonize a land that promised so much.

Hackluyt says, "It is the goodliest soil under the cope of heaven, the most pleasing territory of the world. The continent is of a huge and unknown greatness, and very well peopled and towned, but savagely. If Virginia had but horses and kine, no realm in Christendom would be comparable to it." He thus characterizes the natives: "They are a people gentle, loving, faithful, void of guile, cruel, bloody, destroying whole tribes in their domestic feuds; using base stratagems against their enemies, whom they invited to feasts and killed."

Some might be disposed to consider this old writer a wag, but his description was doubtless a correct one, as it seems to be a very good general description of human nature in all countries, and in all ages.

In the preface of a book printed in London, anno 1626, entitled "Purchas his Pilgrimage or Relations of the World," the author breaks out into the following: "Leaving New France, let us draw neerer to the sunne to New Britaine, whose virgin soyle not yet polluted with Spaniards lust, by our late Virgin Mother was justly called Virginia, whether shall I here begin with elogies or elegies? whether shall I warble sweet carols in praise of thy lovely face thou fairest of virgins which from our other Britaine world hath won thee wooers and sutors, not such as Leander whose loves the Poets have blazed for swimming over the straits betwixt Sestos and Abydus to his louely Hero, but which for thy sake have forsaken their mother earth, encountered the most tempestuous forces of the aire and so often ploughed vp Neptune's Plaines, furrowing the angry ocean, and that to make thee of a ruder virgin, not a wanton minion but an honest and Christian wife."

And so the worthy Pilgrim continues for several pages without a stop; but we would as lief drink a quart of beer without taking breath as undertake to read it all. In the narrative he goes on to say, "In the river of Tamescot they found oysters nine inches long, and were told that on the other side there were twice as great. Moreover, the people told our men of cannibals neere Sagadahoc with teeth three inches long, but they saw them not."

At this point the annotator was interrupted by a remark from a green-looking passenger, in a blue coat with brass buttons.

"Stranger," quoth he, "you appear to take great diversion in that book you're a-reading."

In reply, Crayon read the last quoted paragraph aloud. The listener opened his eyes, puckered his mouth, and wound up with a long whistle.

"Oh, Chowan! Three inches long? Well, that's what I call a Gatesville story."

"My friend," said Crayon, with severe gravity, "there is frequently as much rashness exhibited in the rejection as in the assertion of a belief. For example, we must all admit that nothing has been created in vain. It is equally susceptible of demonstration that the oyster was created expressly to be swallowed whole. Now we must either be prepared to allow that oysters eighteen inches long (which we have seen) exist contrary to a fixed law of nature—a false note in the universal harmony—or we must believe that there are men big enough to swallow them properly."

"Stranger, I've a suspicion that you're from the North."

"Why so, my friend?"

"Because the people up there are so bookish and larned that they'll believe almost any thing."

Brass Buttons walked away, and our traveler returned to his notes.

After several abortive attempts to establish a colony on Roanoke Island, the coast of Carolina was abandoned, and it was not until 1653, forty-six years after the settlement of Jamestown, that a colony from Virginia settled permanently on the Roanoke and the south side of Chowan. Ten years afterward, the Governor of Virginia appointed

William Drummond to take charge of the young colony, and the Lake of the Dismal Swamp still preserves the name of the first governor of North Carolina. At a later date one of the appointees of the British Crown thus characterizes his subjects: "The people of North Carolina are not to be outwitted nor cajoled. Whenever a governor attempts to effect any thing by these means he will lose his labor and show his ignorance. . . . They are not industrious, but subtle and crafty—always behaved insolently to their governors; some they have imprisoned, others they have drove out of the country, and at other times set up a governor of their own choice, supported by men under arms."

In fact, their whole colonial history is a narrative of turbulence and high-handed resistance to their British rulers, up to the commencement of the Revolutionary War; and in summing up her history, it appears that upon the soil of North Carolina the first colony of Englishmen was planted; the first child born of English parents in the New World. She may also claim, with propriety, to have shed the first blood, and to have spoken the first word, in the cause of our national independence—at the Battle of Allemance, fought in May, 1771, and through the Mecklenburg Declaration of Independence, put forth in May, 1775. The fact that so unruly and impracticable a colony should, when left to herself, have become so exemplary and conservative a State, is, in itself, a noble monument to the spirit, patriotism, and wisdom of her people.

The mid-day breeze now curls the broad bosom of the Chowan, and its shores are teeming with life and activity. Numerous bald-eagles sail overhead, while the surface of the water is dotted with boats of every description, from the cypress canoe, paddled by a lonely sallow-faced angler, to the ten-oared barges that carry out the cumbrous seines. White smoke curls up from groups of cottages on shore, where busy crowds, composed of whites, blacks, and mules, wage unceasing war upon the shad and herring. Colerain is at length reached and passed, and now the vessel's prow is turned eastward. Behind her the sun sets in a haze of golden glory. A long, low wooded point is turned at last, and at the head of the handsome bay sits Edenton—queen-like, one might say, but in a small way, and the view is all the prettier for not being in any way interrupted by those forests of shipping which usually mar the appearance of sea-port towns.

The landing of this steamer is the great event of the day for the Edentonians, and our hero had no difficulty in finding his way to the principal hotel of the place. Here he got a comfortable supper, at which fish of all kinds figured largely. Not so easy was it to secure a bed, for the County Court was in session, and the house was full. Now, in regard to county courts, they are much the same all over the Anglo-Saxon world, and the only notable peculiarity of the county courts in this region is the unheard-of number of buggies and stick-gigs that are collected about the court-house taverns on the occasion.

The glimpse that our traveler had obtained of the fisheries in coming down the Chowan had so excited his imagination on the subject, that he deferred his intended exploration of the town of Edenton next morning, and shouldering his knapsack, started on foot in quest of a fishing-beach, of which he had received information from his landlord.

Pursuing the beaten road for some distance, he at length turned into a by-way, which seemed to lead toward the point which had been indicated to him. Like all the by-ways treated of in moral allegories, this soon led our pilgrim into serious difficulties. Too perverse to turn back, and, in truth, being rather attracted by the gloomy grandeur of the swamp forest, he pushed boldly into a wilderness of reeds, tangled green briar, and cypress-knees. After half an hour of plunging and tearing, he was at length brought up on the shore of the Albemarle Sound. The scene which here presented itself was unique and beautiful, one peculiarly Southern in its features, and more easily pictured than described. In fact, Porte Crayon was decidedly blown, and here was an opportunity of resting for half an hour, without acknowledging his condition even to himself. When he had completed the sketch to his satisfaction, he re-commenced his walk, skirting the Sound for the distance of a mile or more, and, issuing from the swamp, at length gladly found himself on *terra firma,* in full view of the Belvidere Fishery.

Fatigue, hunger, and mud were all forgotten in the animated scene which here met his eye. In the foreground was the landward boat moored to the beach, while her swarthy crew were actively engaged in piling up the seine as it was drawn in by the exertions of four lively mules at the windlass hard by. In the centre, upon a bank a little elevated above the water, rose a group of sheds and buildings, alive with active preparation. Beyond these the seaward boat appeared, while upon the surface of the water, inclosing the whole beach in a grand semicircle, swept the dotted cork line of the seine. To complete this scene of bustle and animation on land and water, the air furnished its legions of fierce and eager participants. Numerous white gulls, fish-hawks, and eagles hovered or sailed in rapid circles over the narrowing cordon of the seine, at times uttering screams of hungry impatience, then darting like lightning to the water and bearing away a struggling prize in beak or talons.

It was wonderful to observe the brigand-like audacity with which these birds followed up the nets and snatched their share of the prey, sometimes almost within arm's-length of their human fellow-fishermen and fellow-robbers.

Our hero hastily unslung his knapsack, whipped out his pencil, and, seating himself upon the outer windlass, made a note of this busy and picturesque scene; and having thereby partially gratified his artistic yearnings, he lost no time in introducing himself at headquarters. Here he was received with that frank hospitality which characterizes the region, and ere long was seated at the dinner-table, where boiled rock, stewed cat-fish, white perch, and broiled shad disputed the claim on his taste and attention. Unable to decide by the eye, he tried them all twice round, swearing with devout sincerity at each dish that it was the most delicious morsel he had ever tasted. About the close of the meal a grizzled woolly head appeared at the door, and its owner, flopping his greasy wide-awake upon the sill, humbly craved audience with the manager.

"Well, what is it, Uncle?"

"A little somethin', master, if you please."

A bottle of very superior whisky, which had been set out in compliment to the stranger, was at hand, and the manager, pouring out half a tumblerful, gave it to the petitioner.

"Sarvant, master—sarvant, gent'men," and as the precious liquor, in obedience to the laws of gravity, went down, Uncle Sam rolled up his eyes with an expression of devout thankfulness that would have become a duck at a puddle.

"There now, you old reprobate, don't you call that good whisky?"

"Please God, masters," replied Uncle, with a low bow and a bland smile, "I often hear you gent'men talk about good whisky and bad whisky, but I never seed any dat wasn't good, 'specially ef ole nigger was dry. Ke! he! he! sarvant, gent'men."

But we must not tarry too long at table. The approaching cries of the mule-drivers at the windlasses warn us that the seine is gathering in, and on sallying forth we perceive that the dotted semicircle of cork line is narrowed to the diameter of fifty paces. Both boats are at hand, their platforms piled high with the enormous masses of netting, like great stacks of clover hay. The windlasses have done their part, and the mules discharged from their labors, as they are led away by their conductors, celebrate the event with cheerful brayings. All hands now leave the boats, and, at a signal from the chief, dash into the water waist deep to man the rope. A train of women, armed with knives and bearing large tubs, is seen hastening down the bank. Within the circuit of the net one may already see a thousand backfins skimming rapidly over the surface of the water. Every eye is lighted with excitement. "Hard cork!" shouts the captain. "Mind your leads thar!" yells the lieutenant. "Hard cork! mind lead! ay, ay, Sir!" roar the fifty black, dripping tritons as they heave the heavy net upon the beach. Behind the cork line where the seine bags the water now is churned to foam by the struggling prey, and the silvery sides of the fish may be seen flashing through the strong meshes. The eager gulls shriek at the sight, and sweep unheeded over the busy fishermen. One more hurrah, and the haul is landed, a line of wide planks is staked up behind, the net withdrawn, and the wriggling mass is rolled upon the beach—ten or fifteen thousand voiceless wretches, whose fluttering sounds like a strong rushing wind among the leaves.

"To the boats! to the boats!" and away go the men; now the boys and women rush knee-deep into the gasping heap. The shad are picked out, counted, and carried away to the packing-house. The rock are also sorted, and then the half-savage viragoes seat themselves in line, and begin their bloody work upon the herring. With such unmerciful celerity they work, that the unhappy fish has scarcely time to appreciate the new element into which he has been introduced ere he is beheaded, cleaned, and salted away.

If you now raise your eyes to look for the boats, you will see them already far on their way out in the Sound, the voice of their captain mingling with the cries of the disappointed gulls. In the operations of the fisheries there are no delays. Success is in proportion to the promptitude and energy displayed in every department and from the beginning of the season to the end they are driving day and night without intermission. The powers of endurance are as heavily taxed as in the life of a soldier campaigning in an enemy's country.

After a delicious supper on various dishes of fish, washed down with yeopon tea, our traveler retired to bed, blessing the man that invented sleep.

About midnight he was aroused by the hand of the manager on his shoulder: "If you wish to see a night haul, now is your time, Sir; we will land the seine in fifteen or twenty minutes."

Mr. Crayon sprung to his feet, and hastily donning his vestments, repaired to the beach. Here was a scene similar to that which he had witnessed during the day, except that the picturesque effect was greatly enhanced by the glare of the fires that illuminated the landing. The wild swart figures that hurried to and fro carrying pine torches, the red light flashing over the troubled waters, the yelling and hallooing suggested the idea that these might be Pluto's fishermen dragging nets from the Styx, or maybe a dance of demons and warlocks on a Walpurgis Night.

But such half-drowsy fancies were contradicted by the dark quiet background, where one could see faint twinkling lights marking the spot where some vessel rode at anchor, and the dim unbroken line of the horizon, from whence sprung, high over all, the vaulted arch of heaven studded with stars. How calmly and solemnly they looked down upon this scene of midnight turmoil!

Oh, beautiful and benignant guardians of the night, should not men sleep when you are watching! Oh, radiant, dewy eyes of heaven, what earth-born loveliness can vie with yours! And yet I do bethink me now of one whose eyes, mayhap less bright, beam with a gentler light, warmer and nearer. Oh, high and mighty princes of the air, when the soul plumes her flight toward your mystic and illimitable realms, how groveling appear all human pursuits and aspirations! How the vaulting spirit sinks, reeling back—

"Take care, master; you well-nigh fell into the shad bar'l."

"Whew!" ejaculated Crayon, "I believe I was asleep. Thank you, Uncle, for the timely warning;" and so he staggered back to bed, and tumbling down in his clothes, slept oblivious of heaven and earth until he was called to breakfast.

The product of these fisheries constitutes a most important item in the wealth of this region, and during the fishing season (which begins about the middle of March, and lasts until the middle of May) their success is a subject of as general conversation and all-absorbing interest to the inhabitants as is the yearly overflow of the Nile to the Egyptians.

There is scarcely an estate bordering on the Sound furnishing a practicable beach where there is not a fishery established. The number is limited, however, by the fact that these natural advantages are less frequently afforded than one might suppose. The water is often too shallow, bordered by extensive tracts of swamp, or filled with obstacles which prevent the proper dragging of the nets.

To establish a first-class fishery requires from five to ten thousand dollars of outlay, and although enormous profits are sometimes realized, the great and certain expense of carrying on the business, and the uncertainty of its results, bring it to a level with the ordinary industrial pursuits of the country. As adventurous and uncertain means of obtaining wealth are invariably more seductive than those of a character more ordinary and more certain, it has been supposed that the fisheries have exercised an unfavorable influence upon all other branches of industry in their neighborhood; but the numerous, extensive, thoroughly cultivated, and elegantly improved estates in the vicinity of Edenton would not seem to justify this idea.

Now for a more practical account of the fisheries. At the Belvidere, the seine used was twenty-seven hundred yards in length, and twenty-four feet in depth. This enormous length of netting is packed upon platforms laid on the sterns of two heavy ten-oared boats, which are rowed out together to a point opposite the landing beach, about a mile distant. Here the boats separate, moving in opposite directions, and the seine is payed out from the platforms as they row slowly toward their destined points—the seaward boat following a course down the stream and parallel to the beach, the landward boat curving inward toward the shore at the upper end of the fishery; thus heading the shoals of fish as they journey upward to their spawning grounds. The top line of the seine is buoyed with numerous corks, while the bottom, which is attached to the lead line, sinks with its weight. When the seine is all payed out, heavy ropes, made fast to the staves at its ends, are carried in to the great windlasses at either end of the fishing-ground, at this place about eight hundred yards apart. The aggregate length of the seine with these ropes is not less than two miles and a half. During the time they are winding in the rope the oarsmen have a respite from their labors, and are seen enjoying it, lying in groups on the sand, and generally in the sun, like terrapins. Here they may snore until the staff appears, when they are called to their posts to take up and pile the netting as it is drawn in. The process of winding being now continued by lines tied to the lead line of the seine, which, as they successively appear, are attached to consecutive windlasses nearing the centre. The boats follow to receive the net until they arrive at the innermost windlasses of one-mule power, which are not more than sixty or eighty yards apart. Here, as before described, the men handle the rope themselves, land the haul, take up the intervening net, and put out immediately to do it all over again. The whole process takes from five to seven hours, averaging four hauls per day of twenty-four hours.

The shad and herring are the great staples for packing. The miscellaneous fish are sold on the beach, eaten by the fishermen and plantation negroes, or are carted with the offal to manure the adjoining lands.

The refuse fish commonly taken are sturgeon, rock-cats, trout, perch, mullet, gar, gizzard-shad or ale-wife, hog-choke or flounder, lampreys, and common eels. Other varieties are sometimes taken, and among them the bug-fish, which, from its singularity, merits a particular description. In size and general appearance this fish resembles the herring, although there are external marks by which the practiced eye may easily distinguish them. The head of the bug-fish is more rounded than that of the herring, and its back and sides marked with irregular bars of a dark lead color, but its characteristic peculiarity is only discovered on opening the mouth, in which it carries a sort of parasitical bug. This singular animal belongs to the aquatic crustacea, bearing some resemblance to the shrimp or common crayfish, but not enough to be confounded with either, even by a casual observer. It is nearly colorless, and semi-transparent, like the fish found in subterranean waters which have never been exposed to light. This bug, however, has eyes which are black and prominent, and six legs on a side, each terminating in a single sharp hook, by which it retains its place in the fish's mouth. When drawn from its native element the bug-fish dies very soon, and is usually found with its mouth closed so tight that it requires a knife to force it open. The size of the occupant is proportioned to its domicil, and this fact alone proves conclusively that it is not an accidental or temporary tenant, but a permanent dweller in the fish's mouth. It is often found alive some time after the death of its carrier, and shows signs of life twenty-four hours after its removal from the fish. It makes no attempt at progressive motion either in the water or on land, but simply moves its legs and tail as if it had never been accustomed to a separate existence. The fishermen relate a number of curious stories about the bug-fish and its parasite, but as no opportunity offered to substantiate them by actual experiment, the author forbears to repeat them.

Mr. Crayon has taken the pains thus particularly to describe to us this queer fish, in the belief that naturalists have heretofore overlooked it. If this should prove to be the case, our traveler claims the honor of having added a scrap to ichthyological knowledge, and takes advantage of the privilege usually accorded, by naming the fish the *Harengus Porte Crayonensis*.

A first-class fishery employs from sixty to eighty persons, all negroes except the managers. These are for the most part free negroes, who live about in Chowan and the adjoining counties, and who, as the season approaches, gather in to the finny harvest as to an annual festival.

Although they depend almost entirely upon this employment for a livelihood, it is doubtful whether they could be induced to undergo the tremendous labor it involves, were they not passionately fond of the sport and excitement. If generally inferior in appearance to the sleek, well-fed slaves of the neighboring gentry, there are not wanting some fine-looking specimens among them, both male and female.

For instance, there is Betsy Sweat, herring-header at the Belvidere, who might serve some sentimentalist as the heroine of a romance. In her person lithe and graceful as a black panther, an expressive eye, a mouth indicating refinement and vigorous character uncommon in her race, and whether with keen-edged knife and admirable skill she whipped the heads off the silvery herrings, or with flaming torch in hand she rushed up the bank and stood waving it over the busy beach, she did every thing with an air that reminded one of the great

BETSY SWEAT

tragedienne Rachel. What though Betsy was an abominable slattern, smoked a short-stemmed pipe almost incessantly, and would drink numerous consecutive jiggers of raw whisky without winking? The true romancer seizes the great and salient points of character, overlooking trivial defects, or noting them only as eccentricities of genius. It is said that Guido Reni could take a vulgar porter at the street corner, and from him draw a magnificent head; so may the skillful writer, by the power of imagination, make heroes and heroines of big negroes and beggars' brats. The world admires and weeps, but unfortunately the real blackamoor remains unwashed, and the poor child's head uncombed, as before.

We might now take a walk through the extensive cooperage and packing-rooms, but these subjects are too practical and smell rather fishy for the journal of a picturesque and sentimental tourist; we must, therefore, look out for more congenial subjects. Ah! here is something that promises better: a train of Gates County buggies, conducted by natives from the interior, come to buy fish.

The buggy, so called probably in derision, is a cart covered with a white cotton awning, drawn by a bony, barefooted horse with one eye. This is not a Cyclopean monster, as one versed in the classics might imagine, for the eye is not located in the middle of the forehead, but on one side, and the animal, on an average, is rather below the medium size. Nor were we able to ascertain whether Gates County furnished a one-eyed breed of horses, for our visitors from the interior are not communicative, their silence being apparently the result of diffidence. But they are acute observers, and sharp as a mowing-scythe at a bargain.

"That chap with the sorrel head would make a rare sketch."

"Neighbor," said the manager, "if you will sit for your portrait to this gentleman I'll make you a present of that fine string of rock-fish."

The native paused and looked at Crayon, who was busy pointing his pencils.

"I don't see," said he, tartly, "that I am any uglier than the rest of 'em."

"Certainly not, my friend," said Crayon, "you misapprehend my motive entirely. I merely desired your portrait as a remembrance, or rather a specimen—or a—" Here our artist closed up, and the manager snickered outright.

"I'll tell you what, Mister, you needn't think to make a fool of me; if you'll jest take a lookin' glass, and picter off what you see in it, you'll have a very good specimen of a bar."

"But, neighbor, don't go off at half-cock; here's another superb rock I'll add to the bunch."

The indignant countryman hesitated, and weighed the fish in his hand. "Well, you may take me if you can catch me while I'm bobbin' around, but I can't stop for you."

Having spent several days at the Belvidere, a hospitable invitation induced our traveler to move his quarters to the Montpelier Mansion, and his sketching operations to the fishing-ground belonging to that estate. The Montpelier beach is only about a mile distant from the Belvidere, and has the advantage over all others which he visited of being beautifully shaded by a growth of lofty trees.

Henry Hoffler, the master-fisherman at Montpelier, is a model of his class, and a character not to be passed over without a proper notice.

A NATIVE

In physiognomy and manner he reminds one of a "jimber-jawed" bull-dog—one of those fellows who never let go. With an indomitable perseverance and sturdy honesty invaluable in an executive officer, he is a shrewd, skillful, and experienced officer in his vocation.

No one knows better than he how to interpret the signs stenographed on sky and water, or can more certainly foretell, from wind and weather, the probable results of a haul; no one readier than he to face an unpropitious gale, or who can more skillfully bring a seine to land through a roaring surf.

Like all strong characters, Hoffler has his instinctive aversions, which have been indulged in until they have acquired, perhaps, an undue prominence. Loungers about the fishery he regards with inexpressible contempt, and endeavors to express it by calling them "Arabs"—a term of opprobrium not very clear in its meaning. His hatred of eels is an exaggerated sentiment, entirely disproportioned to the importance of its unfortunate objects. He carries a cane for the express purpose of killing them, and no sooner are the duties of landing a haul attended to than he gives way to his feelings, and falls to thrashing them, right and left, without mercy, swearing against them with the only oath or exclamation he ever makes use of, "My blessed! I wish the seed of 'em was destroyed." Hoffler talks but little, and what he says is to the point; doubly impressive by being delivered in alternate squeaks and grunts—soprano and basso by turns. Round a corner one might mistake him for two men. Like William of Deloraine,

"Though rude, and scant of courtesy,"

there is a strong undercurrent of good feeling in the old fisherman's character, and a kindly twinkle in his eye, that fully make amends for the rugged surface.

As our hero approached the beach, this redoubtable personage advanced to meet him, and giving his hand an agonizing grip, thus saluted him:

MY BLESSED!

"Good-mornin'; make yourself at home; look about."

"Thank you," replied Crayon. "I perceive you have just landed your nets, and have had a good haul."

Hoffler made no reply, but looked in his face for a moment, and then ran off to head an eel that was about escaping into the water. Jimmy, the cooper, who had laid down his adze to stare at the new-comer, now hurried out of the shed.

"Hoffler, I say—easy in time— Hoffler, I've often heard you talk about Arabs, but that's one of 'em, sure enough."

"My blessed!" said Hoffler, "did you hear him? Whar did he come from? The man don't know a net from a seine."

The seven or eight days that followed passed pleasantly enough at the fishery. There was, indeed, a sufficiency of the exciting and the picturesque to have interested both sportsman and artist for a much longer time. The visitor soon begins to feel a personal interest in the game. The hopes, the fears, the successes and disappointments of the fishery become his own. When the seine is out of sight upon the Sound he may sleep, sketch, or shoot gulls at pleasure; but when the back fins of the prey are seen playing about within the narrowing circle, he must needs throw down gun or pencil, and rush to the landing. When it happens that the seine is torn by the passage of a vessel, and the fish escape, he joins heartily in anathematizing the scoundrelly captain whose inconsiderate keel has wrought the damage, and concurs with facility in the general opinion that but for the break this world have been the greatest haul on record.

There is, too, sufficient variety in the incidents of each day to prevent the interest from flagging. Sometimes it happens that such immense shoals of fish are inclosed that the great seine can not be landed at once, and it becomes necessary to cast smaller nets within the large one, to bring them ashore in detail. Sometimes they bring in sturgeon or rock-fish so large that there is reason to fear they may break the net in their struggles. Then negroes are sent in armed with spears and long-handed hooks to kill them and bring them to land singly. The most diverting incidents attend this part of the sport. The wary black wades into the water up to his waist, and, watching his opportunity, strikes the hook into the back of a stout sturgeon. The fish darts off, Cuffee holds on, and a struggle commences for life on one side and fame on the other. The fish leaps and flounders, the black pants and pulls. The spectators applaud one party or the other according to their sympathies, rending the air with shouts and laughter. The sturgeon makes a desperate plunge and jerks the pole out of Cuffee's hands—overwhelmed with reproaches, he splashes along in pursuit, and at length recovers his hold, but as he grasps it, loses his balance and disappears under the water. Presently he reappears, still hanging on to the hook. Two or three fellows rush in to his assistance, but the general voice cries, "Stand back! fair play!" By this time the negro's blood is up, and disdaining the advantage of a weapon, he leaps upon the sturgeon's back, unmindful of his rough saddle. The furious and bewildered fish darts away and lands himself and rider upon the sandy shore. Cuffee springs to his feet, and seizing his antagonist as Hercules hugged Antæus, bears him out of reach of his native element and slams him triumphantly upon the ground.

"Aha! got you now, you mizzible long-winded cuss!"

The grinning victor is applauded, and receives an extra dram as his reward.

Without noticing Hoffler's especial enemies, the Arabs, the society on the beach is varied daily by the arrival of legitimate and character-istic visitors. There is the Yankee sea-captain, whose vessel rides in the offing, a shrewd, entertaining fellow, who can tell quaint stories

of sea-faring life, and quiz the provincials, who come down with their
buggies to get a thousand herring and a few dozen *pearch* or so.

AUNT ROSE

Then there comes old Aunt Rose, with a basket on her arm, to be
filled with cat-fish or "some o' dem red hosses," as she styles the
suckers. Aunt Rose is communicative enough considering the amount
she has to communicate. You drop a dime into her basket and civilly
inquire her age.

"Lord bless you, honey, how does I know? I was borned over on
toder side of de Sound—white folks over dar knows. Lemme see,

when ole miss's mother was married I was den a right smart gal—dat makes me a risin' o' sixty, or seventy, or maybe bout a hundred—any way, white folks over de Sound knows."

When more exciting entertainment was wanting, one could help old Hoffler to kill eels—not in his absurd way by beating them with a bludgeon, but more considerately by sticking a knife through their tails, making a groove in the sand, and laying them in it on their backs, or dropping them alive into a barrel of pickle.

"Mr. Crayon, Mr. Crayon! could you have so far forgotten personal dignity and the common sentiments of humanity? This comes of a man traveling off by himself without the elevating and civilizing companionship of the softer sex."

Porte Crayon looked at us fixedly for some moments.

"I do think," he at length replied, "that if entirely deprived of the society of women, men would in a short time relapse into barbarism; but I also think your sentimentality about the eels extremely ridiculous."

If, at length, the sports on the beach grow stale from custom, the sojourner may find something to interest him in the adjoining country. Bordering on the Sound and around Edenton are many handsome residences and well-improved estates, whose names, Belvidere, Montpelier, Mulberry Hill, etc., in a country almost as level as the surface of the water, exhibit the disposition of the human mind to cherish pleasant illusions in the midst of adverse circumstances.

Here, on an April day, drinking in the perfumed air, the earth around him just bursting into luxuriant bloom, making the simple consciousness of existence a soul-filling delight, the stranger first begins to realize his ideal of Southern life—a life that for the Northern world exists only in books and dreams. But to complete our picture in a more satisfactory manner, let us dwell upon it a little longer— let us live through a day together.

Imagine yourself a guest in one of those hospitable mansions. Shall we begin the day at sunrise? If so, then you must imagine yourself in bed, the sun bidding you good-morning through a screen of honeysuckles or rose bushes; you lie half conscious of existence, recalling a night of moonlight, mocking-birds, and pleasant dreams. Presently, with noiseless step, a servant glides into your room, and you hear the fresh water gushing into your pitcher, suggesting thoughts of Moorish fountains, and then you catch a glimpse of the retreating shadow carrying off your boots. Again you relapse into dreams. How long it matters not; but the blissful trance is at length broken by a soft voice—"Breakfast is ready, Sir." The idea of breakfast is a stimulant, and you start up. A fresh-washed, bright-eyed boy of five years old stands beside you, joyful messenger, hopeful scion of a gentle race, practicing the sweet courtesies of social life ere his tongue has lost the lisp of infancy. "Thank you, little master; I'll be there anon."

Now you may make your toilet without more circumlocution. After coffee and hot cakes, seasoned with broiled shad, ham and eggs, or any other delicacy of the season that may have been incidentally alluded to on the preceding evening, you are ready to begin the day. A visit to some of the neighboring fisheries is suggested. It promises nothing new, but the trip itself will be agreeable. The visit is considerately determined upon. Then shall we go by land or water? The buggy stands at the gate, and the boat is anchored off the beach. The roads are smooth, and the trotter paws the ground impatiently. The breeze is freshening over the Sound, and the yacht will carry us gallantly.

"Let them put up the trotter. Ned! get the boat ready."

A stout sailor-looking black draws up the craft and rigs the mast in a trice. "Push off, good-by!" and away we dart, like a white gull, into the middle of the Sound. Our vessel moves like a race-horse, tacking in and out, with a spanking breeze on her quarter. Sometimes leaving the fisheries on the northern shore almost out of sight, then bearing down upon them so near that you might hail the foreman to ask, "What luck?"

So we go down the Sound some eight or ten miles, far enough to have a good run back before the wind. But it would not be neighborly to return without calling in to pay our respects and to inquire after the success of our friends. So we run in to a landing, are warmly welcomed, of course, invited up to the office, where we take some refreshment, also, of course. [N.B. The water in flat countries is considered unwholesome for strangers, and is not highly esteemed by the natives themselves.] Then, in a cheerful, friendly way, we begin to compare our fishing experiences. How many shad and how many herring we've averaged; what they are doing at Benbury's; what hauls Cheshire has made, and how Wood is getting on. A week's visit is sufficient to make one feel himself a full partner in any of the fisheries, and the visitor always speaks of our beach and our hauls. Now it is time to go.

"But, gentlemen, you must positively stay to dinner. We can offer you no great temptation; only a fiisherman's fare, the best we have, and a hearty welcome."

That might tempt a prince; but we've arranged to dine at home, and so we take leave, and are presently driving before the wind at the rate of two-forty, or thereabout—we can't be very exact, as we have no thermometer. After dinner we may drive to Edenton or not as we feel disposed. For my part I prefer lounging about the shore, taking a siesta, perhaps, under an arbor of wild vines.

Gorgeous in purple and gold the sun sinks beneath the distant horizon. The breeze has lulled, and the calm water reflects the violet-tinted sky like a vast mirror. With a wild and pleasing melody the songs of the distant fishermen break the stillness of the evening, and the eye may now trace the whole circuit of the seine, dotted for a mile or more on the glassy surface of the Sound.

But mark that dead cedar, half clothed in a gauzy robe of vines; how entreatingly it seems to stretch its skeleton arms over something at its foot, like hopeless, half-frantic Niobe, shielding the last of her children. Here, indeed, is a little grass-grown space, respected by the plowman, and two old tombs almost hidden by the overhanging vines. Push these away, and there is still light enough to enable us to read the quaint inscriptions.

HERE LYES INTERRED Y^e BODY OF
HENDERSON WALKER, ESQ^r., PRESIDENT OF
Y^e COUNCIL AND COMMANDER IN CHEIF OF
NORTH CAROLINA, DURING WHOSE
ADMINISTRATION Y^e PROVINCE INJOYED
THAT TRANQUILITY WHICH IS TO BE WISHED
IT MAY NEVER WANT. HE DEPARTED THIS LIFE
APRIL Y^e 14TH, 1704. AGED 44 YEARS.

ON THE NORTH SIDE OF THIS TOMB LIES THE BODY
OF GEORGE LILLINGTON, SON OF MAJOR
ALEXANDER LILLINGTON, WHO DEC^d. IN Y^e 15 YEAR OF
HIS AGE, ANNO 1706.

HERE LYES THE BODY OF
ANNE MOSELY,
WIFE OF EDWARD MOSELY, ESQ.,
SHE WAS DAUGHTER OF MAJOR
ALEXANDER LILLINGTON, ESQ., AND THE
WIDOW OF THE HON^{ble}. HENDERSON WALKER,
ESQ., LATE PRESIDENT OF HIS MAJESTY'S
COUNCIL OF NORTH CAROLINA.
SHE DEPARTED THIS LIFE
NOVEMBER 18, ANNO DON^y. 1732,
AGED 55 YEARS & 5 MONTHS.

The tombs are situated on a point of land, not far from the water, and sufficiently elevated above it to command an extensive prospect in every direction. Altogether, we have seldom seen a more romantic spot for a burial-place. The unpretending tablets are still in good preservation, having been treated leniently by time, and bearing no marks from the hand of that wanton desecrator, man. Are our brethren of North Carolina more elevated in moral civilization than their neighbors, or have the voiceless prayers of the old cedar prevailed?

By a singular coincidence we happened here on the 14th of April, the anniversary of the Governor's death. A hundred and fifty-two years had elapsed since he had made his honored exit from the stage of life. Here was suggestion enough for thought, but a man's reflections while sitting on a tomb-stone will scarcely be appreciated by one lounging on a cut-velvet sofa, so we will discreetly pass them over. Nathless we tarried there until the chill moon marked our shadow upon the trunk of the blasted cedar, and the mocking-bird, whose nest was in the old grape-vine, began his evening song.

But in these listless wanderings we must not overlook our central point, the old historic town of Edenton. This place was established in the year 1716, and was originally called Queen Anne's Creek, which name was afterward changed to Edenton, in compliment to Charles Eden, the royal governor of the province, appointed in 1720. The early records of the courts are said to contain matter of great historic interest, but these are now at Raleigh, the capital of the State. Porte Crayon told us privately that he was glad of it, and also intimated that he infinitely preferred fresh shad to musty records. This, from a pretender to scholarship, is an audacious admission; but the good-natured public will, perhaps, excuse him.

We will, however, on our own responsibility, venture to quote two suggestive items from Wheeler's History:

"From an old custom-house book, now in possession of J. M. Jones, Esq., of Edenton, it appears that in July, 1768, the ship Amelia cleared hence, with an assorted cargo, among which were three bags of cotton."

"By some strange freak of circumstance, many years ago, there was found at Gibraltar a beautiful picture, done in a skillful style, enameled on glass, 'A Meeting of the Ladies of Edenton Destroying the Tea, when Taxed by the English Parliament.' This picture was procured by some of the officers of our navy, and was sent to Edenton, where I saw it, in 1830."

It is to be regretted that Porte Crayon did not get a sight of this painting, that the world might have heard more of it, and that the patriotism of the ladies of Edenton might have been blazoned beside that of the men of Boston, which has figured in so many bad wood-cuts.

The modern Edenton is a pleasant little place, of some fifteen hundred inhabitants, who seem to take the world very philosophically. It contains a number of neat, old-fashioned residences, and several of more recent construction, that would figure handsomely in the environs of New York.

The court-house green, sloping down to the water's edge, and shaded with fine old trees, is one of the chief attractions of the village. The ivy-mantled church, St. Paul's, was built about 1725, and is evidently the pet of the place. The handsomely improved cemetery around it gives ample evidence of the wealth and cultivated taste of the community.

"To speak further," says Mr. Crayon, "of those matters which were especially pleasing to me—the quiet streets and deserted wharves—might be deemed superfluous by those who think a town without commerce is dead and half dishonored. But to one thoroughly disgusted with the haste and hubbub of large cities, there is an air of blest repose, of good-humored languor hanging about these old towns that is positively enchanting." But, like the voyager on the stream of life, we are not permitted long to linger on the green spots where pleasant flowers bloom. We can but cull a boquet in passing, enjoy its evanescent bloom, retain a few dried and colorless impressions in the leaves of a book, and hasten on our way, happy if the interval is short between the fading twilight of regret and the fresh dawn of expectation.

Porte Crayon had his knapsack packed and buckled down, but as the steamer which was to convey him to Plymouth was not expected until late in the afternoon, he determined to take a parting look at the fisheries, to shake honest Hoffler by the hand, and once more bid adieu to his kind and hospitable entertainers.

"Hoffler!" said Jimmy, the cooper, "easy in time: I've found it out. That's none of your Arabs; that's the author of *Harper's Magazine!*"

"Don't tell me, Jimmy; Boss said he was a man of mark—had traveled; but, my blessed, he don't know a net from a seine!"

The Piny Woods

Ye gods of quiet and of sleep profound,
Whose soft dominion o'er this country sways,
And all the widely silent places round,
Forgive me if my trembling pen displays
What never yet was sung in mortal lays.

THOMSON.

NEARLY the whole of the eastern part of North Carolina is covered with pine forests, extending from the swampy country bordering the sea-board as far back as Raleigh, the capital of the State. This section is sparsely populated, but little improved, and although it furnishes the greater portion of all the resinous matter used in ship-building in the United States, it has hitherto been little known. It is called by the Carolinians "The Piny Woods," and we must prepare to follow our persevering traveler, Porte Crayon, in his wanderings through this primitive and lonely region.

At Plymouth we find him seated on the porch, at Enoch Jones's Hotel, looking as lazy and listless as if he were a citizen of the place. Plymouth, we believe, is the county town of Washington, situated on the opposite side of the Sound from Edenton, a short distance up the Roanoke, and contains a thousand or twelve hundred inhabitants.

It is the successful commercial rival of Edenton, and plumes itself on its business activity, not without reason, for Crayon reports that its wharves were crowded with six or seven sloops; and during the day he staid there, no less than three vessels loaded with lumber hauled up to take in grog and then passed on their way. The shores of the Roanoke in the vicinity are low and swampy, and although the village is not unpleasing to the eye, it contains nothing of sufficient interest to detain the traveler long. How Porte Crayon came to remain here for thirty-six hours, happened in this wise.

He had been extremely desirous to obtain a passage to Roanoke Island, and having failed to do so on the other side of the Sound, had hopes of being able here to find a vessel outward-bound. Accompanied by his obliging landlord, he visited several taverns and doggeries near the river, and at length found the commander of a lumber sloop, whose vessel was to sail seaward at early dawn next morning. Crayon felicitated himself on this fortunate rencontre, and the captain cheerfully agreed to take a passenger, at the same time dropping a modest hint about rough fare. A Roanoke Islander, who was returning home by the same vessel, also volunteered to attend at the appointed hour with his canoe at the steamboat landing, to take our hero aboard the vessel, which lay out in the stream. This was most satisfactory. The agreement was forthwith sealed with a glass of "something all round," and Crayon returned to his quarters in a state of pleasurable excitement. That night he dreamed of taking a glass of grog with Captains Barlow and Amidas. Then the bronzed and feather-beaten faces of these worthies faded away, and still wandering in dreams, he was in an extensive grove of live-oaks.

"I delight in dreams," quoth Crayon. "In dreams only can the soul realize its full capacity for feeling. When cold, tyrannical reason sleeps, fancy may revel unchidden and unchecked, like a joyous child when a captious, repressing step-mother is away. What though the dreamer's hunger is never satisfied, and his thirst never quenched —what though his bliss is fleeting as the gilding of a morning cloud —tell me, ye that know, wherein our waking life is better?

"But to return to my dream: straying through this grove of live-oaks for some distance, I at length came upon an open space where stood an Indian encampment. All seemed to be filled with life, yet all was silence. As I passed along in the midst, apparently unnoticed, I saw groups of grim-painted warriors leaning on their bows and war-clubs; others reclined in front of their lodges, smoking; while others were employed in sharpening their spears and feathering their bone-pointed arrows. Copper-colored children rolled and tumbled over the grass, and leather-faced squaws were variously occupied in all the domestic drudgeries of the camp.

"I paused at length before a lodge whose superior size and decorations proclaimed the dwelling of a chieftain. As I gazed in dreamy wonder the grass-woven screen which served as a door was pushed aside, and a maiden of exquisite beauty came forth. As she stood for a time in thoughtful silence, I had opportunity to consider the matchless beauty of her face, and the faultless symmetry of her form, which, if it could not be improved, was but little marred by the barbaric splendor of her costume. Her tunic was of woven bark tissue, white as paper and light as silk, curiously and beautifully wrought with many-colored shells. Her dainty feet were half hidden in embroidered moccasins, her wrists and ankles clasped by bands of shining gold. A richly-ornamented sash bound her delicate waist, and a necklace of gold and white coral hung about her neck. Though her attire was that of an Indian princess, her skin was of dazzling whiteness, and

VIRGINIA DARE

her dimpled cheek flushed with the freshest rose. Her round, wondering eyes were of a tender blue, and the plumy circlet on her head rested on a luxuriant mass of flaxen hair, that fell in wild ringlets over her graceful shoulders, and downward until it became entangled with the shell-wrought fringe of her girdle.

"At the appearance of this bright vision there was a general movement in the camp, and the warriors approached her with looks of mingled love and reverence. More than one young brave, of tall and goodly person, gallantly betrophied with eagles' feathers and bears' claws, advanced trembling as if to proffer service, but a gentle wave of her white hand sent them crest-fallen and disappointed back.

"Then a more aged man approached, who, by his dress, might have been a priest or prophet. He was profusely decked with golden ornaments; a broad gold ring hung in his nose, and in the wide slits in his enormous ears were twined two living green snakes, whose loathsome beauty seemed fitly to decorate the hideous head that bore them. As he advanced with more audacity than the rest, the maiden's childlike face changed its expression of thoughtful dignity to one of disgust, and half of terror. Yet, as if unused to fear, she stamped her little foot like an angered fawn, and waved him off with quick and imperious gesture. Sullen and vengeful was the scowl that darkened his face as he retired; but neither respect for the great brave, nor awe of the mighty necromancer, could repress the gleam of satisfaction that lightened the faces of the younger warriors at this discomfiture.

"The beautiful princess went her way alone, by a path which led to the forest shade. Unseen and unregarded as a spirit in the land of the living, I followed her springing footsteps—half wondering, half worshiping. When she had gone a long way from the camp, and reached a secluded spot in the forest, she paused and stood in an attitude of anxious expectation. Her suspense was of short duration, for presently an arrow, bound with flowers, fell at her feet. She started, a flush of pleasure overspread her face, and ere she could stoop to take up the messenger of joy, a princely youth came bounding through the woodland and knelt at her feet. With a look full of idolatrous love, he bowed himself; but she raised him up, and ere long her flaxen tresses were nestled lovingly upon that manly breast.

"Then a thought flashed upon me like a gleam of sunshine in a shady dell. 'It is, it is! it must be she! she did not perish with the rest! She was saved—saved, sweet, exotic flower! to bloom so gloriously in the far wilderness amidst these savage weeds of humanity—to reign a queen over these rude beasts—to be worshiped, perhaps idolized! Ah me! with such a divinity it would not be very hard to turn idolator. Could I be speak now, to claim kindred with her—first-born of English blood upon this mighty continent—Virginia Dare—to hear, mayhap, from her sweet lips, something of the fate of that lost colony; something to fill that mournfulest blank in the pages of history.'

"Too late; for suddenly a yell broke on my ear,

'As all the fiends from heaven that fell,
Had pealed the banner-cry of hell.'

A hundred shadowy forms came rushing through the forest, and foremost of all the ring-nosed prophet, with snaky eyes bent on the youthful lovers. 'Accursed juggler!' I cried, 'this is your villainy.

But your blasting eyes shall never see their capture!' With superhuman energy I leaped upon him, and as we fell he uttered a frantic scream —which woke me.

"I found myself standing in the middle of my room at Enoch Jones's, and became aware that an obstreperous shanghai in a tree hard by was crowing for day. If I could but have spoken to her," continued Crayon, "I should have been content to die, and have been a happier man for the rest of my life."

Hurrying on his clothes, and slinging his knapsack, our hero hastened to the place of rendezvous on the banks of the river. He arrived a little before the appointed hour, and finding no one to meet him, shouted, called, and signaled in vain, until the time was past. He then visited the half dozen tenantless sloops lying at the wharves, thinking it possible that the *Empire* might have changed her position during the night; and, finally, wearied with the fruitless search, he lay down upon a bale of cotton and slept. About sunrise the wharf-master came down, and informed him that the faithless skipper had weighed anchor about midnight, and by this time was probably far out on the Sound. Sloth and philosophy are said to be near akin, but it required the assistance of both to enable Crayon to keep cool on the reception of this intelligence. To his honor be it said, that he succeeded in his efforts. He only shrugged his shoulders, and mildly expressed a hope that the sloop with her commander might sink to the bottom of the sea, and then, feeling amiable as Uncle Toby, returned to the hotel.

The attempt to get off by this line having proved a failure, Crayon ascertained that the stage-coach for Washington started early on the following morning. Here was a chance, but what was he to do in the mean time. The loungers on the tavern porch spent the morning in discussing the merits of a dispute between Williamston, a little place up the Roanoke, and the proprietors of the steamboat line. The Williamstonians desired the extension of the line to their city. The boats thought it wouldn't pay; hence the controversy. As there was not much in the subject, it died out about the heat of the day, and then followed a dead calm. This was disturbed at intervals by a dog-fight; a negro brat tumbling down the steps; and, finally, about twelve o'clock, by a drunken fellow who called for "licker." The request was negatived. Boosey obstreperously insisted. The landlord stood firm, and there was great hope of a row. But just at the crisis of the dispute, Boosey basely yielded and retired—so completely does drunkenness undermine a man's high moral nature.

After dinner, Crayon repaired to the wharf and sat upon the cotton bales again, from whence he watched two boys fishing. They caught nothing, and our hero sunk to sleep.

Toward evening the tavern porch got more lively. Some one had set a negro boy to trying the speed of a trotter up and down the level street, and this entertainment collected all the available idlers and horse-fanciers in the vicinity.

MAJOR BULBOUS

"That hoss," said the stage-driver, addressing himself to Mr. Crayon, "that hoss reminds me of a hoss that old Major Bulbous used to drive in that old stick gig of his'n. I see him once," continued the narrator, "atwixt G—— and E——, where I druv a coach for a while, a-coming up through the Piny Woods, in sich a pickle as I never see a man before or sence. At fust I thought it was one of these steam-engines tearing along the road by itself, but as he come alongside I see it was the Major in his gig. His skin was pretty full, he was driving like thunder, and his gig all afire. 'Halloo, Major,' says I, 'stop!' But he only cussed me black and blue. Then one of the passengers cried out, 'Halloo, old fellow, whar did you come from?' 'From hell,' says he, giving his hoss the whip. 'Well, I should have thought so from appearances,' said the passenger. By this time the Major was out of sight, leaving a streak of smoke behind him, perhaps a quarter of a mile long. No doubt the gig caught fire from a cigar, for he was much in the habit of smoking as he traveled."

"And what became of him?"

"Why, they say, in passing through the swamp near his house, the wheel stuck a cypress-knee and flung him out into the water. The horse run home with the gig in a blaze and made straight for the barn-yard. By good luck the gate was shut, or he might have set the whole premises on fire. They say the Major didn't get drunk for well-nigh a month arterward."

From Plymouth to Washington the road is generally good, and the coaches make very fair speed. Nevertheless, the leisurely habits of the people during the necessary stoppages for watering and changing teams, give ample time to note the peculiarities of the country. Its features are monotonous in the extreme, varied only by alternate swamp and piny woods; the former bordering the water-courses, the latter covering the sandy ridges between.

These forests are of the long-leafed pine, the *Pinus palustris* of the Southern States. From them is gathered one of the great staples of North Carolina—the turpentine. And although this product and its derivatives are, in our country, almost in as common use as bread and meat, very little is known of the manner of procuring them. We will therefore endeavor to describe it accurately, relying upon such sketches and observations as Crayon was enabled to make during his tour.

These trees at maturity are seventy or eighty feet high, and their trunks eighteen or twenty inches in diameter near the base. They grow close together, very straight, and without branches to two-thirds of their height. Overhead, their interlocking crowns form a continuous shady canopy; while beneath, the ground is covered with a thick, yellow matting of pinestraw, clean, dry, level, and unbroken by undergrowth. The privilege of tapping the trees is generally farmed out by the landowner, at a stated price per thousand, say from twenty to thirty dollars. Under this privilege the laborer commences his operations. During the winter he chops deep notches in the base of the tree, a few inches from the ground, and slanting inward. Above, to the height of two or three feet, the surface is scarified by chipping off the bark and outer wood. From this surface the resinous sap begins to flow about the middle of March, at first very slowly, but more rapidly during the heat of summer, and slowly again as winter approaches. The liquid turpentine runs into the notches, or boxes, as they are technically called, each holding from a quart to half a gallon. This, as it gathers, is dipped out with a wooden spoon, barreled, and carried to market, where it commands the highest price. That which oozes out and hardens upon the scarified surface of the tree is scraped down with an iron instrument into a sort of hod, and is sold at an inferior price. Every year the process of scarifying is carried two or three feet higher up the trunk, until it reaches the height of twelve or fifteen feet—as high as a man can conveniently reach with his long-handled cutter. When this ceases to yield, the same process is commenced on the opposite side of the trunk. An average yield is about twenty-five barrels of turpentine from a thousand trees, and it is estimated that one man will dip ten thousand boxes.

The produce is carried to market on a sort of dray or cart which holds but two barrels, consequently the barrels are always seen setting about in the woods in couples. The trees at length die under these repeated operations. They are then felled, split into small sticks, and burned for tar. The dead trees are preferred for this purpose, because when life ceases the resinous matter concentrates in the interior layers of the wood. In building a tar-kiln a small circular mound of earth is first raised, declining from the circumference to the centre, where a cavity is formed, communicating by a conduit with a shallow ditch surrounding the mound. Upon this foundation the split sticks are stacked to the height of ten to twelve feet.

The stack is then covered with earth as in making charcoal, and the fire applied through an opening in the top. As this continues to burn with a smouldering heat, the wood is charred, and the tar flows into the cavity in the centre, and thence by the conduit into the ditch, or into vessels sunk to receive it.

In a country endowed by nature with such unlimited plantations, yielding their valuable products for so small an amount of labor, one might expect to see some signs of wealth and prosperity; yet here all appearances seem to indicate the reverse. Human habitations are few and far between; and when found, are but little better in appearance than the huts of our Western borderers. An accurate observer, however, may see about the dwellings in the Piny Woods many little peculiarities indicative of an older civilization. They almost always have fruit trees about them, and a trellis supporting an extensive scuppernong grape-vine. There are besides four characteristic indispensables to every cottage: a well-sweep with a cypress-knee bucket, in shape and size like a slouched hat; a group of slim fodder-stacks, made of cornblades tied to high stakes; three sweet potato hills, carefully protected, and a tall pole hung with empty gourds to entertain the martins. This unfailing care to provide for the comfort of these social chattering little sojourners impresses the stranger favorably in regard to the inhabitants of this region, and if circumstances should throw him upon their simple hospitality he will not be disappointed.

After traveling some twelve miles by the coach Crayon resolved to see more of the country than could conveniently be viewed from his seat beside the driver; consequently he shouldered his knapsack and thenceforth pursued his journey on foot. Turning from the main road into the first bypath that presented itself, he was soon wandering *ad libitum* among the turpentine-trees. It is impossible to resist the feeling of loneliness that creeps over one on entering these silent forests, or to repress a sentiment of superstitious dread as you glance through the sombre many-columned aisles, stretching away on every side in interminable perspective. When the trees have been recently blazed, the square-cut markings, white on the black trunks, strikingly resemble marble grave-stones, and the traveler may imagine himself in a vast cemetery. In the older workings, if he should pass near the hour of twilight, he may see misty white, horned ghosts, starting and staring from every tree—silence and monotony, like two evil spirits following every where, suggesting uncouth and dreary fancies.

Our hero at length came to an old milldam, grown up with cypresses, presenting altogether so unique a picture that he tarried to sketch it. His drawing was nearly completed when he remarked the slanting rays of the sun upon the trees, and not without some feeling of uneasiness he hastily put up his work and resumed his journey. He had not walked more than a quarter of a mile, however, before he had the pleasure of seeing a clump of gourds towering over the trees. The house which our hero approached had a lonely, dilapidated look, and even the gourds on the martin pole appeared to be tenantless.

His doubt as to whether the place was inhabited was soon resolved by the appearance of a small man, who rushed from the front door pursued by a tall virago with a broomstick in her hand. The high-toned clatter of the woman's tongue and the rapid thwacks of the stick, with which she belabored him over the head and shoulders, completely drowned the man's voice in any prayers or remonstrances he might have attempted. His principal defense, therefore, was confined to dodging, at which he seemed well practiced.

Porte Crayon, being naturally of a chivalrous temper, was on the point of rushing forward to espouse the cause of the weaker party, but in consideration of the general impropriety of mingling in domestic feuds, and the particular manner in which the woman handled the broomstick, he restrained the generous impulse, and withdrawing himself from sight behind a tree, remained a quiet spectator of the scene. As the couple made the circuit of the inclosure in front of the house he was also enabled to understand the cause of the difficulty.

It seemed that the man having got through the proceeds of the last sale of turpentine, instead of gathering more, as he was ordered, had robbed two of madam's sitting hens and sold the eggs, the proceeds whereof he had invested in whisky. This last charge was denied at first, and only admitted when a second tour of the yard was nearly completed. The broomstick was then discontinued, and the Amazon retired into the house, whence issued at intervals a smothered blast from her yet unsatisfied tongue.

The little man, with a dejected countenance, seated himself upon a lame wood-horse, appearing upon the whole, however, as if he was rather pleased that it was all over. Just then a solitary martin perched himself upon the pole, and after some consideration entered one of the gourds. A moment after there was a furious chattering that might have been heard a hundred yards off, and the gourd began to swing to and fro. At length two birds, with a cloud of dried twigs and feathers, tumbled out of the opening and fell fluttering to the ground. So fierce was the combat that they had nearly fallen a prey to a hungry-looking gray cat that was watching near. At this the little man began to laugh, when the woman reappeared at the door, and, in a loud voice, ordered him to go to his work. Without looking up he rose, and entering a log building hard by that looked like a turkey pen, he commenced pegging away merrily at a pair of shoes.

From motives of delicacy Porte Crayon did not wish to remain longer a witness to these family differences, and as soon as he could do so unperceived, made his escape. But where was he to go? That was a serious question. What he had just seen was rather calculated to mar the prospect of a night's repose. But Crayon was an old stager. "A calm," said he, "generally succeeds a storm; I will return to the old milldam, finish my drawing, and then come back to claim their hospitality. In the course of half an hour the clouds will have rolled away." Carrying out the resolve, he returned to the gate a second time just as the sun was setting. No sooner had the proprietor laid eyes on him than he threw down his lap-stone and hurried to meet him, with a countenance beaming with delight.

Scarcely allowing the traveler time to tell his needs, he overwhelmed him with proffers of hospitality. Pleased with the free cordiality of this welcome, our hero still entertained some unhappy forebodings, which the next moment sufficiently justified. The heroine of the broomstick, armed this time with a large wooden spoon, and wearing an awful scowl on her countenance, came forward.

"No man can't stay here to-night," said she, in a voice that rang like the shriek of a Pythoness. "You nasty, good-for-nothing, sneaking creeter, have you the drotted impudence to ask a stranger to stay in your house when your own family is starving? You hain't had a mouthful of meat for a week. Let the man go to Squire Smith's, where he can get something to eat."

Crayon hesitated, and then humbly taking off his cap, inquired how far it was to Squire Smith's.

"It don't make any difference how far it is, you can't stay here."

"For God's sake, stranger, don't go," whispered the cobbler. "It's good five mile, and you'll git lost in the swamp sure as you're born."

Crayon winked at the cobbler.

"Madam," said he, respectfully, "if I am to go on, will you have the goodness to give me a drink of water?"

"Water's plenty, at least sich as it is," said she, pointing to the bucket in which floated a gourd. Crayon crossed the threshold, helped himself to a drink, and then took his seat on a three-legged stool. The matron cast a furious look at him, and with three consecutive kicks sent as many dogs howling out of the cabin.

Our hero rose—"Madam, I am a stranger in this country, and don't know the paths. It is now nearly dark, and I expect to lose myself in the swamp; but rather than put a lady to any inconvenience, I will even run that risk. I bid you good-evening."

Here he offered his hand, which was rather reluctantly accepted, and, on withdrawing it, managed to leave half a dollar sticking to the lady's palm. The cobbler, who had stood aloof during this scene, now ventured to put in a propitiatory word.

"Perhaps," said he, "if the gentleman must go, I might go with him as far as the Squire's."

"Go mend them shoes, you mean, sneaking brute. Didn't you promise 'em for to-morrow morning—you sorry onreliable pretense of a man? If the gentleman can't go without you to show him the way he had better stay, that's all; and if he can make up his mind to put up with our poor entertainment, I reckon it's rather late for him to go, anyhow."

During this speech Crayon unslung his knapsack, hung it on the bed-post, and made himself generally at home. Several cotton-headed urchins had now gathered in, and stood staring at the newcomer with all their eyes. Attracted to the door by the sound of horse's hoofs, our hero next saw a strapping girl, about sixteen, astride of a gray pony without saddle or bridle, driving up a couple of cows. A profusion of coal-black hair hung in elf locks about her neck and face, and her great black eyes danced like a rabbit's. In fact, she was pretty—a softened image of her mother without the broomstick.

"Sal! Sal! you abominable hussy, git off that hoss. Don't you see the strange gentleman?"

Sal's countenance fell; she bounced from her seat, stuck her finger in her mouth, and, by a circuitous path, gained the back part of the house.

Presently Crayon observed the cobbler very earnestly making signs to him from his workshop; he accordingly entered, and took a seat opposite him on a roll of sole leather.

"I am mighty glad, Sir, you've made up your mind to pass the night with us. It goes agin me to see a stranger turn from my door; but Lord bless you, Sir, you know women—they will talk." Here the speaker gave Mr. Crayon a facetious and significant wink. "P'r'aps there's no meat, but I'm goin' to town to-morrow to lay in a supply. The fact is, I'm 'mazin' fond of talkin' when I meet a friendly, sociable gentleman. I should judge you've been round some; 'pears you know a thing or two. So do I. I've been in pretty nigh every State in this Union. I traveled round when I was a jour'; then I served in the army a while. I was with the volunteers in Mexico. I was in all them battles, and entered the city of Mexico with General Taylor."

"Scott, you mean," suggested Crayon.

"Scott it was. Sence Taylor was 'lected President I got 'em mixed. And so, afterward, I fou't at Buena Vista under Scott or Taylor, one or t'other, but I disremember which. I never was any great scollard, but I've smelt powder in my time."

"I don't doubt it," said Crayon, dryly.

Just then there was a blast from the house—a demand if he "was finishing them shoes," preluded by the ordinary string of epithets. Whack! whack! whack! went the hammer, spasmodically.

"Never mind—pretty nigh done!" he cried. Then repeating his facetious wink, he continued, in a lower tone, "You know women, Sir. Pshaw! I never mind 'em; they will talk, and to stop 'em is onpossible. But I do like to talk myself with a sociable, friendly man, when I get a chance. But when I was the army—we was then before Rackinsack la Palma—the Colonel says to me, says he, 'Squibs, I've got great reliance on you, and there's a certain thing I want to have done—' But maybe, stranger, this here's gittin' dry. Wait a minute."

Having reconnoitred the house, he slyly took out a pint bottle which had been deftly hidden in the leg of an old boot, and, drawing the corncob stopper, handed the liquor to his guest. He merely wet his mustaches, and returned it.

"Here's luck!" said the cobbler, as he threw his head back, half closed his eyes, and stuck the bottle neck into his mouth. With a spasmodic jerk he suddenly withdrew it; his eyes stared horribly, the whisky gurgled in his throat and trickled from the corners of his mouth. The hand of the Amazon reached in and took the bottle. Crayon expected to hear it crash against the house, but he only heard a string of some ten or fifteen disrespectful adjectives, followed by the noun *"Hog."* The presence of the stranger probably prevented any overt breach of the peace and dignity of the household. As soon as she was gone, Squibs made a ghastly effort at a wink.

"Hang the woman, she's got it! Mister, you should have kept a better look-out, and give me warnin'. Not that I mind her—pshaw! I don't care that; but she has a prejudice against licker, as if what little I drink would hurt a man. But we don't care. They must have their say, or they'll bust."

"Dad, come to supper," said a cotton-headed boy.

The supper of corn bread, sweet potatoes, and yeopon tea was enlivened by a continuous stream of animadversion upon the character and conduct of the master of the house, setting forth his nastiness, meanness, good-for-nothingness, and other similar qualities, in the clearest light. His wife, who had been deceived into marriage under the impression that he was an industrious, thriving person, had been cruelly awakened from her dream of felicity to find herself an abused, starved, and barefooted mother of five barefooted children. He would neither mend shoes for the neighbors nor for his own family. He would scrape a couple of barrels of turpentine now and then, carry them to town, waste half the proceeds before he got back home with his scanty supply of meat and groceries. As long as these lasted he would never lift a hand to any thing.

The only defense made by Squibs was confined to a few miserable winks at his guest. He at length ventured to remark that turpentine was very low now—scarcely worth scraping.

"Low!" said she, with flashing eyes. "Low! What's the price of eggs?"

After the bursting of this shell there was comparative quiet. The ample chimney blazed with pine-knots. Pallets were laid in a dark corner for Sal and the children; another was placed in front of the fire for the stranger, to which, minus his coat and boots, he speedily retired. The elders sat quietly in the chimney corner smoking their pipes. The pine-knots threw a cheerful light over the room, and a cricket ventured from beneath the hearth-stone, and tuned his tiny pipe for a song.

Squibs at length took up one of the traveler's boots, and studying it with the air of a connoisseur, remarked, "This here is a city-made boot."

The matron gave a contemptuous recognition of the remark; and then glancing at the article in question, observed, "Them boots is too long for the gentleman" (pointing with her pipe to a wrinkle in the leather); "his big toe only comes to thar."

"No," said the cobbler, "you're mistaken, mammy. His toe comes to this pint."

"No sich thing," replied she, positively; "for it's plain to see whar the eend of his toe humps up the leather."

Strong in the consciousness of truth and professional knowledge, the cobbler sustained his point. "Why, dad burn me, woman, have I made shoes for twenty years not to know where a man's foot comes to in his boot?"

The matron seized an iron-shod poker, and sent forty thousand sparks roaring up the chimney. "And a mighty deal of good it has done your family, hasn't it? But come, I'll leave it to the gentleman himself if I ain't right."

Thus appealed to, Crayon rose on his elbow, feigned to examine the boot, and unhesitatingly decided in favor of the lady.

"There, now—didn't I know it! A pretty shoemaker you are, to be sure!—an ignorant, lazy vermin!"

Squibs winked, and heaved a deep sigh. "I used to think once that I knowed something about a boot," he faintly persisted.

"And you've at last found out you know nothing," said she.

"The last tag is pizen," rejoined he, winking.

Her concluding snarl was lost as they retired to the bed in the far corner. The cricket began to sing again; and Sleep spread his peaceful mantle over the troubled world.

Crayon arose next morning refreshed and strengthened. As he took leave of the family his host proposed to accompany him for a short distance to put him in the right road to Washington. When they were about to separate, the traveler thanked him for his kind entertainment, and delicately offered pecuniary remuneration. This the little shoemaker nobly declined.

"Sir," said he, "I'm always proud to see a gentleman at my house, and always give him the best I've got; and I do love a good talk."

"But, my friend," said Crayon, offering a dollar, "I must insist that you take something."

"Stranger, it makes me feel bad to have money forced on me this way." Crayon dropped his hand. "But," continued his host, "if you should force a trifle on me for the women thar, I couldn't be so uncivil as to refuse."

The dollar was transferred. Squibs eyed the coin with satisfaction, and then cast a foreboding glance toward the house. "Sir," said he, "couldn't you change this gold dollar into two halves for me?"

The request was complied with, and they parted; our traveler taking the road to Washington.

Washington, the county town of Beaufort, is situated on the head of the Pamlico Sound, at the mouth of the Tar River. It is a flourishing place of four thousand inhabitants, and drives a smart trade in the staples of the State—turpentine, cotton, and lumber. It has several extensive establishments for sawing and planing lumber, and for converting the brute turpentine into its various derivatives. An exterior view of the town presents nothing but a few steeples, peering out from a thick grove of trees, and the street views only continuous archways of verdure. In fact, its modest white wooden houses are completely buried in trees; and when the weather is hot the effect is highly pleasing. The only sketchable object here is a private residence, at the end of the main street, with beautifully-improved grounds; and at the principal hotel, the only item deserving particular commendation was John, the head servant. Pope says,

"Honor and fame from no condition rise;
Act well your part—there all the honor lies."

By this rule, John should have both fame and honor.

Next morning early, our traveler embarked in the steamer *Governor Morehead,* a small boat, of rather queer build, which navigates the Tar River to Greenville, twenty-five miles distant. There were but seven or eight passengers on board. The morning was delightful, and Captain Quinn gave Crayon a breakfast that seems to have won his heart completely. In fact, he never alludes to it without complimenting the Captain in the warmest terms.

The Tar River, as far as they traveled, presented the dark-colored water and low, swampy shores common to all the streams in the lower country. But few traces of improvement or population were visible in passing, and the evidences of trade were confined to a few flats loaded with lumber and cotton, and propelled with poles. The river is narrow, crooked, shoaly, and only navigable for flat-bottomed boats.

At Greenville our traveler again took to the road, on foot. In its general features this country resembles that over which Crayon had passed. There are the same interminable pine forests, boxed and scarified by the turpentine-gatherers, with the barrels standing about in couples among the trees, and frequent tar-kilns in process of erection, or smoking and smouldering toward completion.

As you approach the line of railroad, running from Weldon to Wilmington, across this portion of the State, signs of life and improvement begin to be manifest. The groups of fodder-stacks about the barns are larger, the old dwellings are in better repair, there are many new ones of a more modern and more pleasing style of architecture, and one more frequently meets the native going to or from market, on his two-barreled cart, drawn by the long-tailed, shoeless horse.

Having arrived at a village about four o'clock in the afternoon, our hero determined to tarry for the night. As he lounged upon the tavern porch his curiosity was excited by seeing a crowd of shabby-looking white men and negroes collected in an open space behind the stable. He presently joined them, and soon perceived there was a cock-fight on the tapis. Two of the negroes, who carried meal-bags, had just liberated a pair of cocks therefrom, which they placed in the hands of the two gentlemen who were to play a principal part in the affair. Number One of the parties was remarkable for his bad clothes and an indomitable shock of carroty hair. His appearance was rather improved by taking off his coat, which he did preparatory to handling his fowl. This was a large spangle—a noisy, robustious fellow, whom it took two to hold while the trimming was going on.

His proposed antagonist, a keen-looking black, on the contrary, sat perfectly quiet upon the hand of a sallow, long-nosed covey with sleek black hair, and rather flashily dressed in a green coat with brass buttons. As there is an absurd prejudice existing at the present day against this elegant sport, it is more than probable that many are ignorant of the manner of conducting it. We may be pardoned, therefore, for entering somewhat into detail in describing the preliminaries. The cocks are generally matched by weight. This being ascertained, the pitter takes him in hand, and with a pair of shears trims all the superfluous feathers from his neck, tail, and back, thereby rendering him lighter and more active, but effectually destroying his beauty. The spurs are sawed off near the leg, and upon the stumps a pair of sharp-pointed steel gaffs, about three inches long, are carefully tied. To dispose these artificial spurs so as more surely to strike the adversary and to prevent self-inflicted wounds, is one of the delicacies of the art only to be acquired by long practice and profound study. It was delightful to see the air of professional gravity with which these worthies went through the business of trimming and heeling, and the respectful admiration elicited by their skill from the assistant by-standers, including negroes.

All preliminaries having been satisfactorily adjusted, Green-coat called upon the spectators to set their bets. This was accordingly done, the amounts ranging from a dime to a quarter, although several desperate characters went as high as a dollar.

The pitters entered a circle formed of plank staked up, the specta-tors ranged themselves around outside. The cocks were held up together, to see if they were ready for the combat; they answered, "Ready!" by pecking fiercely at each other's eyes. The seconds then retired to opposite limits of the circle, and set their principals upon the ground. These strutted about for a moment; eying each other askance, and then, flapping their wings, poured forth clarion notes of mutual defiance. This was the signal for the onset; they advanced, squared themselves, and incontinently pitched into each other. For a moment they struck rapidly, hitting and dodging like practiced boxers; but becoming entangled, they presently tumbled over together, the black above. "Hung!" exclaimed Woodpecker; "handle 'em." "Stand back!" shouted Green-coat, "he's in the feathers." "You're in my wing," persisted Woodpecker, attempting to seize the combatants. He was resolutely grappled by Green-coat; while the black, taking advantage of the delay, was endeavoring to pick the spangle's eyes out. The excitement at this moment was so intense that a hatless lackey, who had a quarter on the spangle, broke into the ring. He was jerked out in a trice, and order restored. The combatants were separated, and it was discovered that no damage had been done; but blood was rising, and before pitting a second time, Woodpecker nodded fiercely across the ring to his opponent, and said, in a voice husky with suppressed passion, "I'll go ye another dollar!"

"Done!"

There was no preliminary strutting this time. As soon as they touched the ground the eager duelists rushed to the combat. After some smart rapping without apparent result, the cocks seemed to be getting a little blown. The spangle got his head under the black's wing, and they both stood panting for some minutes in this position. The spangle appeared to be seriously revolving something in his mind, and it was perceived that blood was dripping from his neck. At the third round the result of the spangle's cogitations transpired. Instead of meeting the black's advance, he took to his heels. The black pursued him to the barrier, giving him a rap behind which helped him over, and away he went, pursued by half a dozen boys and negroes, with mingled shouts of derision and merriment. "Kill him!" "Cut his head off!" "Dunghill!" "Used up!" were the expressions which followed the ignominious bird. The victor behaved much like a gentleman. Leaping upon the barrier, he saw his recreant adversary in full flight. Disdaining to pursue—for the truly brave is never truculent—he hopped back into the pit, proclaimed his victory, as it was his bounden duty to do, and then quietly suffered himself to be taken and disarmed.

The losers were either vituperative or calmly philosophic under their misfortunes, reasoning curiously upon causes and effects. The winners were loud and unconfined in their joy.

Woodpecker stood for several minutes lost in thought, then stepping up to his successful opponent, he drew out two ragged one-dollar bills on the Bank of Cape Fear and forked them over. Making an effort to swallow the lump in his throat, he said,

"Adam, I've been deceived. That spangle winned his fight last year at Gaston, when Jones fit Faulcon—Virginia agin North Carolina—a thousand on the odd. True, he wasn't cut nary time, and so I gin two dollars for him arterward, and kep him on a walk ever sence; but I'll break every darned egg, and kill every chicken of the breed, I will!"

Jack the horse-boy won a quarter from that old dogmatical despot, Uncle Jonas, the chief waiter at the tavern. Jack screamed and turned somersets on the straw. So elated was he that he forgot his condition, and as Woodpecker passed, Jack hazarded a joke.

"I say, Massa, dat rooster of yourn run like first dip."

The defeated rolled his eyes vengefully upon the grinning ebony. "Look'ee here, boy, I've ben deceived in that 'are chicken. I've lost my fight. But I'm not a-goin to be made game of for all that, especially by a nigger."

Jack hastily took himself elsewhere.

We ventured, in civil and somewhat covert manner, to rebuke Crayon for having assisted at so cruel and disreputable an amusement.

"I do not see," he replied, "why it is considered more cruel than angling or partridge-shooting; and the people one meets at such places are, in all respects, the same as those who, under our admirable system, play the most prominent part in the government of the country. For example, would it not be difficult to tell whether the originals of this sketch were the heroes of a cock-pit or an election day?"

Crayon arrived at Goldsborough about midnight, and shortly after took the Central Railroad for Raleigh, about fifty miles distant. He went to sleep when the train started, and when he awoke, about sunrise, was just entering the elegant capital of North Carolina. A comfortable 'bus transferred him from the dépôt to Guion's Hotel, where, with a little warm water and an alkali, he proceeded to wash his hands of tar, pitch, and turpentine. We will now leave him to repose for a short time in the famous City of Oaks.

Guilford

"List his discourse of war, and you shall hear
A fearful battle rendered you in music."
                                        SHAKSPEARE.

"THE capital of North Carolina bears the appropriate and beautiful name of Raleigh, in honor of the accomplished and chivalrous 'Sir Walter, the man of wit and the sword,' under whose auspices the first colonies were planted on our shores. The town is comparatively of recent date, its site having been established by a convention met at Hillsborough in 1788. In 1810, it contained only six hundred and seventy inhabitants, but its permanent population at present is estimated at between two and three thousand. On a commanding but gently sloping eminence, the young city sits embowered, in a grove of stately oaks, like a rustic beauty, whose ornaments are awkwardly worn and unskillfully put on. Incongruous, incomplete, but nathless fair and pleasing. Thus appear her broad tree planted, unpaved avenues. The superb and costly capitol with its forms of Grecian elegance, rising amidst a grove of forest oaks, and in an inclosure grown up with weeds and traversed by narrow ungraveled paths, and its stately entrances encumbered with huge wood piles.

"Around this central point the town is built upon several streets densely shaded with double rows of trees. The private residences for the most part resemble country houses, each standing isolated in the midst of its ornamented grounds, profuse in shade-trees, shrubbery, and flowers, reminding one more of a thickly settled neighborhood than a town. The avenue leading from the capitol to the Governor's house is more compactly built, and is the theatre of all the commercial life the place affords.

"On an eminence near the town, imposing from its extent and position, stands the State Asylum for the Insane. A building worthy the taste and public spirit of any State.

"By the burning of the old capitol in 1831 Raleigh lost the statue of Washington by Canova, a gem of art of which the Carolinians were justly proud. The hero was represented in a sitting posture, costumed as a Roman general, holding tablets in one hand and a style in the other, as if about to write; we believe the intention of the sculptor was, to represent him as Washington the statesman and lawgiver, while his recent military character was indicated by the sheathed sword beside him. The conception was beautiful, the work skillfully and elegantly wrought, but there was nothing in it especially to touch the American heart or understanding. The soft Italian, whose genius was inspired by dreams of the Greek ideal commingling with shapes of modern elegance, who pined even in brilliant Paris for the balmy air and sunshine of his native land, beneath whose magic chisel the frigid marble warmed and melted into forms of voluptuous beauty, had neither the soul to conceive nor the hand to carve the iron man of '76."

As Porte Crayon warmed with his subject he rose from his chair and paced about our writing-table like a chained bear. "That task," continued he, "yet remains to be accomplished; there is no statue of Washington existing, there never has been one."

"You forget that which adorns the square in front of our Federal Capitol," I mildly suggested.

"Get out! it is scarcely worth criticism—a pitiful heathen divinity set to be scoffed at by the children of the image-breakers—a half naked Olympian shivering in a climate where nudity is not, and never can be, respectable."

"But there is the statue in Richmond."

Crayon paused for a moment as if to cool off.

"Houdon," said he, "made an effort in the proper direction, and the unaffected approbation which his work has elicited proves it. That it has been greatly overpraised, is not chargeable to a want of taste in our people, but simply to the fact that they have no means of comparison. It is the best we have, and is estimated accordingly. But although the costume and design of the statue are good, there is nothing in that affected pose to remind one of the most striking characteristic of Washington's person,

'The lofty port, the distant mien,
That seemed to shun the sight, yet awed if seen.'

"A French writer says: *'Malgré l'opinâtreté des hommes à louer l'antique aux depens du moderne, il faut avouer qu'en tout genre les premiers essais sont toujours grossiers.'* The truth and common sense of this assertion is applicable, in a greater or less degree, to every subject to which human effort has been directed. If it seems not to have been sustained by the progress of the fine arts at all times, the exception may be fairly referred to the fact, that the genius of certain peoples and periods, instead of being devoted to the legitimate task of developing into beauty and grandeur the ideas of its own times, perversely turns for inspiration to antiquity, rejecting the healthful freshness of the present to feed morbidly on the decay of the past; wasting its native vigor in feebly imitating, instead of aspiring to the nobler task of creating. Why may not the ridicule that in literature is attached to the faded imitations of the ancient poets—the Venuses, Cupids, nymphs, and shepherdesses—be as fairly turned against the wearisome and incongruous reproductions in marble of gods, heroes, and senators, with modern names, and modern heads on their shoulders?"

"Bravo! Porte Crayon turned lecturer! You bid fair to rival Ruskin in the crusade against the Greeks and Romans. You and he are harder on them than were the Goths and Vandals."

"But, my dear P——, permit me to explain. You have misunderstood the drift of my remarks—"

"Encore, Sir Critic. You administer the chibouk like a very Fahladeen."

"Now pray be quiet, and I'll tell you an anecdote appropriate to the subject:

"A provincial society of literati, somewhere in France, wished to compliment Voltaire, and voted that his statue should decorate their hall. A young artist of great merit, a native of the province, was commissioned to execute the work. The sage, who was never averse to flattery in any shape, complacently sat for the bust, and an excellent likeness was modeled. The artist was now at a loss how to complete his work. The antique *furore* was then at its height in France, and Hogarth's caricature of a nobleman personating Jupiter, with a big wig, ruffled shirt, and a thunder-bolt in his hand, scarcely surpassed in absurdity many of the serious productions of that ridiculous era. The artist was an honest fellow, and was at his wits' end in endeavoring to reconcile common sense and the spirit of the times. Embroidered cuffs, shirt ruffles, and knee breeches, would not do in marble at all. The wardrobe of antiquity was ransacked, but nothing found to fit Voltaire. Fortunately the severely classic taste could dispense with all costume, even the fig-leaf, so our artist modeled his figure after the Antinous.

"But to see that lean, leering face, that preposterous curled wig and scraggy neck, set upon a round, graceful, fully-developed figure, was inadmissible; the incongruity was too glaring. The head, which had been pronounced a perfect likeness, could not be changed, so he went to work again, and, with much labor, reduced the figure to the meagre standard of the face. The completed statue resembled Voltaire, no doubt, but it also looked like a chimpanzee, or the starved saint done in stone in the Museum at Florence, or the wax-work figure of Calvin Edson at Barnum's—a sculptured horror, a marble joke. The society was outraged. The statue, instead of being inaugurated, was kicked into a cellar; while the unhappy victim of classic taste lost his labor and reputation together, nor is it likely that posterity will ever repair the injustice."

Having passed several days very pleasantly looking at the outside of things in Raleigh, our traveler continued his journey westward, by the North Carolina Railroad. This road traverses the best portion of the State. The face of the country is pleasantly diversified with hill and dale. The sombre vesture of the pine woods is changed for the rich and varied leafing of the upland forest, while evidences of agricultural improvement are manifest on every side. Then, as we pass along, we hear the old familiar names of Revolutionary memory; names that make the heart leap in recalling the wild, romantic details of the Southern war, all the more thrilling that they have escaped the varnish of spiritless limners, and are not heard in the common babblings of fame. But still, in the humble cot and squirely mansion, the memory of these brave deeds and glorious names is fondly cherished.

"Come hither, Curly-pate; what paper was that you showed your

THE PARTISAN LEADER

mother just now that delighted her so, and got your pocket filled with ginger-cakes?"

"That, Sir, is a picture of Colonel Washington chasing Tarleton. Mother says I am a great genuis."

"Why, Beverly, be quiet. I said no such thing."

"Indeed, madam, this drawing is an astonishing production. The attitudes of his horses are decidedly classic, and seem to have been studied from the Elgin marbles. The boy will doubtless be a great painter some day."

"No, I won't. I'll be a soldier, and lead a regiment of horse like Colonel Lee."

"Get away, then; take your tin sword, and make war upon the mullin stalks."

Still rolling westward we pass Hillsborough, the county town of Orange, then the Haw River. At length we approach Greensborough, the county town of Guilford. Here we must tarry to visit the battle-field, which is but a few miles distant.

The town of Greensborough contains about two thousand inhabitants, and is a place of some trade. Except two or three private residences and two seminaries, its buildings, public and private, are poor; and, in short, there is nothing about its exterior either to prepossess or interest the passing traveler. Its two seminaries for the education

FEMALE EDUCATION

of young ladies are said to be in a flourishing condition. In North Carolina there are a number of institutions, colleges, etc., for the education of ladies, all in high repute and well attended. Indeed nowhere does this important subject seem to have received more consideration than in this State.

On arriving at Greensborough our traveler ascertained that the site of Martinsville, the old Guilford Court House of Revolutionary times, was five miles distant. As it was too late in the day to set out for a visit, he passed the afternoon in sauntering about the village, and the evening in poring over "Lee's Memoirs." At an early hour next morning he mounted a horse and trotted off toward Martinsville.

Porte Crayon at length arrived at Martinsville, and the results of his visit we will give in his own words.

"It was," said he, "with a feeling of indescribable interest, mingled with something of awe, that I reined up my horse in the midst of a group of ruined chimneys and decayed wooden houses, all, save one, silent and deserted. There was no human being in sight of whom to make inquiry, but I knew instinctively that I was upon the field of Guilford. The face of the country answered so well to the descriptions which I had read, and there had been apparently so little change since the day of the battle, that there was no difficulty in recognizing the localities. Unmarred by monuments, uncontaminated by improvements, the view of the silent, lonely fields and woods brought the old times back, so fresh, so real, so near. Come, wizard fancy, with thy spell of gramarye! fling me a picture of the fight!

"The hills are again crowned with armed battalions. The rolling of drums, the startling bugle call, the voice of command, break the silence of the budding forest. There, swarming in the thicket, near the edge of the wood and behind the protecting fences, are the unskillful militia, valiant in pot houses but unreliable in the field, hearkening, with fainting hearts, to the mingled threats and encouragement of their leaders, ready to fire and run away at the first burst of battle.

"Manœuvring on either flank are the snorting squadrons of Washington and Lee, whose flashing sabres have already tasted blood. In the distance are seen the serried lines of the grim Continentals, men of reliable mettle, who can hear the battle going on around them and bide their time; who, unmoved and scornful, see the panic-stricken herds of friends fly past them, and then rush gallantly to meet the bayonets of their enemies.

"The cannon are posted; the ready artillerist holds the lighted match. Alternately anxious and hopeful, the American commander reviews his order of battle. It is all wisely considered and complete. For the result, 'Trust in God, and fire low!'

"The hour of impending battle is always terrible. To the commoner mind the question of life or death is presented with awful distinctness, while the nobler soul is torn with more complicated emotions: "Shall victory or defeat be ours? honor or disgrace? a liberated country or a despot's bloody sword?'

"Hark! the rolling of the English drums! Like an electric shock it shakes the thousands that stand expectant upon the embattled hill! Now the coward's cheek blanches, as with impotent and trembling haste he fumbles his musket lock. Now the warm blood rushes to the brow of the brave, and with fiercer eagerness he grasps his sword hilt. The head of the advancing column is already in sight. The sun's rays glance upon their burnished arms:

> " 'And more. Behold how fair arrayed
> They file from out the hawthorn shade,
> And sweep so gallant by!
> St. George might waken from the dead
> To see fair England's banners fly.'

"As the column deploys in the open ground, white wreaths of smoke rise from the wood, and the thunder of cannon proclaims that the battle is begun. Then, as the audacious Briton, in long scarlet lines, advances steadily to the attack, the crash of small arms is heard along the American line. Soon the tree-tops are hidden with the rolling smoke, and the volleying musketry of the English, mingling with the continuous roar of the American fire, swells the terrible anthem of battle.

"The American lines are broken, and the tide of war rolls on until the intrepid assailants meet, in the Continental line, foes more worthy of their steel:

> " 'The war which for a space did fail,
> Now, trebly thundering, swelled the gale.'

"Then, then Virginia, it was a joy, that even defeat and disaster can not blight, to see that haughty battalion of Guards flying in wild disorder from the wood, while thy fiery horsemen, with hoof and sabre, trampled them in the dust!

"I rose in my stirrups, and gave a shout that made old Guilford's echoes ring again, and alarmed a plowman on a hill half a mile off.

"So bidding adieu to fancy, I set off to see the plowman, wishing to make some more particular inquiries about the localities. I found him intelligent and disposed to be communicative. He indicated the different points where the hardest fighting had been, showed an old tree which had been struck by a cannon-shot, and said that in plowing, even at this day, he frequently turned up bullets, bayonets, and portions of arms and accoutrements that had withstood the tooth of time.

" 'One day,' said he, 'as I was plowing near my house thar, my little daughter found in the furrow a complete musket-lock, much rusted and standing at full cock. That,' continued the countryman, 'set me to thinking more than any thing I have yet seen. It looked more like fighting. The man that cocked that gun was killed perhaps before he had time to pull the trigger.

" 'Many a time, Sir, when I am idle, I take that lock in my hand and look at it, until I feel curious like, as though the battle that was fought so many years ago was somehow brought nearer to us.'

"This quaint talisman that wrought so powerfully on the imagination of the unlettered plowman, might even set more learned men to thinking.

"Taking a friendly leave of the countryman, I returned to Greensborough in time to dine and meet the cars for Salisbury."

Picnic in the Gold Region

"Earth, yield me roots;
Who seeks for better of thee, sauce his palate
With thy most operant poison. What have we here?
Gold, yellow, glittering, precious gold."

SHAKSPEARE.

"I PRAY, come crush a cup of wine, rest you merry." What's this? An invitation to a May-day picnic. The earth has already put on her summer livery, wearing it daintily and fresh like a bran-new gown. The southern breeze blows balmily, all perfumed like a sweet damsel just come from her toilet. The birds sing like fifers, and the meads, bepranked with flowers, vie in beauty with our fashionable hotel carpets. Woods, breezes, birds, and flowers—all nature joins in the invitation.

At an early hour on the third of May a numerous and brilliant company took the cars at the Salisbury dépôt in answer to the foregoing invitation. There was broadcloth and beauty in proper proportions, and a profusion of flowers, wit, and merriment. The disembarkation at Holtsburg developed still further the intentions and resources of the party. Numerous mysterious hampers were transferred from the baggage-car to the platform of the station-house, and a brace of Cuffees, bearing instruments of music, made themselves a part of the company.

This couple reminded one of Don Quixote and his Squire done

FINDING GOLD

in ebony. Alfred, the fiddler, was a lathy, long-armed, knock-kneed black, with a countenance that vied in ruefulness with that of the Knight of La Mancha; while Simon, the tambour-major, was a short, wiry, jolly-faced fellow, who thumped his sheepskin with a will. Of these, however, more anon.

The idea of "dancing on the green" is eminently poetical, but quite absurd in practice; the managers of the picnic had therefore wisely determined to take advantage of the springy floor of the Holtsburg station-house. This was pleasantly situated near the silvery Yadkin, in the midst of a beautiful woodland, and a more fitting locality could not have been selected. They were at first somewhat disconcerted at finding the station-house entirely occupied with bales of hay; but this untoward circumstance was so turned to account by the ingenuity and energy of the gentlemen that it was afterward esteemed a lucky hit. The bales were rolled out on the platforms, arranged around the room, and piled up at one end, where they served admirably for tables, seats, couches, galleries, and added greatly to comfort and the appearance of the scene.

The early part of the day passed most agreeably in rural walks, music, dancing, cards, and conversation. Then the mid-day feast was spread and eaten, of course. Every body pronounced every thing delightful, every body was pleased, and every body was quite right. The bright Champagne foamed in o'erflowing bumpers. The corks flew about like shot in a sharp skirmish. Much store of wit and mirth, which, like the music in the bugle of Munchausen's postillion, had remained congealed by the frost of ceremony, now broke forth spontaneously, under the melting influences of wine. The fiddler struck up a merrier tune, and even Alfred's rueful visage seemed to catch a gleam of jollity. The tambourine boomed and jangled with redoubled power as the excited Simon rapped the sounding sheepskin consecutively with knuckles, kneepan, pate, and elbow. Alfred's legs and arms worked like the cranks of a grasshopper engine, going at thirty miles an hour. The spirit of the dancers kept pace with the music until the approach of evening warned them to get ready for the train which would bear them back to Salisbury. Things were packed up, and the necks of several bottles of Champagne, discovered among the stuff, were broken off to pass away the time while they waited for the train.

"What a delightful day we've had! How charmingly every thing has passed off! not an incident to mar the enjoyment!"

Just then Alfred appeared on the platform, his trembling knees knocked together, his bosom heaved like a blacksmith's bellows, his face was ashy pale, and his eyes rolled upward with a mingled expression of terror and despair. For some moments he was dumb; but his attitude and accessories told his story—a grief too big for words. In one hand he held an empty bag, and in the other his tuneful friend and companion, the fiddle. But in what a case! splintered, smashed, mammocked, bridge and sounding-post gone, the tail-piece swinging by the idle strings.

Simon looked on aghast.

"DAT FIDDLE DONE RUINGED"

"Somebody done sot on her!" he exclaimed.

Alfred at length spoke: "Da! dat fiddle is done ruinged!" and again relapsed into dumbness, while two big tears gathered in his eyes. The hearts of the spectators were touched, and they crowded round the unhappy negro.

"Why, Alfred," cried one, "it can be mended."

"Never, massa, she'll never sound agin."

"Pass round your hat, Alfred." That was a woman's voice. God bless the ladies! May their kind hearts never know sorrow!

The hat circulated, and substantial sympathy showered in it so freely that there was presently enough to buy two fiddles. A glow of happiness overspread the minstrel's face, and as he acknowledged and pocketed the contents of the hat, he glanced again at his mutilated instrument.

"I specks I kin mend her up yit."

Now Simon was an interested spectator of these proceedings, and when he saw the turn things had taken he grew thoughtful and began to scratch his head. Anon he disappeared, and after a short time returned with tears in his eyes, uttering groans and lamentations.

"Well, Simon, what has befallen you?"

"Oh, master," replied Simon, with a tragedy countenance, "I wouldn't a had dis to happen for five dollars; jis look at dis tambourine—busted clean through."

"How did this occur, Simon?" said the gentleman, examining the broken instrument.

"Why, master, I don't know exactly how it come; but I specks somebody put dere foot in it."

"I would not be surprised," returned the examiner, "if some one had put his foot in it. Now, Simon, you perceive the frame of the tambourine is perfectly sound, and the cracked sheepskin can be easily replaced. Your estimate of five dollars damages is excessive. In my judgment, a judicious expenditure of ten cents will put every thing *in statu quo ante bellum*. Here is a dime, Simon."

During this discourse the tambour-major looked very sheepish and restive, but habitual deference for the opinions of the dominant race induced him to accept the award without demurrer, only observing, as he joined in the general laugh,

"I mought as well not a-broke it."

Meanwhile one of the company had got hold of the broken tambourine-head, declaring that the events of the day deserved to be written on parchment.

A call was made upon the company for poetical contributions, which was answered by a shower of couplets. A committee appointed to collect and arrange the proceeds reported the following:

VERSES WRITTEN BY A PICNIC PARTY ON THE HEAD OF
A BROKEN TAMBOURINE WITH A CORKSCREW.

"Of all the year, the time most dear
Is buxom, blooming, merry May;
In woodland bowers we gather flowers
From morning fair to evening gray.

"Time we beguile with beauty's smile,
  And sweetly while the hours away,
Champagne sipping, lightly tripping,
  Like lambs skipping in their play.

"Music sounding, mirth abounding,
  Old care drowning in the foam
Of sparkling bumper—fill a thumper
  And we'll drink to friends at home.

"Pray mind your work and pop the cork,
  Just take a fork if corkscrews fail;
'Think'st thou, because thou'rt virtuous,
  There shall be no more cakes and ale?'

"To ladies eyes 'neath southern skies,
  To those we prize on earth most dear,
Another brimming goblet fill—
  But, hark! the warning whistle near.

"Drink quick—'tis time to close our rhyme—
  To Holtsburg's halls a farewell—hic;
To Yadkin's bowers and fragrant flowers—
  Quick—*transit gloria mundi*—sick."

A WINTER IN THE SOUTH

Third Paper

"Yet still even here content can spread a charm,
Redress the clime and all its rage disarm;
Though poor the peasant's hut, his feast though small,
He sees his little lot the lot of all,
Sees no contiguous palace rear its head
To shame the meanness of his humble shed."

GOLDSMITH.

JONESBOROUGH, where our travelers decided to fix their head-quarters for a season, is the oldest town in East Tennessee, and is otherwise a place of some historic interest. Here the first log court-house in the State was hewn out of the virgin forest, where justice was dispensed to the hardy pioneers—possibly not less sound and impartial because wanting in the forms and technicalities of more imposing courts. Here the forest soldiers and statesmen convened to devise plans of war and policy against the common enemy, and when triumphant success had rewarded their valor, they met here in factious wranglings and fights to dispose of their new-found independence.

In this neighborhood, too, if we credit the inscription on a venerable beech tree,

D. Boon
cillED A. BAR on
Tree
in ThE yEAR
1760

"This country," quoth Squire Broadacre, "which has hitherto been so little known or regarded, has a history, interesting as a tale of romance, and, doubtless, a rich store of oral tradition might be gathered from its intelligent, friendly, and hospitable inhabitants."

"Winter is fast approaching," replied the artist. "The books we may read at our leisure—a good fire and hot punch will thaw out the traditions fast enough, even with the thermometer at zero; but those mountains, which rise so grandly to the eastward, we must visit while we may. A week's delay may wrap their lofty summits in snow and ice, and render the roads impassable."

"Ah," said Tiny, "what fun we will have rolling down the hills— they look so smooth and blue!"

"My daughter," replied the Squire, "those mountains which appear so soft and beautiful from here, as you approach them will be seen covered with ragged forest, broken with frightful precipices and horrid thickets, impenetrable even to the bears and wolves that roam their rugged sides."

"And what becomes of the pretty blue?"

"It gradually fades away as we get nearer, my child. It vanishes and is not—even like the delusive veil through which youth and in-experience views the future. Ah, the blue mountains—the blue mountains which rise before us in the morning of life—rough and wearisome enough they are when we come to climb them!"

"But," said Larkin, stiffening himself, "I would not wish it other-wise. I prefer the mountains and the way of life even as we find them. There is a manly delight in cutting one's path through the tangled thickets, breasting the steep ascent, and leaping upon the breezy pinnacle, there to snuff the air that warms while it cuts."

"Disappointment—" said the Squire.

"Disappointment!" repeated Bob, interrupting him, "develops and strengthens the character. It knocks the rust off one's faculties, and shows the pure metal like the blows of a hammer. It invigorates the moral system, as a plunge into cold water does the animal."

"Jim Bug, what is your opinion of these matters?"

Jim made a low bow. "Pluck and luck, master, will carry a man through most any whar."

After spending about three minutes in silent meditation the Squire remarked that Jim was right, and the observation worthy of antiquity. It was consequently arranged that the two gentlemen should start for the Black Mountains next morning, while the ladies, who found themselves in comfortable quarters, should remain where they were.

To this they the more readily consented as they had a deal of sewing on hand wherewith to occupy their time, and Jonesborough furnished greater facilities for shopping than they had expected in so remote a locality.

With the appointed morning came clouds and rain, with every appearance of a long continuance; so the journey was postponed until the next clear day, while the travelers consoled themselves with such good cheer as the Eutaw afforded, and those in-door amusements of which their party had ample store.

The heavy rains which for a week continued to deluge Jonesborough at length ceased, and about mid-day on the second of December the clouds which had so long obscured the cheerful sun rolled away. Our friends had made all their arrangements in anticipation of this event, and no sooner did the signs of a general clearing up manifest themselves than Jim Bug was dispatched for the horses. To this requisition that worthy and ingenuous veterinarian Tom Dosser responded by sending a white horse and a black mare, whose appearance was not particularly prepossessing, and whose qualities will be set forth in the course of the narrative. The animals were fully equipped, even to the stout blue blanket with a hole in the middle, the ordinary riding-cloak of East Tennessee.

Simultaneously with the horses appeared the gentleman who had kindly volunteered to bear them company on their trip, Mr. Jones of Jonesborough. With as little delay as possible the Virginians took leave of their ladies, mounted their steeds, and the trio rode gallantly forth, sitting stiff in their stirrups, ready for any desperate adventure that fortune might vouchsafe to them. The Tennesseean was a tall man, and slender withal, with a keen black eye and dark beard, clothed, externally, in a slouched hat and blanket cloak, which reached nearly to his feet. He was substantially mounted on a powerful gray, and rode generally in advance, thus doing the honors of the country, and indicating the safest way through the mud holes. Squire Broadacre, astride of Dosser's white, followed next, his portly person buttoned up in a tight-fitting overcoat, his plump legs bandaged with drab leggings tied with green strings, and his grave, dignified face shaded by the brim of a black fur hat a little the worse for wear. An umbrella, which had done its owner some service, was carefully tied behind his saddle, and a span-new red cowhide served to admonish the white when perchance the sight of a comfortable barn-yard or a group of jolly haystacks induced him to slacken his pace too decidedly. The rear-guard consisted of Bob Larkin, mounted on the black, behatted and blanketed after the Tennessee fashion, with a short rifle strapped on his back, and an extremely fat pair of saddle-bags flapping the flanks of his beast at every step.

Thus our adventureres rode out of Jonesborough like knights equipped for high emprise, followed by the admiring eyes and fervent good wishes of all the ladies, to say nothing for the boys and negroes.

And now, having fairly started them on their journey, it becomes the duty of the chronicler to inform the world what they went out to see.

Had they started earlier in the day, we might have commenced somewhere in New Brunswick, and have given a lengthy account of the Appalachian system through all its ups and downs to where it gets swamped in Georgia and Alabama; but as the golden sun has already begun to shoot his rays aslant upon the mountains, and the shadows of Tom Dosser's ponies caper like huge giraffes upon the level ground, we must be brief. The chain of mountains known at different points as the Iron, Great Smoky, and Unaka, forming the eastern boundary of Tennessee, and the prolongation of the Blue Ridge from thirty to sixty miles to the eastward through North Carolina, forms an extensive irregular inclosure, hemming in half a dozen of the western counties of the latter State with walls five thousand feet high. The space thus inclosed is not a valley, as one might naturally suppose, but literally a vast basin filled with mountains, immense anomalous spurs heaved up at random, so crowded together that the streams seem to find their way among them with difficulty, while their summits in many instances considerably overtop those of the external ridges.

Pre-eminent in this vast assembly are the Black Mountains in Yancey County, which, according to measurements made sometime since by Professor Mitchell of North Carolina, and more recently by Professor Guyot of Boston, are ascertained to be the highest mountains in the United States, attaining an altitude of six thousand seven hundred and sixty feet above the ocean tides, nearly five hundred feet higher than the famous White Hills of New Hampshire.

The fame of these mighty peaks had reached the ears of our artist, and so fired his imagination that they had become the frequent theme of his sleeping and waking dreams. Now so near the realization of these romantic fancies, no wonder that he rode apart, silent and serious, with fascinated eyes fixed upon the landscape before him.

But at length the Tennesseean draws his rein before the gate of a modest-looking country residence, pleasantly situated almost under the shadow of one of the advanced spurs of the Iron Mountains. Here we are on classic ground. Soon after the war of our Independence, young Tennessee, with characteristic impatience of parental authority, undertook to flout her respectable mother, and set up for herself before she was of age under the name of Franklin or Frankland. In those days the people of the settlements did not understand the art of revolutionizing by ballot, or blackguarding a dynasty out of power through the newspapers, but, having recently delivered themselves from a kingly yoke by force of arms, were more ready to resort to the *"ultima ratio regum,"* and had faith in bullets and cold steel. Thus it was that the frequent collisions between the authority of the old and new governments were not always bloodless. The last and most famous of these fights took place in 1788, when Colonel Tipton, the chief of the North Carolina party, was besieged in this house for several days by General Sevier, then Governor of Franklin.

As the details of this ignoble strife will add nothing to the renown of the brave and patriotic men who were unfortunately engaged in it, we prefer to pass them over in silence. For while the sterner duties of the historian may require that he should note impartially the evil and the good that men have done in their day and generation, we, in our idle and pleasant wanderings, choose rather to remember the old Governor only as the hero and patriot, and in our recollections of the spot, to associate the pleasant cottage on Sinking Creek with its present accomplished and hospitable occupant.

It rained heavily during the night, but the morning rose blustering and bright; our adventurers were upon the road betimes, and erelong found themselves amidst the ragged defiles of the mountains, with a keen wind blowing in their faces. But in return, the dreary, leafless landscape of the lower country had disappeared, and their road followed the course of a dashing, sparkling, amber-tinted stream, shaded by forests of perennial beauty. There were waving groves of the silver pine mingled with lofty firs and hemlocks. There was the varnished holly, gemmed with its scarlet berries, and the snaky laurel, whose dense evergreen masses oftentimes obstructed the road—a wilderness of rich and graceful foliage, defying the icy breath of winter. About noon they halted upon the summit of the Iron Ridge, just on the dividing line between the States. Here they got the first and most imposing view of the Roane, which stands like a mighty sentinel guarding the entrance to a land of giants. Dark-browed and frowning he lifts his head into the calm, blue heaven, inspiring mingled joy and terror. It is a scene to make its mark indelibly upon the memory.

From thence our travelers descended by a winding and romantic road into North Carolina. From the eastern foot of the Iron Ridge their road led them over hill and dale, through field and forest, around the base of the great mountain; but still over the ever-varying landscape the "awful form" of the Roane predominated, and it was from his lonely and mysterious heights they saw the last golden rays of the sun fade out.

"Good-evening neighbor! How far to Grey Briggs's?"

"Well, four or five miles, p'raps—and are you the men that have lost a horse?"

"No! thank Fortune, we've only lost a little time."

"Well, now, if I might be so bold, where might you gentlemen be from?"

"From Jonesborough, friend, and we're going to see the Mountains."

THE MOUNTAINEER

"From Jonesborough, I wonder! Well, is there any thing encouraging down your way?"

"Nothing particular, except that they have discovered a brass mine down in Buncombe lately."

"Well, now, that'll be waluable and handy like—to counterfit gold money with and make breast-pins."

"But it's getting dark, and we've a lonesome road before us—good-evening, neighbor."

So our friends put their horses to a trot, and within the next mile encountered a party of three jolly fellows, who had evidently had a recent bout with John Barleycorn or some of his kindred. These gentlemen rushed upon our travelers, whooping and yelling like a troop of Comanches, and when within grappling distance, each singling his man, they simultaneously proposed a horse trade. With equal abruptness and unanimity the travelers requested them to go to a very warm place, and kept on their way without drawing rein. The soberest of the trio balanced himself upon his pony and shouted after them that he had no doubt they were horse-thieves, but the country was up, and they would be sarved with justice in due time.

A cold, bright December moon now lighted the dreary path, and a biting wind whistled through the naked forest. From his place among the stars the dark Roane still looked down upon the benighted horsemen.

"I begin to feel a creeping dread of this mountain," said Larkin, "as if it were in reality some monstrous ghoul-like creature, following and watching us."

"Bob, my boy," quoth the Squire, "if your toes were as cold as mine your thoughts wouldn't run upon such nonsense."

"Lights ahead!" exclaimed Jones. "That must be Briggs's."

So it was, and without much circumlocution our travelers dismounted and took possession. The women went to prepare beds and supper forthwith, while the strangers readily accepted the place of honor in front of the wide-mouthed, roaring chimney. In the course of time both horses and riders were fed and made comfortable, and the mountaineer's household gathered around the fire, discoursing of the Roane, the corn crops, and the weather.

"Speaking of corn," said Briggs, "reminds me of a time I wonst had with a painter in this very mountain."

"Tell us about it by all means," said the Squire.

"P'raps you gentlemen wouldn't believe that a man of my make could outrun a painter in a fair race?"

Now Briggs is a stout, broad-shouldered man, with a long back and short legs; he has a rugged, weather-beaten face, square head, and a nose prominent and red withal—but this latter circumstance most probably has nothing to do with his running.

After scrutinizing his host the Tennesseean ventured to express a doubt upon the subject.

"Well, I did do it," said Briggs, curtly, "and I'll tell you how it was. I was a smart young feller, you see, and thought myself a man if I wasn't one, and I had a sow that was a kind of a pet, you see. And so this sow had pigs, you see, and would stray off in the mountains every day or two, but most ginerally come home at night. Well, one night she didn't come home, and early in the mornin' I gits up to look for my sow, and as I passed the barn I puts two ears of corn in my pocket to toll her home with. Well, there was a little skift of snow on the ground, and I follered up a ridge of the mountain maybe about two mile, but nothing could I see of the sow, nor yet of her tracks.

"So I thought I'd go a leetle further—about a quarter—and reached a pint of rocks, where I stopped and listened. In about a minute it appeared as if I heard a child cry. 'Good Lord,' says I, 'some of the neighbors' children have got lost in the mountain!' And so I listened agin, and heard it agin, closter like. Then I was sure it was a child, and was startin' off to look for it, when I looked up, and behold! about fifteen steps off, was a full-grown painter standin' lookin' me in the face. Well, I said it was cold, didn't I? but I broke out into a sweat as if it was summer; and what do you think I did?

"Why, I hauled them two years of corn out of my pocket, and fired one at the painter's head. It didn't hit him, but just grazed his ear, and so I flung the other right quick, and didn't stop to see where that hit, but turned and run. Well, as I run I looked backward like, and I see the critter gallopin' on my tracks; and so I run faster, keepin' down the ridge, about a half or three-quarters. But presently I heard the creeter pantin' behind me, and I gathered up a little stronger. I didn't make many tracks in a mile—I didn't; but I was gittin' blowed a little; and as I still heard the cretter jumpin' behind me, I couldn't help lookin' back, though I knowed I'd lose time by it. Well, good Lord! there was the dratted thing not three steps from my coat-tail, a-canterin' along, and not a hair turned. So I give a jump down the side of the ridge, and lit in a laurel, maybe about fifteen yards down; and, the cussed thing, it seemed to a missed me, and jumped up into a tree to see whar I was.

"Now, that laurel thicket was borderin' on a clearin', and I got into that, and the beast was afeard to foller me. But I didn't stop till I got to the house; and that's what I call beating a painter in a fair race."

"But," said the Tennesseean, "I don't think the panther let himself out."

"He did," said Briggs, indignantly. "He done his best."

"And was that the end of it?" asked Larkin.

"No," said the narrator. "I told daddy and brother about it, and they took the dogs and their guns, and went out and killed it. It was a thunderer, I tell ye."

"I'm very doubtful—" said Squire Broadacre.

"What of?" asked Briggs, straightening himself.

THE HORSE-THIEF

"Not of the truth of your story, by no means, but really whether that panther was—"

Here the discourse was interrupted by the furious clatter of horses' hoofs upon the frozen road, and anon a loud hallo in front of the house. Briggs hurried out, and presently returned with three strangers, who, after being assured that all was right, informed the company that they were in pursuit of a horse-thief. Now, there is something delightful in the idea of a horse-thief. He is the intermediate between a common rogue and a highwayman. As highwaymen have long since starved out of this country, if it ever possessed them, the horse-thief is the highest order of rogue known, and he is estimated accordingly.

The pursuers were full of mystery and importance, while every body had something to say bearing on the subject. The Squire stated how the mountaineer had asked him if he had lost a horse, and how the drunken men had called him a horse-thief. The statement was listened to with much interest, and was supposed to have thrown some light on the subject. It proved, at least, that the rogue had been about.

Having hastily refreshed themselves and their horses, the night riders mounted, and their departure was the signal for bed.

Long before the morning sun had showed his face in the frosty vales our adventurers had breakfasted, and were on their way toward the summit of the Roane. The party on horseback, swelled to four by the addition of a friendly neighbor, trotted along briskly in Indian file. At their head strode Grey Briggs on foot, skipping from rock to rock with surprising speed and agility, evidently exhibiting himself before the strangers to substantiate the panther story.

"Go it, old horse!" exclaimed the Tennesseean. "He's after you, with his back up!"

"By George," cried the Squire, "if I ever harbored a doubt on the subject of that race, I have none now!"

"If he traveled at this rate when he was a boy," said Larkin, "it must have been a fast panther that followed him."

As the hill became steeper the guide's pace slackened, and after a while he didn't mind riding a spell.

The distance from Briggs's to the summit is estimated at five miles. The path is through an open forest, steep, and sometimes rocky, but a bold horseman would not hesitate to ride the whole distance up and down. Indeed, the feat has been accomplished by several ladies.

The height of the Roane has been estimated at six thousand and thirty-eight feet. Its summit is generally bare of trees, but covered with a luxuriant growth of grass, which in summer affords excellent pasturage for cattle. This undulating meadow is spotted with tufts of laurel and stunted firs, and traversed by numerous rocky gullies washed by the springs which ooze from the soil in many places; rounding gently toward the wooded declivities of the mountain in every direction except the southwest, where it terminates suddenly in a range of stupendous precipices many hundred feet in perpendicular height.

But the scene which meets the eye while standing on this summit, who shall attempt to describe? Any effort to convey to the reader the sensations experienced by the beholder would indeed be but a vain essay, an idle stringing together of words. Let that pass. Nevertheless, a plain, unambitious catalogue of what is to be seen on a clear day may not be amiss, and we will give it.

The sweep of the vision in every direction is unlimited, except by the curvature of the earth or the haziness of the atmosphere. The first idea suggested is, that you are looking over a vast blue ocean, whose monstrous billows, once heaving and pitching in wild disorder, have been suddenly arrested by some overruling power.

To the eastward the level country of North Carolina beyond the Blue Ridge may be dimly discerned, while the broad cultivated lands of East Tennessee stretch away to the westward, bounded by the distant ranges of the Cumberland Mountains. Nearer at hand the lofty kinsmen of the Roane are pointed out—the Unaka, the Bald, the Yellow, the Table, the Grandfather, and many a haughty hidalgo whose claim to distinction has been overlooked in the crowd.

To the southward, about twenty miles distant, rises the famous group of the Black, where, surrounded by his court, solemn and silent, stands the dark-browed monarch of the Appalachian system, Mount Mitchell. His dome-like crown is black with a dense growth of balsam fir, and now adorned with many a glittering gem of ice and snow. Professor Guyot calculated the height of eight of these peaks, and gives the following as their elevation above the level of the sea:

The Black Dome	6760	Hairy Bear	6606
Balsam Cone	6668	Bowler's Pyramid	6340
Black Brother	6626	Long Ridge	6244
Cat Tail Peak	6615	Deer Mount	6213

The Squire and Larkin sat apart from the company, contemplating this imposing scene in silence. The former at length spoke:

" 'He that ascends to mountain tops shall find
The loftiest peaks most wrapped in clouds and snow:
He that surpasses or subdues mankind
Must look down on the hate of all below.' "

"It is impossible to tell by the eye," said Larkin, "which of these great peaks is the highest; and it must have been a source of deep mortification to the Balsam Cone when Guyot's barometer decided the question and gave the crown of pre-eminence to the Lord of the Black Dome. We may even now trace upon each gloomy front the jealousy and hate of approved superiority. They doubtless talk of it among themselves; and when those who dwell in the valleys overhear their hoarse whisperings they imagine the wind is blowing, and when it storms their unrepressed growling is mistaken for thunder."

"You have a lively fancy, Robert," said the Squire, elevating his bushy brows.

"Indeed," continued the artist, "it would not be difficult to imagine what they say. The Balsam Cone whispers to the Cat Tail, 'Harkye, princely brother. Do you believe these confounded *savans* can measure so neatly with their instruments as to tell whether he or I is the taller? I once held myself above him.' 'Ah!' groans the Black Brother, 'I was once at least his equal; but he has been so puffed up with his cursed pride, I fear he overtops us now in reality. Since Mitchell measured him he has grown three hundred feet from pure conceit.' 'Hist, brothers!' says the Cat Tail, slyly, 'we are too boister-ous. Now do you know I have long doubted whether it was really he the Professor measured, but have good reason to believe it was one of us—myself, perhaps.' 'You?' exclaims the Cone, contemptuous-ly looking down fifty-three feet on the conceited speaker. 'Or perhaps it was you,' suggests the Cat Tail; 'but after all, what mighty difference does ninety-two feet make? Does he think we are valleys for that?' 'A valet, did you say? his valet?' cries the Cone; 'I'd rather be a low morass haunted by terrapins and frogs than such a mountain.' 'Ugh!' growls the Hairy Bear, 'I could tear out his stony bowels until he caved in!' 'Would I were a volcano,' howls the Black Brother, 'that I might spit fire and brimstone in his hateful face!' 'If,' says the Cat Tail, 'we could keep it before the people that he was the wrong mountain, nobody would be the wiser, and one of us might be king.' 'May an earthquake rend him!' roars the Cone. 'Yea, rather than submit to such measures, I would we were all hurled down in common ruin!' "

"Robert," quoth the Squire, "your mountains talk as though possessed of the spirit of modern democracy."

Having passed about five hours in the enjoyment of this magnificent prospect, our adventurers concluded to descend, which feat was accomplished without accident. At the foot they took leave of their friendly guides, and pursued their journey toward Bakersville, said to be four or five miles distant. Owing to the length of the miles, or the bad condition of the roads between mud and ice, they did not arrive at their destination until sometime after dark. Here they were received after the fashion of the country, got a hearty supper, and went to bed, where for ten consecutive hours they lay in sweet oblivion of all sublunary delights and discomforts. They were aroused from this long sleep by a summons to breakfast, and descending the steep stairway which led from their dormitory, found themselves in the presence of their host, the Colonel, and his interesting family.

"Thank Heaven," whispered Larkin, "we are at length in a region where Jew clothiers have not penetrated—those enemies of the artist and antiquarian, who obliterate in their course all that is venerable, original, or picturesque in costume."

"A paradise," said the Squire, "where hoops and crinoline have not entered—those enemies of elegance and grace, those idle occupiers of space."

And then he cast an approving glance upon the Colonel's six blooming, buxom daughters. And indeed they were girls worth looking at; all well-shaped, tall, and handsome, full of fun and frolic, although perhaps a little demure before strangers.

Then there were three boys, the terror of rabbits and ground-squirrels we'll warrant. The youngest, a little rosy-faced, pot-bellied pest, from his stronghold between the Colonel's knees, appeared to rule the household.

"Pap! I want a apple."

One of the boys is dispatched to bring a tin basinful.

"Pap! I want a knife to peel me apple."

"Well, sonney, where's your knife?"

"It's lost. I want yourn."

"But mine will cut sonney's fingers."

"It won't—gimme, gimme hit."

So out comes the big jack-knife, and sonney begins peeling. One of the girls gets a rag ready to tie up his finger when he cuts it. Contrary to the general expectation this does not happen, but the apple pops out of his hand and rolls into the fire.

"Pap! Pap! pick up me apple."

The veteran renders prompt obedience to the order.

"I won't have hit, hit's dirty."

"Only a leetle ashes, sonney," says the old man, wiping it with his sleeve.

"I won't have it. Gimme another."

"Did you ever see such a case," whispered the Squire to Larkin.

"I think I have," replied Bob, with a significant glance at the speaker.

"What!" said Mr. Broadacre, reddening; "do you mean me and Tiny?"

Bob laughed, and went on with his notes.

The Squire continued. "It is ridiculous, and yet touching, to see how completely instinct masters judgment; how the strong bows to the weak; how the crafty is the tool of the simple; how the dogmatism of experience and the stubbornness of age delight to humble themselves before the feeble capriciousness of a child."

The town of Bakersville, being a place of some mark, should not be passed over without befitting notice; for we are persuaded there are many persons, considering themselves very well informed, who are totally ignorant of its locality and resources. It is situated on the main road from Grey Briggs's to Young's, about eight miles from the former place. Its principal street is built up on one side with a rail-fence, and on the other with two cabins, set back from the street. The back streets and alleys, which are laid off *ad libitum,* contain the stables, cowsheds, and hen-houses. The only public buildings worthy of note are an apple-jack distillery, where the best may be obtained for twelve and a half cents a quart, and a spring-house, covering a fountain of cool, pure water, which has no commercial value, although some persons affect to prefer it to the former as a beverage. During the dark of the moon the town is lighted with pine-knots; and its police force, consisting of six big dogs, is at all times uncommonly vigilant and active.

Having discoursed on the subject of the Presidency, the crops, and the horse-thief, until ten o'clock, our travelers, reluctantly quitting the cheerful society of Bakersville, mounted their horses and resumed their journey.

To the southeastward, the dark, towering peaks of the Black were discernible from every eminence, and with the principal object of their journey in view, they urged their steeds forward at a stirring pace. About noon they halted to repose and lunch in a narrow valley, well wooded with beech and maple, mingled with evergreens, and watered by a cool stream. Hard by was a mountain distillery, and on the rail-fence inclosing it sat a little dried-up old man, clad in a bobtail hunting-shirt.

What with his queer hat and keen eye, Squire Gouge mightily resembled a crow perched upon the fence, and as the crow is known to be the smartest animal that wears feathers, our friends presently ascertained that the resemblance was not merely superficial. Squire Broadacre opened conversation with the proprietor by asking some civil questions in relation to his business.

These the distiller answered with much politeness, and then proceeded to inveigh bitterly against the perverse morality of the North Carolina Legislature, exhibited in the passage of certain laws interfering with the free traffic in spirituous liquors.

"But," said Mr. Broadacre, "is it not the duty of the Legislature to watch over the morals of the State, and pass such laws as are required to improve them?"

"No! that haint hit," replied Gouge; "hit's this: they go thar to set traps for public offices, and thar they eat and git drunk among themselves, until they're nigh done for; and when they're 'bout to break up, some to save their conscience and some to fool their constituents, they pass sich bills as this durned quart law."

"What is your objection to the quart law?" asked the Squire.

"Why, hit's this. Formerly neighbors mought come, take a civil drink together, and go their ways; now they can't buy less nor a quart. Now a quart of licker is too much for any man; and a poor man don't like to fling away what he has paid his money for, so he is bound to git drunk, and hit's the Legislater's fault."

"But can't he do without it entirely?" said the Squire.

"Was a man sott on this yearth to drink nothin' better nor persimmon beer?" asked Gouge, scornfully. "No! God gin us these things to be used, and not to be abused. Now scripter says God looked upon all he had made and said it was good, and ef so be he hadn't intended us to drink licker, he wouldn't ha' gin it to us."

"God did not give us brandy or whisky, but only apples and corn."

"True," said the distiller, "neither did he gin us bread nor pies, nor yit any thing jist as we use it; but he gin us the ingredients and the smartness to make what we wanted out 'en 'em, and hit's the same as if they were his gifts."

"Man," said Mr. Broadacre, "was created pure and upright, and has of himself sought out many inventions and debased himself thereby."

"True as gospel, stranger; but tell me how do you know that apple-brandy comes under the head o' them inventions, any more than the quart law does, or p'raps the woolly hoss?"

"Then you believe in encouraging drunkenness and making brandy, in spite of my arguments!" exclaimed Squire Broadacre with heat.

"I never git drunk myself," replied Gouge, "nor encourage my neighbors in it, but I can make more out of my apples this way than any other; and didn't Noey set to making wine as soon as he got out of the ark?"

"And got drunk and exposed himself," said the Squire—

"And," persisted Gouge, "wasn't his sons that respected him blessed, and him that made game of him wasn't he cussed and made a nigger of?"

"God help us," quoth the Squire with an air of vexation, "he fights like a raccoon in the water. Good man, what do you ask for a quart of your best?"

"Twelve and a half cents," said Gouge.

"Larkin, my boy, go fill our decanter and let us go on our way."

The three horsemen rode along for some time in silence, till at length the Squire spoke:

"I very much doubt," said he, "the feasibility of legislating a State into greatness or a people into virtue; and am inclined to believe that most of the patent schemes to attain either object have been productive of more evil than good. The causes as well as the cure of most social evils lie too deep to be reached by direct legislation. They are either inherent in the character of a people, or the result of long training and education. Now when we have seen our Legislatures one after another deliberately pulling down the wisely-contrived barriers wherewith our ancient virtue and liberty were fenced about, preferring the vile, capricious sovereignty of the many to the calm, equitable rule of the law—studiously contriving to withdraw the masses from their honest and peaceful employments, to embroil them in a warfare where the choicest weapons are chicanery and lies— flattering that they may lead them, corrupting that they may use, training them at the polls, educating them with newspapers—and after all that, passing laws to make them virtuous—one scarcely knows whether to feel more indignation at the wicked recklessness which has raised the storm, or contempt for the imbecility which amuses itself in thus darting straws against the wind."

Having delivered himself of the foregoing, the Squire commenced belaboring his hack as if he had been a legislator, and started off at such speed that he was soon out of sight. Our travelers at length arrived at Young's, from the door of whose house they had a magnificent view of the whole chain of the Black Mountains. Larkin took advantage of the halt to sketch the imposing scene, while at the same time the Squire's horse, equally bent on improving his leisure moments, treated himself to a roll in the mud.

Mr. Broadacre and the Tennesseean entered the house to see what information they could get in regard to their route. Now the good man to whom they had been recommended was gone somewhere to a husking, and madam, who was extremely communicative, told them so much more than was possible that they departed knowing less than when they arrived. Under the circumstances, it was resolved to go on to Burnsville, and to Burnsville they went as fast as their horses could carry them, arriving about sunset.

Being warmed and fed, in due time they held a council to plan their movements for the following day. They were informed that they could go to Tom Wilson's, who lived twelve miles distant, at the foot of Mitchell's Peak, and that he would guide them to the summit, which was six miles further.

The information was clear and satisfactory, and the question then arose, could they accomplish the ride, the ascent, and return to Wilson's by nightfall? It was necessary that this should be done to enable them to return to Jonesborough by the day appointed.

Their host insisted that it was impracticable. Larkin said by a neat calculation he could prove

AGGRAVATION

that it was possible. The Squire, who was sipping a hot toddy, swore that it should be done. The Tennesseean said it would be done. And so they went to bed.

Next morning they were in their saddles by daylight, and went clattering down the frozen road at a hand-gallop. Their ranks were swelled by a recruit from Burnsville, a handsome, wiry young Carolinian, mounted on a spirited sorrel. The more the merrier. Away they dashed, crushing into ice-bound mud-holes, splashing through shallow fords, galloping up hills and trotting down. Ah, it was glorious! What though the sky was overcast and the earth powdered with snow! what though the morning breeze cut like a knife! There was life and courage in every draught. Then they had set themselves a task, and staked their manhood on its accomplishment; forward, forward! The horses smoked like hot cakes, the riders' beards and ear-locks were white with frost, warm fires gleamed temptingly through the open doors of the cabins, and glimpses of white-clothed tables loaded with smoking viands wooed to repose and luxury. But no; have we not said it?—Forward!

Now they ride the Caney River, whose waters roll clear and cold as liquid ice; now on the further bank their dripping steeds clatter over the pebbles. The ninth mile-board from Burnsville is past, the road has dwindled to a mere bridle-path half lost among thickets of dogwood and laurel. Now their confident advance is checked, for they must grope for the path as it wanders alternately through the stream and among the bushes. At length the Tennesseean rises in his stirrups and shouts triumphantly. Near the banks of the stream, in a grove of lofty firs, rises a column of blue, curling smoke.

In a few minutes the riders drew rein in front of a cabin fresh hewn from the forest. A short distance from the door stood a stalwart woodman leaning on a rifle, and attended by two dogs. In the door behind him was a group composed of a white-haired sire, two women, four children, and a boy.

But we have not time to go into particulars. This is Tom Wilson, of course; that's his father, his wife and children, his wife's sister, perhaps; and the boy is his factotum.

"Quarter to ten o'clock," said Larkin.

The travelers made known their wishes in few words.

Tom Wilson scratched his curly pate. "Well, I hain't no mighty much to do no time; so I s'pose I ken go. But you'd better light and take a bite of something to eat."

No. They had already breakfasted, lightly to be sure; but they were bent on the accomplishment of their undertaking, and preferred going on immediately. Now Tom Wilson is not a man of "mighty many words," and so, accoutred as he was, he plunged into the bushes "and bade them follow."

As they advanced, the guide proposed his plans for the ascent. They could ride to the upper place a mile distant, and leaving their horses

TOM WILSON

there in comfortable quarters, accomplish the rest of the way on foot. The Squire looked at his fat legs, and raised himself considerably in his stirrups, as if to calculate his weight. When arrived at the upper place, Wilson informed them that they might even carry the horses a mile further if they wished. The Squire preferred it, and the animals, obedient to rein and whip, turning their heads reluctantly away from the fodder stacks, trudged along up the narrow path.

This soon became so steep that every nerve of man and beast was strained to its utmost tension in the effort to hold on their way. The rider was obliged to use hand and foot to keep clear of the rocks and branches on the upper side, while the slightest misstep on the part of the horse would have sent them rolling a thousand feet into the dark gorge below. The snow, which had slightly powdered the lower country, was more decided as they ascended, and increased the hazard of the journey. Every two or three hundred yards a stream would spirt across their path, covering every thing near with ice, and they were then obliged to dismount and carefully lead their animals over. In this way they at length reached a cove from whence there seemed to be no exit upward, except by flight. Making a virtue of necessity, it was agreed to leave the horses here; so they were unsaddled and securely tethered among the bushes, where they could entertain themselves eating moss and twigs until their companions returned.

Tom Wilson, who, during these proceedings, had stretched his stalwart form upon a snow-covered bank, now rose and led the way. Nothing loth our adventurers followed, at first with words of cheer, quick-spoken jests, then silently, then panting and sobbing audibly. Still they strove with hearts of controversy, until the last breath seemed to be leaving their bodies, and they sunk in the path from pure exhaustion. No one had strength to chide his comrade, and all were glad of a chance to stop.

"This is what Professor Guyot calls 'work for a giant.' It is too much for a fat, easy-living man of my inches," groaned the Squire.

"This is no tavern," cries the guide; "we've yet a mighty ways to travel."

And again they breast the slippery steep. After many consecutive efforts they attained a level spot covered with beech-trees. Tom Wilson struck the butt of his gun on the ground, and announced that this was the Bear Garden. "But," he continued, "there hain't no mighty many bar here now," and having thus spoken he again made tracks through the snow. Passing over this level, the path ascends rapidly through tangled thickets of rhododendron and dark forests of balsam fir. The travelers toiled upward in sullen silence, betraying with long-drawn sobs the fatigue which had not yet been acknowledged in words.

After some time the guide showed them a mark upon a tree which indicated that there was water at hand, and with a little search they found a spring bubbling from under a rock. Having partaken freely of this welcome refreshment, our friends suddenly discovered that they were furiously hungry.

It was in fact half past one o'clock. They had breakfasted at five, and in the haste and excitement of starting had eaten but sparingly. In addition, the rapid ride and the frosty air had put the keenest edge upon their appetites, yet unfortunately not a biscuit had been provided. According to the calculation of the guide, the summit was yet a mile and a half distant, and rating their speed by what had been accomplished this was full an hour and a half. Then an hour at least on the summit and three to descend. The prospect was appalling.

Although no one dared to acknowledge fatigue, it was reckoned no disgrace to be hungry, and the complaints on that score were loud and manifold. The guide at length spoke up.

"Men! if we stop here ciphering and grumbling, we'll never see the top of the Black."

The remark was well-timed, and stirred up the dying embers of that enthusiasm which had hitherto sustained them.

"Old Virginia never tire!" shouted Larkin, springing up the slippery path.

"Tennessee is always thar!" yelled the wiry Jones, following with good heart.

"Old North State is generally somewhar when you look for her!" cried Burnsville.

Now Squire Broadacre didn't say any thing, but tugged and toiled after them as well as he could; nathless he thought to himself that if those plump legs of his were elsewhere under some well-loaded dinner-table, he wouldn't begrudge a cool hundred.

Having worried on in this way for half a mile or more the enthusiasm again died out, and now unrepressed complaints of hunger and exhaustion were heard from all.

"Thanks to fortune!" cried Larkin, "I've found something to eat in my pocket."

This announcement was received with eager looks and exclamations by his companions.

"Here are five chestnuts. Let me see, one for each man."

They were served round, and no one had the self-denial to refuse his portion; but each devoured his nut with a satisfaction that was ludicrous, although most sincere. Burnsville, however, uttered an exclamation which wouldn't print well, and rested his head upon his hands with a look of bitter disappointment.

"What ails you now, neighbor?" asked Tom Wilson.

"Ah!" replied he, with a groan, "mine had a worm in it."

> "But the darkest night will have a morning,
> The longest lane will have a turning."

They at length reached the foot of a knoll covered with laurel and stunted fir, where they halted to rest. The guide informed them they were then within two hundred yards of the summit of the Black Dome.

This inspiriting news set them again in motion, when the Squire, who was seated at the foot of a tree, called out,

"It is useless, boys for me to strive. Time has made his mark upon me, and I can go no farther even if my life depended on it. I will lie here until you return. Only remember, if Tom Wilson finds any thing to eat on the top, to send me down a share."

"How now! what's the matter? what's the matter?" cried one and all.

"Nothing at all, boys. Go on, go on, see the top. As for me, I have already passed the summit point in life's highway, and am only fit to go down hill."

"But, uncle," said Larkin, "I have with me a mechanical power that will lift you to the top in a jiffey, the true lever of Archimedes."

"How now, you scamp! Why didn't you show it sooner?"

"Because," said Bob, "it is only good in a pinch, but ruinous in a long chase. If I had showed it earlier we would never have got to this point."

The Squire gave a vigorous whistle as he recorked the flask, and immediately rose to his feet.

"I believe," quoth he, cheerily, "I can still go up hill a little further."

In a few minutes they stood upon the summit of Mount Mitchell.

Around and beneath them rolled dense masses of vapor, shutting out all terrestrial objects except the rounded knoll on which they were standing. Above, the deep-blue sky was visible, and the sunlight beamed clear and cold upon the stunted shrubs and fir-trees cased in glittering ice.

The summit had been recently cleared by the axe, and in the centre a sort of rude observatory was constructed of pine logs ten or twelve feet in height.

A little circle, of a hundred paces diameter, comprehended all that our adventurers saw from the top of the Black Mountains; yet the triumph of accomplishment illuminated every face, and for a space fatigue and hunger were both forgotten.

As their blood cooled these feelings of exultation passed away, and Nature again began to urge her claims with redoubled force. Burnsville wrapped his blanket about him, and, sinking down at the foot of the observatory, fell into a sort of stupor. A round of brandy stimulated the others to join in an attempt to light a fire. Every thing was wet and frozen; but, by perseverance, they at length accomplished it. The crackling flame did not bring consolation, for although it warmed them, it also suggested cooking, and there was nothing to cook. Hollow-cheeked despair began to settle upon the faces around.

"Uncle," asked Larkin, "is there any nourishment in leather?"

"I have heard," said the Squire, "how the defenders of beleaguered cities have subsisted on soup made of jack-boots; but why do you ask?"

"I observed the fat frying out of your boots, Sir, and it smelled very savory."

"They have been well greased lately; but, my boy, it would never do to eat our boots: without them we could never get down from here."

Burnsville, roused from his trance, now joined the circle, his lips blue and his face wearing a savage expression.

"Gentlemen," said he, "unless we get some refreshment we will never have strength to get down this mountain. There's one thing can save us, and I've made up my mind to it."

The greedy eyes of the party were centred upon the speaker.

"There's Tom Wilson's yaller dog: he's young and fat, and, by blood! if we can do no better—"

At this moment Wilson drew near with an armful of fresh fuel.

"Men! an ideer jist struck me. There's a cabin a little below here, p'raps about a quarter, put up for travelers that come here in the summer to see the sun rise. Now, there might be something thar a man could eat."

"Hurrah for Tom Wilson! Hurry down, and let's have it! Quick, quick!"

"There might, at least, be some hoss feed," he continued.

"Bring it! Bring it! Corn, oats, chop, bran, any thing!"

Tom scratched his head thoughtfully. "I know there's some hay and corn cobs there, for I see 'em about three weeks ago."

"I speak for half a dozen cobs," said Jones; "red ones I prefer, but I am not finnikin."

Tom carefully whistled up his dogs, and sending them ahead presently disappeared in the cloud on his hopeful errand. Hope had thrown our adventurers into a state of excitement, and they eagerly fell to conjecturing the chances of the forage. Some thought of one thing, and some of another; but no one had ventured to suggest any thing above corn meal.

"Great Lord!" exclaimed Burnsville, "suppose he should find a ham!"

"Young man," said the Squire, sternly, "upon what ground do you base such an absurd idea? You do wrong to trifle with the feelings of desperate men. Besides, in our present condition nothing could be more unwholesome. I hope he'll not find any ham."

Hark! there was a shout. The yellow dog came skipping out of the cloud, and, unconscious of the fell designs which had been entertained against him, went nosing around in the most friendly manner. Wilson soon followed carrying something on his shoulder.

"By all that's blessed, a frying-pan. We can cook the dog anyhow, or make boot soup. What luck? What luck?"

"Oh, only sort o' tol'able. I've got some hoss feed, a peck of corn or thereabouts, and some salted bran."

"Hurrah! That's glorious!"

In a moment the guide was surrounded, and every body was munching raw corn as if it was a prime delicacy.

This gave Tom an opportunity to wash the pan and put about a quart of corn to parch.

"Hands out, men. Leave the corn git done, hit's more wholesomer that a way than raw. I begin to be afear'd," he continued, "that you raley would eat my dog, and that's why I got this corn; for, you see, the cabin was locked, and I had to break in, and so make myself liable to the law. But I wouldn't like to lose that pup, I wouldn't. He's mighty keen on a bar trail. Now the corn hain't done yet; jist leave me gin it another turn."

To see the eager hungry boys seemed natural enough, but to see Squire Broadacre watching the pan and grabbing up the "captains" as they hopped out on the snow, was rather ludicrous.

"Ah, Bob, you terrier, you were too quick for me that time."

"Uncle," quoth Bob, handing over a handful, "I was gathering it expressly for you."

"Thank you, my boy, I will remember your heroism."

The browned and smoking mess was now turned out upon the handkerchief and duly mixed with a handful of salted bran to give it flavor. Our adventurers went into it with speechless gusto, while the good-humored guide browned several additional pansful, and then went back to replace the utensil in the cabin where he had found it.

"Blood of my body!" exclaimed the Squire, "I am still unsatisfied, and I haven't the power to give my jaws another wag."

"A sip of brandy, a brief repose, and try it again."

Indeed, although parched corn is a most savory and nourishing mess for a hungry man, it requires an uncommon amount of energy, perseverance, and power of jaw to get enough of it.

After an hour's hard work, performed with intense satisfaction, the whole supply was devoured, and the travelers declared themselves ready for the descent; but how stout and cheery they were—how jolly and boastful!

"Ah!" quoth the Squire, "for a man of my age and figure to have ascended the highest mountain in the United States."

"To eat a pint of parched corn," suggested Larkin,

"Fond of high living," said Jones.

And down they went spouting wit and poetry, shouting and laughing, apparently as fresh as if just starting out. The horses were regained before nightfall, the dangerous paths crossed, and when they reached the banks of Caney Fork the valley was shrouded in the gloom of night.

Giving the reins to their sagacious steeds they reached Wilson's cabin at seven o'clock, after an absence of nine hours and a quarter.

Having already described one meal at length, we will not dwell upon the supper at the cabin, nor tell what buckwheat cakes and biscuits, what pork and fried chicken, what stewed pumpkins and cabbage, disappeared from the groaning board, nor enumerate the cups of milk, coffee, and persimmon beer that were swallowed during the meal. Mrs. Wilson declared it did her good to see 'em eat—in fact it did every body good; and then, when stuffed until they were nearly blind, and set before the fire to dry, it was a treat to hear the jokes and stories of the day's adventures.

One of the ancients has said, "No man can be considered fortunate until he is dead." The moderns say, "Never halloo until you're out of the woods." We may add an apophthegm of our own, "The troubles of the day are never over until one is in bed." Now it happened that our friend Burnsville's experience verified the aptness of these sayings, especially of the latter. When it was proposed to retire he commenced as usual with his boots, but found to his extreme vexation that they were immovable. After a reasonable amount of tugging, swearing, and upsetting of chairs, he got out his knife for the purpose of "ripping their blasted soles out of 'em." To prevent the desperate deed the company interfered, and Wilson asked permission to try his hand on 'em. Overruled by the general voice, the patient yielded, and stretched himself upon the puncheon floor with the air of a man about to have his legs amputated. Two of his companions seized him by the shoulders, while Wilson took one boot in his hands and placed the other against his knee.

"Now, all together—Yeo-heave-oh!"

Tom bowed himself and pulled till every muscle quivered with the exertion, but the leathern hoof was immovable.

"Hold on!" cried Burnsville, groaning. "Let me cut it; you've loosened every joint in my leg, and filled me with splinters from these blamed puncheons."

"Waggle your heel and toe back and forth," cried Tom, setting himself again.

This time the boot came off, and, by repeating the operation, the the other foot was uncased in like manner. The young man managed to crawl into bed, while Wilson consoled him with the following observation:

"Your jints 'ill tighten up by mornin', and the boots hain't hurt a bit."

As the next day was Sunday and our friends intended to ride no further than the town of Burnsville, they slept late and lingered about the cabin for some time after breakfast. While they sat discoursing upon the subject of mountains in general, Johnsey, the first-born and heir apparent of Tom Wilson's cabin, recently washed and combed, entered. Stationing himself in front of Larkin, he regarded the stranger for a space with a look of intense respect mingled with curiosity. Presently, as if he had made up his mind to it, he approached and thus addressed him.

"Look'ee, mister, is them saddle-bags of yourn full of money?"

"Perhaps so, Johnsey," said Larkin, "and if you will stand still for about five minutes longer, you shall have some of it—a dime at least."

Fifth Paper

"Nurse of a people in misfortune's school,
Trained up to hardy deeds—a manly race
Of unsubmitting spirit, wise and brave."
THOMSON.

EAST TENNESSEE is one of the most delightful countries in the world. Possessing a genial climate, a fertile soil, abounding in all those natural resources whose development and use constitute the true wealth of a state, her virgin forests, lovely rivers, and majestic mountains, offer, at the same time, a rich and varied feast to the romantic tourist. Her annals, although they might now be comprehended within the memory and experiences of a single life extended but a little beyond the allotted term of threescore years and ten, are swelled with many a page wherein the statesman and philosopher may find food for thought and theme for speculation. They furnish us the records of a people who, having won a fair heritage by their courage, have cultivated it with industry and governed it with wisdom—a people who have fought their own battles, plowed their own land, and made their own laws. We may also find there names, familiar as household words, of men, types of their race, who, sustained by native force alone, have led in war and peace, and attained the highest distinctions in the camp and in the cabinet, whose fame, too large for the narrow limits of a State, now belongs to our national history.

In these days one may see a great many queer sights in Tennessee. He may discern the prints of the deer-skin moccasin and the French kid slipper side by side. Overlooking the mud-chinked cabin of the pioneer, carefully imitated from the handiwork of Daniel Boone, he may see the elegant villa from a design by Downing or Vaux. Strangely contrasting with the simple garb and manner of the olden time, he meets every where the luxury and polish of modern refinement. There are colleges, railroads, piano-fortes, electric telegraphs, and fancy stores. Old folks have already begun to shake their heads at these things, but old folks are always shaking their heads at something. Whether or not they will be of any advantage to the State, we can't presume to say; yet, after a rambling visit to the soil, and a cursory glance at the records of our recent battle-fields, we can not perceive that the Tennesseean of the present day is in any way unworthy of his gallant ancestry

"For every virtue, every worth renowned,
Sincere, plain-hearted, hospitable, kind;
Yet, like the mustering thunder, when provoked—
The dread of tyrants, and the sure resource
Of those that under grim oppression groan."

Driven by the storms of fate to seek a refuge on our shores, the exiled Mitchell was charmed by the appearance of this fair and peaceful land, and found a temporary home in one of its most secluded districts. The advent of such a man naturally excited the curiosity of his uninformed and unlettered neighbors, and numerous speculations as to the why and wherefore of his coming were indulged in. It was suggested that he might be a land-jobber, "one o' them book-larnt fellers in sarch of metals," maybe a counterfeiter. But the life of the stranger seemed to justify none of these surmises, and the wiseacres remained for a long time completely mystified. At length one of them, whose business had carried him as far as Knoxville, obtained the clew to the mystery. At the next log-rolling it was duly promulgated. "Their quare neighbor had had a quarrel with the British Government, and had come to Tennessee to git shut of 'em."

"Well, forever!" exclaimed an old hunting shirt; "British Government, did you say? Why, is that blasted old concern a-standin' yit? Well, may I never! British Government! Now I thought old Jack Sevier and Gineral Jackson had busted hit up long 'go."

But we must turn again to our legitimate business, and look after the welfare of our adventurous travelers.

Immediately on the return of the gentlemen from the mountains, the whole party set about preparing for their departure from Jonesborough. The trunks were all packed, shawls and bonnets on, and the ladies had even gone through their preliminary leave-taking, when the coach which they had expected to convey them drove up hopelessly and disgustingly crowded. Those who have been placed in similar circumstances will not be surprised to learn that Squire Broadacre left the room where the ladies were discussing their disappointment, himself looking red and vexed, and that a few moments thereafter he fell upon Jim Bug, loading him with abusive epithets, and flourishing his cane over his head in an awfully threatening manner.

To this Jim submitted with respectful deference, looking as unconscious of the cane as an Italian dog when menaced with a stone. When the Squire got through, however, Jim spoke up:

"I think, master, it's 'bout time you was leaving me that coat you got on—it's all ripped under the arms."

The Squire's eye twinkled, and, examining the coat, he exclaimed, in a milder tone, "Why, you observant rascal, so it seems; but hark ye, if you wish to save your mistress's life, go immediately and hire a carriage that will take us to Russellville; any thing with wheels will answer, even though it were an ox-cart."

Their friend, Tom Dosser, was again appealed to, and, through his civility, they were presently provided with a vehicle of the tin cart species for the passengers, and a dismantled buggy to carry the baggage. With this substantial but not particularly elegant equipage, they took the road next morning, hoping, as they bade adieu to Jonesborough, that they had left behind as agreeable impressions as they carried with them.

Their journey to Greenville, twenty-five miles distant, was not signalized by any event worthy of record, except that the younger folks got their mouths puckered up eating persimmons, which are very plentiful along the route. They entered this cozy little town about sunset, and were comfortably entertained at an old-fashioned country tavern. As Russellville, the point where they expected to take the cars, was only twenty-five miles farther, they made themselves easy, and did not resume their journey next morning until after ten o'clock.

Notwithstanding their previous experiences in mud, they had made no calculations for such a day as this proved to be. Long before their journey was accomplished night overtook them, and with it a cold, driving rain. In spite of this and the pitchy darkness, they worried on until at length their vehicle was stuck so fast in a mud-hole that every effort of their horses to extricate it was unavailing.

Larkin, who has a noble voice, now commenced hallooing at a venture, and, to their joyful surprise, the signal was presently answered by the barking of dogs and the appearance of a light near at hand. Bob immediately started off through the mud and darkness to communicate with the signal, and in a short time returned, accompanied by a gentleman bearing a light, followed by a couple of stout negroes.

With this timely assistance they were delivered from the mud-hold, and, following the lantern, they presently halted before the door of a comfortable country mansion. The necessity of the case was so evident that ceremony was entirely forgotten. Without question or explanation the travelers and their baggage were transferred to the house, while the horses, snorting with delightful anticipation, trotted off to the stables.

The ladies were, without delay, ushered into the warm and cheerful precinct of the family room; while the gentlemen, less fortunate, were shown into a handsomely-furnished parlor, where two or three fussy negroes were engaged in kindling a fire. A glass of gooseberry cordial, if it did not facilitate the burning of the fire, served at least to quicken the blood of the benumbed and wearied tourists, and warm their thoughts into cheerfulness.

Their host was a tall, fine-looking man between thirty-five and forty years of age, with an uncommonly intelligent face and a frank and easy bearing, which indicated at once acquaintance with the world and a position of superiority among those by whom he was habitually surrounded. His family consisted of an amiable and comely wife and four children, the eldest a boy about thirteen years old. At the supper-table our friends ascertained that they had wandered several miles from their road, and were still a considerable distance from their journey's end; but beguiled by the hospitable attentions of their entertainers, they soon ceased to regret the accident, and at length went to bed forgetting that they were under the roof of a stranger. As the next day was cold and rainy and Mrs. Broadacre slightly indisposed, the Squire easily yielded to the warm solicitations of his host, to tarry with him for several days.

As the travelers were recently come from the realms of fashion, the ladies were soon immersed up to their eyes in the discussion of modes and patterns; while the gentlemen, with lighted cigars, retired to another room discoursing on the weather, the roads, crops, and public improvements. Then as these themes (hackneyed, indeed, but both convenient and necessary in the incipiency of social acquaintance) were disposed of, and as each began more properly to estimate the character and capacities of the other, the conversation between the Squire and his host became more genial and interesting. The discussion of temperance societies and public education drew from the Colonel some reminiscences of his school-boy days so pleasant and instructive that we can not refrain from giving them at length.

"I learned to read and write," said he, "in an old school-house on Indian Creek under the shadow of the Bald Mountain. You have no doubt seen similar ones in your travels—a rude log-pen, floored with puncheons, with a single opening, which served as a door, but entirely without windows or chimneys. In the centre of the room was a hearth formed of stones and earth, where, in winter, a huge log-fire blazed and fumed, the smoke (when it was not blown in our eyes) rising and gathering in a dense cloud under the high pitched roof, and escaping through the wide crevices at the eaves. Ranged in a hollow square around this fire the scholars sat on rough-hewn benches conning their well-thumbed primers, or blue-backed spelling-books, with vociferous diligence.

"Our school was divided into three classes—big boys, little boys, and girls—and presided over by a pig-nut-faced professor, who maintained his state on a split-bottomed throne, and with a sceptre of hickory, tough, limber, and far-reaching. In this wigwam of science, deep-hidden in the shade of primeval forests, did I acquire the rudiments of learning, and experience the incipient sorrows of knowledge.

"When I grew older I was sent to the academy in the town of X——, where I boarded for several years with an affectionate and credulous relative, and chiefly distinguished myself for idleness and audacious mischief. When I was about sixteen the academy boys organized a literary society of which I became a member. The idea was a capital one. We were required to read, deliver select orations, write original compositions, and take part in debating such questions as were selected by the society. What though our speeches were not models of elocution nor our essays of composition? our efforts were sincere. What though we often discussed questions which we were about as capable of understanding as a litter of blind puppies might be? in that we did not greatly differ from most of our grown-up public assemblies. Yet it was surprising to see with what superior zeal those who had been most idle and derelict in the school set about the accomplishment of these self-imposed duties, and what meek and ready submission the most rebellious schoolboy accorded to the laws which he himself had helped to make. Of this my own case, perhaps, furnished the most striking example:

> " 'The genuine offspring of revolt,
> Stubborn and sturdy as a wild ass' colt.'

"From earliest boyhood a recognized leader in mischief, marauding, and rebellion, in my class an habitual bungler and defaulter, I entered the society with but an humble estimate of my own capacities, and no very exalted reputation among the more orderly and studious of my fellows. To the surprise of all, however, I showed myself punctilious in the observance of order, and exhibited in the performance of my allotted exercises a sprightliness of mind for which my best friends had not given me credit, and I had the satisfaction of perceiving that from week to week I was growing mightily in the estimation of my companions, and ambition for distinction in my new career was gradually awakened within me. To astonish where I had formerly been laughed at, to lead where it was believed I could not follow, to alarm the jealousy or conquer the admiration of those who, in the good-natured confidence of superiority, had pitied me—this was stimulus enough. I forsook my idleness and rowdyism, and labored night and day. I labored successfully; for in a short time I began to be spoken of for president of the society.

"In the mean time the society was going on most prosperously: its meetings were conducted with the greatest order and decorum; its constitution and by-laws were observed with religious reverence, and were frequently the theme of animated discussion. Its presiding officer, elected every four weeks, was treated with punctilious deference, and was on his part jealously exact in requiring the observance of parliamentary forms, and stern in rebuking every thing that savored of levity or disrespect.

"The result of these elevating influences could not fail to be observed in the conduct of the boys both in and out of school. Parents and elders remarked and approved of it; several young gentlemen who had already embarked in the learned professions solicited membership, and were admitted. We were invited to march in a Fourth of July procession, and the nimble fingers of many a bright-eyed lass were busied with the blue rosettes that distinguished our body on that day. Thenceforth the title to membership of the Literary Club was a distinction not so easily obtained, and the adopted badge (a blue ribbon in the upper button-hole of the left lapel) was worn with a becoming pride which effectually refutes the ignorant philosophy of those who affect to despise the pomp of dress and ceremony.

"At the next meeting it was proposed, and warmly urged, that the ladies should be admitted to our sittings as listeners and spectators. Notwithstanding the recent effusion of feeling consequent on the blue rosettes, the motion was laid on the table. This failure excited much indignation among the girls and some feeling in the bosom of our society, but the high predominance of law stilled all murmurs there.

"At length I was nominated for the presidency, and next week the election was to come off. My opponent was Jack Loring, a keen, pragmatical little fellow, older than I; a better scholar, and a favorite with the teachers, but too conceited to be popular among the boys. Jack lived in the country and brought apples to school; how he must have sweated under the loads he brought that week! He could also flatter the clever and assist the dull in their tasks. I didn't know how to electioneer, and, under the circumstances, pride made me more reserved than usual. Fortunately I was not before a community of grown-up voters. The boys appreciated my manliness and rewarded it. I was elected by a handsome majority. I received the honor with a calmness of manner that belied the tumultuous pleasure of my soul. I did not sleep that night for thinking of it, and the preparation of my inaugural address robbed me of my usual rest during the whole week. A sense of my prominence took such complete possession of me that I could neither eat nor study.

"When the evening of my inauguration arrived, the older boys were forced to smile as they entered the room. The two tallow dips, stuck in wooden blocks, which had hitherto illuminated the President's desk, were replaced by tall spermacetis in polished brass candlesticks. The desk itself was raised a foot above its usual level, on a sort of dais made of a flat dry-goods box covered with a strip of carpet. I had on a clean shirt and a new neck ribbon, a bit of foppery that I seldom indulged in. The address went off charmingly. I had practiced carefully on the coarse tones of my voice, and got through without a squeak. The glory and usefulness of our society were set forth in a manner to excite enthusiasm; certain improvements were hinted at. There was a disposition to disregard forms and unbecoming familiarity in the speech and manner of some members toward the society: those from the country generally erred in that way. They were reminded of how much 'the divinity that doth hedge about a king' depended on ceremony, and how the dignity and permanent greatness of all associations were based on the respect yielded to their chosen leaders. As all the other inaugurals had been composed of pretty much the same materials, no particular significance was attached to mine; but as it was smoothly worded, and delivered with spirit, it was considered a handsome and creditable effort. Thereafter there was more of pomp and gravity in our proceedings than ever, and I had the satisfaction of hearing it admitted on all sides that the chair had never been so admirably filled. For my part I was indefatigable in devising schemes for the aggrandizement and glorification of the body over which I presided. A flourishing notice of it appeared in the village newspaper, and the question of admitting the ladies was again revived.

"I was deeply interested in the success of this movement. The presence of the fair sex would add lustre to my reign. Then I had a private reason—Molly Morninglory—but this is not pertinent to my story. The proposition was put to the vote and rejected. I was vexed, and under the irritation dignity swelled into arrogance. I fined right and left, and stretched the prerogative of my place to the utmost limit. There was some rebellious murmuring, but in the main the meeting passed quietly. To me it was any thing but satisfactory. I was outraged to perceive that my elevation had not increased my influence;

that position had not brought with it corresponding authority. My nature was aroused on the girl question; while pride forbade electioneering in my own behalf, as the champion of the ladies I found no difficulty in playing the demagogue. Many of the younger members had been my companions in mischief; and, recognizing my leadership in good as well as evil, had followed me into the society. These I could command, but it was necessary to gain other interests. I

IN FAVOR OF MOTION

knew the sweet-hearts of several of the elder boys, and found means to engage their influence. In short, by the next Saturday night I had worked my wires so well that I felt assured of the success of my measure.

After the regular exercises one of my partisans, whom I had previously stuffed, rose, and in a set speech again introduced the question. It was debated with a fury worthy of the ancient factions of Guelf and Ghibelline. Its supporters appealed to the well-known chivalry of East Tennessee; no society was complete without the presence of the fair; her companionship banished rudeness; her approbation stimulated to higher efforts, and was the noblest reward of success. In fine, the society was assured, on undoubted authority, that

> " 'The earth was sad, the garden was a wild,
> And man a hermit sighed till woman smiled.'

"The opponents of the motion professed to yield to none in their admiration of the 'fair sect,' but they had joined the society with the honest intent of improving themselves in speaking and writing; and while they were willing to submit to the criticisms of their schoolfellows, they had no idea of being snickered at by a parcel of girls, nor of having their blunders tattled all over the country. 'They went agin it tooth and toe-nail.'

"The question was at length called, and on counting the votes there was a tie. The constitution provided 'that, in cases of a tie, the presiding officer shall have the casting vote.'

" 'But,' said Jack Loring, 'the chair voted on the question in the first place, and the constitution does not give him two votes.'

"With a supercilious nod to the speaker, I replied, 'The chair does not need to be instructed in regard to its rights and duties. The question is decided in the affirmative.'

" 'It's unconstitutional!' cried Jack, with spirit.

" 'Sit down, Sir! the question is decided'—

" 'I won't sit down!' he retorted; 'I know my rights here, and intend to stand up for them. I appeal to the society.'

OPPOSED TO IT

"My face reddened. 'Your manner, Sir, is disrepectful to the society over which I preside. Secretary, record a fine of one dime against Mr. Loring.'

" 'I'll not pay it!' persisted Jack; 'I'll appeal.'

"Now several members rose:

" 'Mr. President, I would beg leave to suggest—'

" 'Mr. President, please to consider—'

" 'Take your seats!' I cried, haughtily; 'the question is settled, and I'll hear no more.'

" 'Why, Mr. President,' persisted a big chap of the *anti-gunaic* faction, and the son of a noted Whig, 'this conduct is rather tyrannical. It reminds me of General Jackson.'

"The allusion to this great name overthrew the little of self-command and common-sense that passion had left. With an imperial frown and voice of thunder I commanded silence.

"Loring gave a contemptuous whistle: 'Gentlemen, the elevation is too much for him. That store-box is unconstitutional, anyhow. I move it be carried out—'

" 'You mutinous scoundrel!' I cried, half-choking with passion, 'I'll pay you for this!'

"Jack haw-hawed. 'Go it, Rex! He's practicing now to show off before Mary Morninglory next Saturday evening!'

"The next moment Jack Loring and myself were rolling over the floor, sputtering, scratching, and swearing like a pair of tom-cats across a pole. As soon as practicable we were separated; covered with dust, shirt torn, the blood oozing from several scratches on my face, breathless and pale with rage, I mechanically resumed my official seat, while my antagonist was led off to the door to wash his bloody nose.

"As the excitement and confusion subsided there was an interval of silence, and I could perceive in the faces around a prevailing expression of regret and mortification that cut me to the heart. Presently a leading member arose and proposed a committee, to report on the affair, and advise what steps should be taken to vindicate in a proper manner the outraged peace and dignity of the assembly. Upon this, with as much calmness as I could command, I tendered my resignation; but the leaders shook their heads, and I was politely requested to await the action of the committee. While that body was deliberating in an adjoining room, I had full leisure to give heed to the proceedings of a tumultuous assembly in my own breast. The fiercer passions were all there, aroused and clamorous, and it was long before the moderator Reason could obtain a hearing, or bring the house to tolerable order. Should I seize the poker and run a-muck, lathering indiscriminately at friend and foe? Should I take my hat and leave the society, whizzing a few stones through the windows by way of a parting salutation? Though fallen from my high estate, could I descend to such boyish and vulgar resentment? Would not the exhibition of angry defiance be an acknowledgment of my mortification, and resigning my membership an advertisement of my disgrace? After all, was my reputation so hopelessly wrecked that it might not be retrieved? Would not a frank acknowledgment of my error, and a manly submission to the penalties, whatever they might be, win back, at least in part, the esteem I had lost?

"The committee at length returned, and its chairman proceeded to read a formal bill of impeachment against me. I was charged with high misdemeanors in office—arrogance, abuse of prerogative, tyranny, and, finally, a violent and disgraceful assault upon a member. It was admitted that his conduct had been improper, offensive, meriting rebuke; but while it might palliate, it could not in any manner justify my greater offense. It was then proposed that I should be deposed from office, and receive a reprimand from my successor; or, in case I refused to submit to these penalties, that I should be expelled from the society, and resign my blue-ribbon badge before leaving the room.

"This was harder to bear than I had anticipated. The extra circumstance of humiliation attached to either penalty seemed to me wanton and uncalled-for; and I fancied I could trace the motive which prompted it in the triumph and gratified malice which shone in the faces of some, despite their efforts at concealment. The desire to disappoint them as much as possible nerved me to a still greater show of magnanimity. In a lively, good-humored speech, I acknowledged the propriety of the proceedings in my case, lauded the firmness and decency of the committee's report, expressed my entire willingness to submit to laws which I had assisted in making, determined to continue an orderly and interested member of the society, and so to deport myself in the future as to regain the position which, in an unguarded moment, I had forfeited. I wound up by making a formal apology to the house, and offering my hand to Jack Loring. Such magnanimity took every body by surprise, and almost disarmed my enemies.

"The society, however, proceeded to execute sentence. I was regularly deposed by vote, and a successor elected (the chairman of the committee). I was then called upon to rise and receive the reprimand, which I did with as much *nonchalance* as I could assume. It was administered with such mildness that it might have been mistaken for a compliment.

"Now all this seemed very pretty while it was passing, but after I went home that night the enthusiasm of magnanimity cooled off, and a sense of my humiliation returned upon me, burning and rankling like the sting of a venomous reptile. Instead of yielding to time, this feeling increased from day to day until it obtained entire possession of me. The society became hateful; every allusion to it revived the drama of my disgrace. The very attempts of my companions to ignore the events of that unlucky night tinged my cheek with the blush of mingled shame and anger. I had no individual

enemies upon whom I might wreak my vengeance, nor could I now
recall my submission or withdraw from the society without exposing
myself to justifiable ridicule and contempt; yet, in its prosperous and
orderly existence, it stood a monument to perpetuate my ignominy.
From suffering I was at length relieved by the suggestions of subtlety.
I do not know whether a snake is conscious of its power, or whether
it is moved to use its venom solely by a blind instinct. Even as a boy
I was endowed with a stinging wit, a power of ridicule, a shrewd
insight into character and motive that was hardly boyish; yet I
was then scarce conscious of its power, and in bringing it to bear
upon my mortal enemy was certainly led more by instinct than reflection. Thenceforth I became uncommonly busy and officious in the
affairs of our society. My essays took a humorous turn; I was continually poking fun into the gravest debates, and our pompous observance of parliamentary forms furnished me with an unfailing theme
for ridicule. The older members bit their lips, the president would
rebuke me with a smile, but the boys generally received my sallies
with uproarious mirth, pleased with any apology to escape the re-
straints of dignity too rigidly enforced. As the fun was good-humored
and spicy, I soon had imitators who could not discriminate between
wit and buffoonery, nor fairly draw the line between liberty and
license.

"One stormy night, immediately after our adjournment, I visited
my overcoat pocket and exhibited a bottle of whisky, with a package
of sugar and lemons. Their appearance was hailed with applause.
It was a capital idea. Water was heated in the tin bucket, and we
brewed punch enough to make us all sociably boosy. At the close
of the next meeting the punch was repeated; and, at length it came
to be considered one of the regular exercises; other business was
hurried over that we might get at it; and our proceedings gradually
degenerated into broad farce. Committees were appointed to heat
the water and squeeze the lemons while the essays were read; another committee brewed the drink while the debate was going on. In
the midst of a discussion a waggish lad would present a dipperful
to his excellency the president, asking his opinion of its flavor; another would insist that it was unconstitutional for the presiding officer

to take a drink during the time of meeting—and so we went on from bad to worse.

"At our meeting during Christmas week, Black Bob brought in a roasted turkey and a bucket of egg-nog, prepared at my instance. His entrance was greeted with tumultuous applause; the thanks of the society were formally tendered, and the treasurer ordered to pay him half a dollar on the spot. Business was suspended until egg-nog was served round. When resumed, I read a funny essay. The boys laughed. More nog was handed round. Some of the members began to exhibit signs of obfuscation. The name of Black Bob was proposed for membership, to be appointed a standing committee on egg-nog.

"More nog.

"During the debate one asked leave to lean against the wall while he spoke. Another stopped short in his harangue, and, with owlish gravity, asked permission to go out and puke. In short, it was evident from that night that the *morale* of our society was defunct. Its reputation soon followed. People insinuated that there was something more than speechifying carried on at the Academy of Saturday nights; and although our proceedings were kept strictly secret, parents began to feel suspicious, and some went so far as to prohibit their boys from attending our meetings.

"But things had not reached this point without remonstrance and resistance. A strong party had earnestly endeavored to stem the current. Frequent efforts were made to prohibit the introduction of refreshments altogether, and by wordy appeals to our honor and public spirit, to lead us back to that pride of decorum and deference for law which had formerly characterized us. Vain and futile efforts! What chance have virtue and dullness in a contest with fun and frolic? How can a society or a nation ever recover the self-respect once lost?"

"Ay, ay," groaned the Squire. *"Facilis descensus Averni, sed revocare gradum—* You understand, Sir. Go on; go on."

"Some of our steadiest and brightest members had left in disgust; others, formed of more stubborn stuff, resolved to see it out, and continued to meet, zealously performing their exercises, and sturdily refusing to take any part in our disreputable proceedings. Hitherto I had taken pains to appear more as an easy follower than an instigator in this downward progress. I had even pretended to lament it, and sometimes rebuked the most forward; but now, aware of the bad repute of our society externally, and the feebleness of the decency party within, I determined to strike a decisive blow.

"The town, like most others, was infested by a gang of idle, lawless boys, notorious for rowdyism and rascality. Of this troop I had formerly been the acknowledged and admired chief. Since the rise of the Debating Society my myrmidons, headless and spiritless, had disbanded, and were forgotten. One Saturday afternoon I called upon my old Lieutenant, whom I found up a narrow alley sawing boards.

" 'Tad, said I, 'what are the boys about now?'

" 'Cap'en,' replied Tad, 'them fellers often talks 'bout you; but they thinks you've deserted 'em, and they don't like it.'

" 'Couldn't you parade them for me tonight, Lieutenant?'

"Tad's face brightened. 'What fur, Cap'en?'

" 'Never mind that, old friend. But couldn't you muster them out behind the stone wall near the Academy?'

" 'Bust up that durned 'Bating Siety?' exclaimed the Lieutenant, with prophetic eagerness. 'Them fellers is in for that job, certain.'

" 'Perhaps there will be some fun,' said I, with a knowing wink. 'When I meet you there I'll tell you more about it.'

"Tad winked in return. 'All right, Cap'en—honor bright!'

" 'And my old uniform and sword?'

" 'Up in the shop-loft, Cap'en. They'll be on hand.'

" 'All right—all right.'

"My friend and myself then hooked little fingers, and, after half a dozen mysterious wags, we parted.

"In arranging my plans I wished to avoid a resort to extremities, if possible. I expected to have a majority of my friends in the meeting to dissolve the society by a formal vote, destroy the records, and then satisfy the outside band by leading it off to a husking that I was aware of in the neighborhood. When we convened I was startled and disappointed. The decency party was in full force, and wore a resolute, defiant air, as if it had been advised of the meditated blow. I did bethink me then of an indiscretion—a weakness that I had been guilty of. Ah! Molly Morninglory, who would have thought it? But it was too late for vain regrets. My partisans, who had been fierce enough in caucus, I thought looked cowed and undecided. We were short in numbers, too; several on whom I counted surely having purposely absented themselves. These things made me savage; and while the exercises were progressing I slipped out to look after my banditti. At the appointed place, behind the stone wall, I found the faithful Tad, with full five-and-twenty ragamuffins at his back. They were diversely accoutred in reversed jackets, woolen shirts, and military coats belonging to fathers or elder brothers, and armed as variously— with clubs, old swords, rusty bayonets fixed on broom-sticks, and several lockless guns. As I passed along the line, saluting my old comrades, I observed that some had their faces painted, and wore other disguises. Among these I recognized several whom I was surprised to see there—boys of a better class, some of whom had formerly belonged to the society, and had been expelled; and others, whose application for membership had, for some cause, been unsuccessful. As I reviewed this formidable host, burning for action, and only waiting my orders to begin, all qualms of conscience and sickening indecision vanished. The Captain of the Forty Thieves was not prouder of his band than was I at that moment.

" 'Cap'en,' whispered my Lieutenant, 'I've brung your muster coat and sword.'

" 'Well done, old fellow; but keep the boys quiet till you hear me whistle.'

" 'That I will, Cap. But hit's mighty cold out here; hurry 'em up!'

"With a promise to do so, I quickly returned to my seat in the society. My old rival, Jack Loring, occupied the chair, and during my absence the question of abolishing refreshments and reforming our morals was again introduced. A member was in the midst of an harangue, depicting with great feeling the difference between our present rather equivocal position and our past glory—

" 'Oh, blast such stuff!' cried I. 'Let's adjourn.'

"The president flashed up like gunpowder. 'Your motion is an outrageous breach of order. I fine you one dollar.'

" 'Will you take an order on your granny for the money?' I asked, contemptuously.

"Jack attempted to reply, but his wrath choked him.

"I continued, 'There's a husking out at Slowman's to-night. The majority, I am sure, want to go; and as this society has got to be rather a disreputable concern, it's time we had smashed it up. So I again move we adjourn *sine die.*'

"The president recovered his power of speech at length. 'This is a gross contempt of the society,' he exclaimed—'a premeditated insult. I know that man now; he's been at the bottom of all this disorder and indecency from the beginning. Ever since a certain evening which he well remembers he has been scheming to ruin us. He ought to be expelled instantly.

"I put my thumb against my nose and facetiously waggled my fingers at the excited speaker.

"He screamed with rage. 'Gentlemen, shall we put up any longer with the insults of this monkeyfied blackguard?'

"I answered, with provoking merriment, 'The only monkey I see here, Mr. President, has his head sticking out of your cravat.'

" 'Those in favor of his expulsion will rise,' yelled Jack.

"Most of the members had already risen, in anticipation of a row.

" 'Expelled unanimously—expelled with contempt and contumely. Secretary, record it. Go out of the house, you disgraced buffoon; you are no longer a member of this society!'

"With a bow of mock humility I took my hat and went to the door. There was no need for the signal. No sooner had I crossed the threshold than Tad handed me my coat and sword, and facing about I marched in at the head of my ruffians. After the command, 'Halt! Front face!' there was a dead silence. This uncouth, many-headed apparition, so sudden and unexpected, struck the conservatives dumb.

"Waving my sabre above my head, I cried out, 'Three groans for the dissolution of the Literary Humbug of X——!' A yell followed, as if young Pandemonium had broken loose. In the mean time the society's adherents had rallied around the president, and mounting on benches and forms, armed themselves with books, billets of wood, inkstands, or whatever missile first came under their hands.

"At the command to sweep the room a spiteful volley was hailed upon my troops. My lieutenant was floored by a thump from Ainsworth's Dictionary—the first pang, I'll warrant that learning had ever cost him. Another sunk under the blows of a Cæsar, while the sable stream from a pewter inkstand mingled with the blood that spun from the nose of a third. Jack Loring fought like a madman, whizzing his missiles with unerring aim at me wherever I appeared. The minute-book of the society took me between the eyes, and made me see stars. Seizing it eagerly I thrust it into the stove, and there perished the record of my deposition and disgrace. The engagement was becoming serious. Throwing aside the useless and cumbersome guns and swords, several parties clenched and went tumbling over the floor, overthrowing desks and benches, wooling, gouging, and fisticuffing in downright earnest. Their ammunition spent, and giving up all for lost, the society boys began to escape by the windows; but the president and some of his adherents whipped out their apple-peelers, and threatening death to all who approached, heroically stood their ground.

"Believing that I had fully accomplished my object, and wishing to prevent more serious mischief, I had managed by a dexterous use of my sword to put out all the lights but one, which stood upon the president's desk. With another blow I brought down twenty feet of hot stove-pipe, which as it fell, extinguished the last candle, and left the combatants in total darkness. This, with the stifling smoke that presently filled the room, put an end to the battle.

"My company, swelled in numbers by the addition from the society, was again paraded on the Green. We gave three cheers for victory, and then marched off to the husking, singing, "Oh, wha did you come from?' in full chorus. As we withdrew, a brass candlestick struck me in the back, and we were followed for some distance by stones and curses from the indomitable Jack Loring."

When the rain ceased, the gentlemen, escorted by the proprietor, walked around the farm, where every thing that met their eyes betokened plenty and fatness. While they stood admiring a pen of plethoric grunters, Larkin observed a greasy-faced negroling peeping through the boards, and thus addressed him—

"Well, youngster, what do you think of these fellows?"

The youngster grinned admiringly. "We gwine to kill next week, Sir."

"Indeed! and what good will that do you?"

"I allers gits de blathers, Sir."

HAPPINESS

"Ah! Robert," sighed Squire Broadacre, "I well remember the time when that was a source of happiness to me—quite as real, quite as substantial as the more expensive bubbles I have blown since."

"I've no doubt of it," replied Bob, remembering some of the Squire's Western land speculations: "but I should never have thought of moralizing upon pig bladders."

But what doleful sound is that we hear? That's Aunt Charity's hog. The creature has been so overfed and is so fat that it can't stand up, and has lost the power of locomotion entirely. Indeed, it is too lazy to grunt, but lies and whines in that way by the hour. The fear is that it will die of a surfeit before killing-time.

I've never been able to account for the fact," said Squire B., "that the negroes' hens always lay more eggs and hatch more chickens, and their hogs are always fatter than those of their masters. 'Fat as a nigger's hog' has become a proverb with us in Virginia."

On the third day it cleared off, and, taking leave of their kind hosts, our friends made their way to Russellville, where they took the cars for Knoxville, fifty miles distant. In due time they arrived at their destination, with bag and baggage all safe. That all the world has not been equally fortunate, the following authentic and touching epistle will show:

> Mr J—— D—— R. Road Agant
> or J—— S—— thay manager of thay carse
> Russellville
> Es' Tennessee

Mr. S—— as i have ritan To you onst A bowt my trunk And you hav not Anssered my leter i am in great nead of my things And am A going to hav them or thay worth of them if you Wwill drop Mee A line if i have To come To rusilville i Wwill could I B sheure you ort To tak pitea on mee

And send hit To mee A poare disilut Woman you ort mind your mamy was A Woman i Am perising for thay nead of my cloahs this coald Weathr I Am a going to sue for that trunk if i cant git hit Any other weay i caried hit so fare And lost hit at home i met say that negro i think sot hit down or Mr S—— ware mistak my things I nead i cant say my preares out of my book til i git my Blak Trunk that trunk of mine you hav of mine in thay deapo or Wear leaft in they carse i Ast S—— to cheak my trunks And hee Woald doe hit And then I Woald have bean sheure of them I Am giting mad And that will in Jure caus

in hast

your Trobled freand

Sary ann Locks.

AUNT CHARITY

Knoxville was laid off in the year 1792, and named in honor of General Henry Knox, then Secretary of War at Washington. It was fixed upon by Governor Blount as the seat of the territorial government; and after the admission of Tennessee into the Union, in 1796, it continued to be recognized as the capital of the State, until 1817, when the seat of government was finally removed to Nashville. The town is beautifully situated on several high bluffs, on the right bank of the Holston, and contains some five or six thousand inhabitants. It is substantially built, with handsome store-houses, hotels, and private residences, while, among its public edifices, the Asylum for the Deaf and Dumb is especially worthy of note.

The University of East Tennessee, more remarkable for its beautiful location than architectural elegance, stands on an eminence commanding an extensive view in every direction. Although the political sceptre has departed from Knoxville, it is still regarded in East Ten-

nessee as the great centre of commerce, learning, and the arts, and
when the system of railroads, now
in progress, connecting it with
the Atlantic and the Mississippi,
shall have been completed, and
the capacities of the country
around it fully developed, the
most sanguine hopes of those now
interested in its prosperity will
doubtless be fulfilled.

In conclusion, we will insert
some extracts from a letter written by Bob Larkin to his friend
J—— R——:

YOUR TROUBLED FRIEND

"My dear R——: I gave you an account of our glorious trip to the
Black Mountains in my last from Jonesborough. We got here several
weeks ago, and, finding ourselves very comfortable at the Lamar
House, will probably remain some time longer. On our arrival here,
as an especial honor, we were received and escorted to our hotel by
the celebrated General Roberts, a gentleman whose amiable notoriety
extends all over the Southern country. Notwithstanding his formidable title, I am not aware that our General ever wore a chapeau in
the tented field, but believe he has earned the sounding prefix in a
service equally arduous and not less glorious—the service of the
ladies, who, in gratitude, have dubbed him Beau General. But our
Republican Beau must not be confounded with those who have made
the dainty appellation notorious in other countries and other times.
Beau Brummel, for example, only invented the commonplace art of
starching shirt-collars; Beau Roberts has acquired the more difficult
and *recherché* art of doing without them entirely. Brummel was
the slave of his washer-women, and ended by bilking and cheating
them; superior to such meanness, Roberts, having once been wronged,
has turned his back on the whole class forever. Brummel wasted
his estate on perfumers, tailors, and gluttony; Lycurgus himself never
inculcated more sublime contempt for soap, toggery, and victuals than
is daily manifested in the austere life of General Roberts.

"If these external peculiarities do not win our admiration at first sight, a better acquaintance with the General develops qualities which make ample amends for all apparent deficiencies. His life is merged in the love of the beautiful. Scorning the vile pursuits of muck-rakes and place-mongers, his time is occupied in the Chesterfieldian accomplishment of elegant letter-writing, and his income absorbed in fancy stationery and post-office stamps. He pricks his fingers in gathering roses for the fair, and wears out his boots in running useful errands. Yet not, like Jacob, does he serve for one fair Rachel, nor, like some besotted knight of chivalry, does he insult the whole sex to flatter the pampered vanity of one Dulcinea; but rather like the beneficent sun, his admiration shines equally on all; and for his devotion he seems to claim no other reward than an occasional smile of recognition, or the consciousness of having rendered agreeable service.

"In this selfish, gouging, money-making world, it is pleasant to meet with such a character.

"Beginning with so notable an acquaintance, we could hardly fail to find a sojourn here very agreeable. I have already attended two balls, and find the ladies eminently handsome and intelligent, and pretty good dancers in the reel. They entirely ignore hoops and the polka, to the great delight of Uncle Broadacre; and even our ladies, yielding to the prevailing sentiment, have lessened the circumference of their skirts by a foot or so, and figure only in reels and cotillions.

WATER-WORKS

"The city is lighted with gas, and well watered, although but scantily supplied with other liquids. While the water-works of Philadelphia have long challenged the admiration of the world, it must be acknowledged that their machinery is complicated, and maintained at vast expense. At Knoxville, although the quantity of water required is less, it must be raised to a greater height than at Fairmount; and the plan adopted reflects infinite credit on its originator, as being equally remarkable for its ingenuity, economy, and simplicity. I send an imperfect diagram of the machinery, which your knowledge of hydraulics will, doubtless, enable you to comprehend.

"Although there is no Opera-house here, they expect to have a custom-house very soon; and in the mean time the city is not wanting

WINTER SPORTS

in public amusements, especially during the winter. That most fashionable at present is the same that is so much in vogue at St. Petersburg and Paris, known as *Les Montagnes Russes*. Nature here has furnished facilities for this elegant amusement on the grandest scale; and the citizens lose no opportunity of improving their advantages. But the artificial slides of Paris are mere child's play, when compared to these; while danger and broken bones only give additional zest to the sport—for, whether in a fight or a frolic, a Tennesseean, you know, does not stop for trifles.

"And now, my dear fellow, I have a great deal to tell you about myself, and what a quandary I am in. But I can't trust that to paper, and must wait until we meet. . . ."

Sixth Paper

As a man grows old he naturally takes to grumbling and fault-finding. Government, morals, manhood, and beauty, all seem to have degenerated since his day. The green soda-biscuit and patent-yeast rolls of the present are compared with the crisp Johnny-cake of forty years ago. The clean-shaven past of wigs and queues is vauntingly pitted against the bearded and mustached present; powder and pomatum against hair-dye; the cocked hat *versus* the wide-awake. How vastly superior the "tweedle-dum" of the old times to the "tweedle-dee" of the new!

Even in Tennessee we hear the voice of lamentation over a State grown effete in its civilization before the stumps have rotted out of the streets of its cities.

Here's something on the subject of the fashions:

"The plain old-fashioned sons and daughters of this country at that day had no knowledge of such gaudy trappings and ostentatious flummery as bedeck our bucks and belles of the present age. If the first settlers in the then wilds of Tennessee had met with one of our modern dandies, with his superfine cloth pantaloons strapped on at both extremities of his person; his shirt manufactured in four or five different parcels, and fastened around his delicate and sickly-looking frame with tape, ribbons, and gold buttons; a superfine cloth coat upon his back, cut and made after our fashion; a dandy silk hat, with a rim three-quarters of an inch wide, upon his head; and right and left calf-skin boots upon his feet, they would have caught and caged him, and carried him about as a natural curiosity. And if the old ladies of that day had met with one of our slender, pale-faced, fashionable belles rattling in silks and satin; her clothing drawn over her delicate limbs as tight as the skin upon a lean weasel; her waist belted up in buckram until compressed within the circumference of six inches; her snow-white bosom peeping over the top of her outer garments,

LOADING CORN, ON THE TENNESSEE

protected only by the slight covering of gauze, ribbons, and lace; a
monstrous staked and ridered bonnet upon her head, streaming with flounce
and furbelows; a green vail, half as long as her whole person, hanging over
her face and fluttering its ample folds in the winds as she journeyed onward; a bunch of jewelry as large as a wagoner's horse-bells suspended
from each ear and dangling from her shoulders; her dress cut and made
according to the fashions of the present day; her delicate ankles covered
only by a pair of thin flesh-colored hose, at that day called stockings; and
her tender little trampers encompassed within a pair of prunella slippers,
they would have set all the bear-dogs upon her, and ran off and reported
that some nondescript monster or unknown wild beast was running at
large in the forest."

"The old gentleman has had but a limited acquaintance with
fashion-plates and millinery, I should judge," said Mrs. Broadacre.

"What an old-fashioned fright he has described!" cried Annette. "I would not wonder if they had set the dogs on her."

"Ah!" replied the Squire, "it was only written fifteen years ago."

Mrs. B. observed that they sounded very much like some of Mr. Broadacre's own reflections.

Here's something more. Speaking of the times of the early settlement of the State, he says:

"They were then content with the plain substantials of life; cultivated social and friendly habits; lived economically; enjoyed health and happiness, and died in old age at peace with each other and their God. In the administration of public affairs they selected the most competent and trustworthy individuals, without regard to the solicitations of aspirants; for electioneering was wholly unknown among them, and the citizens made choice of public functionaries with no other view than that of promoting the public weal. These were days of primeval simplicity, happiness, and delight; when virtue stood erect in the land, and walked with majestic stride through the public sanctuaries of the country."

Larkin said that Ovid had written much to the same purpose some eighteen hundred and fifty years ago:

"The golden age was first, when man, yet new,
No rule but uncorrupted reason knew,
And with a native bent did good pursue;
Unforced by punishment, unawed by fear,
His words were simple, and his soul sincere;
Needless was written law where none oppressed—
The law of man was written on his breast;
No suppliant crowds before the judge appeared,
No court erected yet, nor cause was heard,
But all was safe, for conscience was their guard."

"Thus sages have written and poets have sung to the same tune from time immemorial."

"And do you not believe they have reason?"

"Quite the contrary," replied Larkin. "If we are to put any faith in the teachings of history, we can not but acknowledge that the political, social, moral, and physical condition of mankind has exhibited, from age to age, a gradual but decided tendency toward improvement. While I am by no means credulous in regard to historic details, it seems that this great truth has been established beyond all controversy. Admit it, and then what are we to think of all these stories of the good old times?"

"Admit it? I admit no such thing."

"Papa," said Tiny, "this is Christmas eve, but I sha'n't hang up my stocking for Santa Claus to-night."

"And why not, my daughter?"

"Because I hung it up last Christmas, and when I came to look at it in the morning, instead of toys it was filled with corn-meal."

"That was most shameful in Santa Claus!"

Tiny replied that she didn't believe in Santa Claus at all; it was just a story they told children.

At this point Jim Bug entered with a waiter of cakes and egg-nog.

"Jim," said the Squire, "do you believe in ghosts?"

Jim answered that he had been too 'spectably raised to believe in any such foolishness; that if a weakness did sometimes come over him of nights in lonesome places, he was ashamed to acknowledge it in day time.

The Squire looked significantly at Larkin.

"That is progress, is it not? Children and negroes too smart to credit the supernatural, while grown-up white folks dote on Mesmerism, Spiritualism, and other isms. In my young days it was different; it was the children and negroes that swallowed the nonsense then— but fill my glass again, and I'll tell you a story:

"When I was a boy there lived on my father's estate an old negro that we called Uncle Ned. At the time I remember him he was old enough to be on the invalid list, and spent his days between his pig-pen, his patch, and his prayers. In his youth he had doubtless robbed many a hen-roost, and swallowed many an unlawful dram. Indeed, there was a story current of his having once been caught in a neighbor's turkey-house, and of his having adroitly excused himself by saying that he had come over to visit the colored ladies, and had mistaken that building for the kitchen. However, as he advanced in years he became extremely devout. One could never address him without hearing the tag end of a sermon, and you rarely passed his cottage without hearing his prayers, interrupted with frequent groans. He was continually wishing for death, and lamentably declared his belief that he was grown so old because the Lord had forgotten to take him.

"Now Aunt Betty, Ned's wife, was a capital cook, and I often applied to her to dress eggs that I had filched and birds that I had killed; and with the addition of an ash-cake of her own baking, many a savory meal have I made in her cabin. My feasts were so often troubled by Uncle Ned's importunate sermons and admonitions that I got very tired of them. I got quite enough of such things from legitimate sources; and besides, I suspected the old rascal, with all his devotion, of being little better than he should be. I never approached a certain old wooden chest in his house without sniffing a strong odor of whisky, and I often saw heaps of chicken feathers under his bed, without perceiving that his stock of live fowls ever diminished. There was also a question of a pig between us; but that is not to the point.

"Uncle Ned's life, although an easy one, was not free from troubles and trials. The archenemy of souls, it seems, had an especial spite at him, and had personally appeared to him in a variety of forms. His experiences on this head were wonderful to hear. He had followed him in the shape of a black cat; had crawled into his cabin like a copper-snake, and tried to bite him; as a huge owl he had perched upon the roof, and scared him with his hootings. When he could do no better, he manifested his disapprobation of the old martyr by spitting at him from among the coals in the fire-place. At length, about Christmas time, the fiend hit upon a more effectual mode of troubling his ancient enemy. That was by whispering a suggestion into my ear. I eagerly adopted the proposition, and lost no time in putting it into execution. As soon as it was dark I slyly possessed myself of the big powder-horn, and approaching Ned's cabin, with cat-like agility crept upon the roof, and leaned over the big stick chimney. The hearth was glowing with a fine bed of coals, upon which sat a coffee-pot and a skillet frizzling with fat sausages. The old woman was fidgeting about the supper-table, while the old man was sitting in front of the fire enjoying the prospect, and, possibly, reflecting on his sins.

"As I carefully dropped a few grains of powder upon the coals, he suddenly drew back his chair.

"'Betty, look da! See debbil sparkin' in dat fire da?'

"'Tain't nothin'; jis' a sign of snow.' And Betty went on with her preparations.

"'Betty,' cried old Ned, drawing still farther from the fire, ''pears to me I smells brimstone!'

"'Tain't nothin',' replied Betty, with less assurance than at first.

"A more decided blaze and smell of brimstone drove the old couple into the remotest corner of the room, where Ned, too much terrified to articulate a prayer, began to groan lustily. In my efforts to repress a sneeze, the next moment I let fall the horn. Whether I rolled or was blown off the roof of the cabin I can not tell, but in my bewilderment I gathered up and ran to the great house as fast as my legs could carry me. I slipped into the sitting-room where the family were gathered, and took a back seat, that my agitation and rapid breathing might not be noticed.

"The next moment there was a sound of hurrying footsteps through the yard, on the porch, in the hall; the door burst open, and in rushed Uncle Ned, staring and speechless. The inmates of the room started to their feet, when the old man's knees gave way, and he sunk at his old mistress's feet, grasping her gown with both hands. Aunt Betty followed, blown and frightened, but not speechless.

"'Oh master! o mistis! Debbil—debbil arter us, sure enough!'

"The old negroes shook as if in an ague fit; but soothing words, with the assistance of a glass of cordial, partially restored their incoherent wits, and Aunt Betty was presently enabled to communicate the cause of their alarm.

UNCLE NED

"While she was cooking supper her old man had observed some signs in the fire he did not like; there was an onaccountable spitting and sputtering, and a strong smell of brimstone, which, he too well knew, indicated the presence of the Evil One. Ned tried to pray, but his tongue clove to the roof of his mouth; when all at once, with a clap of thunder and a cloud of fire, the foul fiend came down the chimney. With one hand he shied the coffee-pot at her head, and with the other hurled the skillet of sausage at her husband; then began with his shovel to toss chunks and coals over the room; and wound up by seating himself, cross-legged, on the old chest, and spitting streams of fire at them. 'On dat very chist whar de whisky was,' sobbed Aunt Betty. 'I often told Ned dat whisky oughtn't be dar. Debbil knowed dat whiskey no business dar.'

WHAT AUNT BETTY SAW

"'They're drunk!' cried my father. 'Get out, you old sinners! How dare you alarm the house with such nonsense?'

"'Their terror is real,' replied my mother. 'George, Sam,' said she, addressing two negro men, 'go down to the cabin directly, and see what is the matter.'

"'Mistis,' answered George, 'I'se afeard.'

"My father took his hat and stick, and, followed by a trembling posse of whites and blacks, went himself to examine the premises. Things were found in the cabin pretty much as Aunt Betty had described them, except that the notorious individual who had made all the mischief was gone. The cooking utensils and supper were scattered over the house, mingled with coals and chunks of fire, and a cloud of sulphurous smoke not yet dispersed. My father looked bewildered, and the teeth of the negroes began to chatter at these unmistakable evidences of the recent presence of his Satanic Majesty.

"Presently Sam stooped to examine an object lying on the floor. 'Merciful Fathers!' he exclaimed, suddenly jumping back, 'it's one of he's horns!'

"'What is it?' asked my father. 'Hand it to me,'

"Sam shuddered. 'Master, tell me to kill myself, and I'll do it; but I wouldn't touch dat—not for my freedom.'

"My father picked it up himself, and on examination it proved to be a veritable horn, much splintered and powder-burned.

"'I smell brimstone orful,' said Sam, staring at the terrible relic.

"'I smell a rat!' said my father, putting the horn in his pocket, and quietly leading the way back to the house.

"As I expected, I was presently called aside.

"'Tony, this is the remnant of my big powder-horn. Explain this matter immediately.'

"I could not tell a lie to my father, even if I had been so disposed; so I told him the story from beginning to end without apology or circumlocution. He tried to look stern, but was evidently at some trouble to repress a laugh.

"'You have committed a grave fault,' said he, 'partly through inconsiderateness, and partly from a spirit of mischief. You have wasted my powder, ruined the horn, and narrowly missed killing a couple of worthy old servants. You must now go and explain to them how this thing occurred, that they may return to their cabin in peace.'

"By this time the whole community, white and black, was in a ferment. The affair was circumstantially explained; the powder-horn was exhibited in confirmation. Some of the negroes shook their heads incredulous; some laughed, and said they knowed Mass' Tony was at the bottom of it. Sam mustered up courage to take the horn in his hand. But the general feeling was one of disappointment that such an eye-stretching story should turn out a joke. As for Uncle Ned, he listened to all this with the air of a man whose perceptions have been obfuscated. Neither bribes nor assurances elicited any further response from him than a mournful shake of the head. He was escorted over to the big kitchen, where, in the course of time, he recovered his usual appetite and spirits; but thenceforth gave up sermonizing, and never could be induced to cross the threshold of his cabin again."

The young people were highly amused with this story, but Mrs. B. took occasion to thank Providence that she had no boys, and also to observe that children who had been spoiled showed the effects of it to the end of their days.

The glasses being replenished, the Squire called on Larkin for a story, who, nothing loth, narrated the following:

"The first Tennesseean I ever became acquainted with I met in Rome, while I was there a pseudo-student of the fine arts. In my free-and-easy intercourse with the artistic fraternity I had frequently observed a tall, fine-looking man, with a mild, intelligent countenance, but withal so silent and reserved that for a time our acquaintance went no farther than a simple salutation when accident brought us together. One evening ten or a dozen Americans happened in, as they say, at the room of a friend. Without, the air was damp and chilly; within, the uncarpeted tile floor and dingy walls were scarcely more suggestive of comfort. There was no fire in the room, except, indeed, our host's *scaldino* (an earthen pot filled with lighted charcoal and ashes), which was civilly handed from guest to guest to thaw their benumbed fingers. Orders were dull with the artists, funds were low, and conversation took a sober turn, until some one remembered it was Christmas eve, when, with one consent, it was determined we must have a spree in honor of the occasion. The *paoli* were accordingly posted up, and a servant dispatched for refreshments. These were presently set before us: a few bottles of thin sour wine, some dry rusk glazed over with white of egg, and a hatful of the sorriest dried figs. The appearance of the entertainment was rather calculated to dampen the spirits it was intended to cheer; but we strove manfully to make merry over it.

" 'Friends,' said one, 'what a contrast between this and Christmas in our own country!' And with that there was a flood of reminiscences poured forth, a gallery of Christmas pictures sketched by lively and graceful fancies.

"My tall acquaintance sat apart, saying nothing, with his head sunk upon his breast, and an expression, not of sadness, nor of despondency, but a dreamy look, as if his thoughts and heart were far away. I felt drawn toward him irresistibly, I don't know why; perhaps there was something sympathetic in his face, perhaps it was simply because I saw he could not even pretend to be merry like the rest of us. Deep down in that unrevealed breast, thought I, there are, doubtless, chords that will ring responsive to a skillful touch. Those who had spoken were from the North, and town or city-bred, and the joys they had pictured were such as they knew of. But it was now my turn; so I painted them a picture of an old-fashioned Christmas in our region. I drew it lovingly and truly, with heart as well as words.

"'Comrades,' I began, 'let me invite you to a country Christmas eve in the mountains. Take a peep into the roomy whitewashed parlor, lighted with flaming tallow-candles, and floored with a striped carpet. In the wide-mouthed fire-place a hickory fire roars and glows like a furnace. A black and turbaned damsel is present, whose time is occupied snuffing the candles and sweeping up the hearth with a turkey wing. Two swarthy elves bring in alternate armfuls of wood to keep up the blaze, always leaving the door wide open behind them. In rushes the wintry wind, flaring the candles, and whirling the hickory-ashes over the hearth-rug; in rushes a brace of shivering dogs, and with them "a sound of revelry" from the kitchen across the yard: squeaking, booming, and clattering in mingled cadence. The dogs are turned out, the wind is shut out, and with it the merry noise of the fiddles; the candles snuffed, the hearth swept, and then *"da capo al fine."* On the right hand sits the landed proprietor, plainly clad, strong-featured, and bronzed; a face that can easily assume the sternness of command, for he has smelled powder on the field of battle, and rules his estate like a feudal lord: yet the companionship of a loving wife and a troop of coaxing daughters has smoothed away all trace of harshness. Opposite to him sits the comely dame, knitting a gray yarn stocking; her demeanor nicely balanced between placidity and fidgetiness; observing sparks on the carpet, ashes on the rug, thieves in the candles, and quietly signaling "Cassy" on the subject. There are some good-looking, gawky boys, or would-be young men, sitting around, talking about horses and guns. There is a great stone pitcher sitting by the fire, covered with a plate. This appears to be under the charge of the proprietor, and nobody knows what is in it; but when he takes the plate off to stir it, as he does occasionally, you may smell hot apple-toddy all over the room. You are disappointed at not seeing the girls, your cousins, of course. The good dame smiles—they are in *déshabillé* —not visible yet; then she leans over and whispers confidentially, "Go in the next room and surprise them." This is a sufficient hint.

You open the door, and glide into the presence of half a dozen bouncing, blooming girls, gathered about a table with crocks of milk, bowls of sugar, eggs, and various *et ceteras*. Now for a moment you may look on and admire that exquisite, unstudied grace of movement and expression which our dear girls are careful never to exhibit in general society. But your heart thumps like a pheasant drumming. You had secretly hoped, but had hardly expected it— but there she is, her face flushed with the frolic, the comb just falling from her hair, which tumbles in luxuriant confusion upon her shoulders, her rosy tapering arms quite bare—beating, with all her might and main, the whites of two dozen eggs into a foam—Cousin Mary, with whom you have walked, and talked, and ridden, and danced so often—she that is such a madcap that the old folks are outdone with her; and so shy and prudish withal that you have often been outdone with her yourself—she that will fearlessly mount the most mettlesome steed and scream so prettily at the sight of a mouse; who sometimes bears herself so proudly that a prince would hardly dare to woo her, then with such winning, girlish gentleness that you think she might be had for the asking.

" 'In short, there sits the little maiden who can tweedle you between her finger and her thumb as easily as she twirls that same egg-beater—can bind you with a thread of pink worsted, and lead you, blind and helpless, as Samson was of old. You forget you are an intruder, but are presently reminded of it by half a dozen affected little screams. Then all the sweet little coquetries, simperings, and pretenses which the engaging sex always puts on in the presence of an admirer are immediately resumed. They try to hide their handsome arms, but don't succeed; to arrange their frolicsome ringlets, but only toss them about the more charmingly. You are scolded, menaced, ordered to retire (a pretty sneak would you be to go!), but you know better, and join the gleeful bevy with laughing assurance.

" 'Then the egg-nog is mixed, and poured into the mighty glass bowl, and crowned with whipped cream; the great silver ladle is produced, a regiment of glasses is mustered, and numerous plates with cakes, nuts, and apples. Then the company unites, and the refreshment is paraded into the parlor.

" 'Then the lass with the turkey-wing and snuffers grins as if she

THE MAID

had an ear of corn in her mouth; the swarthy elves grin as they bring in fresh wood; the shivering dogs yelp with eagerness as they bring in fresh wood; the shivering dogs yelp with eagerness as they rush in for the fiftieth time; the sound of revelry from the kitchen comes fast and furious.

" 'Then the healths go round —first to absent friends, then to the smiling present. The host's apple-toddy is steaming hot and potent. You are now brave enough to whisper sweet things to Cousin Mary, and she looks down and smiles and blushes most bewitchingly. "Now," cries the master, "we must have a dance! Bring in the music." "But," says the considerate matron, "the poor souls in the kitchen—it will spoil their frolic." "What!" replies the master, "because we have the misfortune to be white, shall we never forget our cares and troubles? Bring in the fiddlers! Young folks, take your partners." Yours, doubtless, is already engaged. In come the joyful musicians, grinning from ear to ear, and bowing until they sweep the floor with their greasy hats, anticipating extra drams and half-dollars for their holiday spendings.

" 'Then the dance—
No apish polka, new from France,
But jolly old Virginia reels—
Put life and mettle in their heels.'

"During this description I had watched my tall friend. At first he pricked his ears, then sat bolt upright and listened with kindling eye. When we came to the dance he leaped to his feet.

" 'Whoop-ee! hurrah! Countryman, your hand! Surely you're a Tennesseean?'

TUNING UP

" 'Next thing to one,' I replied, endeavoring to return the over-powering grip.

" 'That sketch,' said he, 'was worth more to me than all the cartoons of Raphael!'

" 'The subject,' I replied, 'is nearer to our hearts.'

"From that hour C—— and I were fast friends, and I found him a man as true as steel. Many a rough adventure we had together afterward—one of which I started to relate; but having used up my time in the preamble, I must defer it until another opportunity occurs. So good-night to all."

With regret our travelers concluded their pleasant sojourn at

Knoxville, and embarked on the steamer *James Williams* bound for Chattanooga. The scenery on the river is bold and pleasing without ever rising to sublimity. But the weather was delightful, the stream was full, and the stern wheel-boat made good speed, and as she frequently landed to put off or take on freight the artists had opportunities of sketching characteristic scenes on shore. At night the young folks had the privilege of the promenade deck by the light of a glorious moon while the elders stupefied themselves with cards and dominoes in the cabin.

The first night on a Western steamboat is not usually an agreeable one. The thundering explosions from the escape-pipes, the jar of the machinery, the rush of the wheels through the water, the frequent signals from the bell, the shouts of command, all confused and half understood, are little calculated to soothe the nerves of those unaccustomed to such sounds, especially if the imagination has been properly stimulated beforehand by newspaper accounts of fires, snags, and bursted boilers. One who has been well brought up, is apt on such an occasion to say his "Now I lay me down to sleep" with especial fervor and emphasis, and to welcome the coming dawn with un-

EMIGRANT ARK

common thankfulness. It is not, therefore, to be wondered at that some of our friends looked a little haggard and sleepy, when they appeared at the breakfast-table next morning; nor is it strange that they laid all the blame upon the narrow, uncomfortable beds which they occupied. All travelers do the same thing. But people soon become accustomed to any thing. The imaginary dangers disappear, the real are forgotten, and in less than twenty-four hours after embarkation the most timid traveler sinks to sleep as free from apprehension as if he were in a church on shore.

That day the *James Williams* passed an ark floating down the river containing an emigrant family and their fortunes. This craft we believe is peculiar to the Western waters, and merits a particular description. It is a huge, flat boat, perhaps a hundred feet in length, furnished with sweeps at each end and a pair at the sides; not used for the purpose of simply propelling her but merely to keep her in the stream, the current being the motive power mainly relied on. In the forward part of the boat the housekeeping for the family was going on. A sallow but resolute-looking matron was stirring the big pot, a buxom girl of eighteen was setting the table. Near the fire sat an aged couple whose bent figures and snowy locks seemed sadly misplaced in a scene that told of hardship and adventure. Around were numerous tow-headed children of various sizes, some assisting in the work, some lolling about on the heaps of hay and provender that occupied the centre of the boat, and two or three little ones sleeping beneath a canvas tent which protected the bedding of the party. Around was stacked in piles a complete inventory of household and kitchen furniture. Chairs, tables, pots, kettles, bedsteads, cupboards, churns, and spinning-wheels. Barrels there were, filled with flour and bacon, with a good store of comfortable quilts and blankets, and a heap of cabbages in one corner.

Toward the stern of the boat the space was occupied by horses, cattle, and farming utensils enough to stock a small farm; chickens, dogs, and a pair of goats completed the motley equipage.

"There," said Squire Broadacre, drawing attention to an athletic figure clad in a hunting shirt of tawny jeans and leaning on a rifle— "there is the representative of a race who have been moving out West for the last two hundred and fifty years. From the day that the first feeble and puling colony was planted on the banks of the Powhatan to the present have they been moving; crawling at first with slow and uncertain progress up toward the sources of the Atlantic rivers, then with more vigorous tread scaling the blue ridges of the Appalachian mountains; adventuring from valley to valley, until from the last summit their eyes beheld the vast fertile plains of the West unrolled like a map of the Land of Promise. These they occupied, advancing, as they grew older, with giant strides; leaping the mighty Mississippi—still onward without a pause, pressing toward the snow-capped peaks of Oregon. Westward, still westward, until the dark rolling surges of the Pacific shout in tones of thunder, 'No more, no more, no more beyond!' The Western country is run out. What a thought! What a bewilderment, a stultification to the American mind to find the leading idea of more than two centuries thus suddenly quenched in a remorseless ocean! Unhappy denizens of the Columbia and California, who have no west. Where will they send their frolick-ing sons, or where marry their superfluous daughters? Where poke off their old-fashioned store goods or young doctors? Where, when debts become pressing and credit fails, will they emigrate to? In short, when the contemplation of realities around them has become wearisome, where will they locate those bright illusions so essential in helping us through this stale, unprofitable life?"

"Ah," sighed Mrs. B., "I can't see the use of living at all in coun-tries where there is no society, no distinctions—"

"And no fashions," suggested Annette.

"Silence, Miss Pertness!" replied the lady. "I was thinking of noth-ing of the sort. Yet I've often wondered how the women occupied themselves in their leisure moments."

"It must be awfully lonesome," said Annette. "It would require an uncommonly handsome beau to persuade me to lead such a life."

"There is a dash of adventure in the life," said Larkin, "which is doubtless the principal attraction for those who embark in it."

On the second night of their voyage our travelers retired early and slept soundly, and on awakening next morning found the boat moored at the Chattanooga landing. A carriage was procured to convey the ladies and baggage to the "Crutchfield House," while the gentlemen followed on foot. The hotel swarmed with people arriving and departing with the trains, east, west, north, and south, hurrying to and fro with eager and excited looks, as if lives, fortunes, and sacred honor hung upon the events of the next hour. All the corners and by-places were filled with groups in earnest conversation, some were handling bundles of papers, others examining maps. Rolls of bank-notes were exhibited, and net purses with red gold gleaming through their silken meshes. In the confusion of tongues the ear could catch the words, Lots—Stocks—Quarter-section—Dépôt—Dividends—Township—Railroad—Terminus—Ten thousands—Hundred thousands—Millions. The Squire, impatient to get his coffee, peeped into the breakfast-room. The waiters were trading coats.

"I tell you what—I'll give you dis coat for a dollar and a half and take your paper at nine months, or ef you like better, one dollar cash on de button—"

"Dem 'rangements don't zactly suit me jis now. I mought be able to raise dat money, and den agin I moughtent—but I'll gib a dollar

A BARGAIN

and a quarter—thirty-one cents cash down and trust for de rest."

"Hum—what skurity on de 'furred payments?"

"Well lem'me see. You 'member dem boots gemmen give me? I let Ike have 'em; he owes me half a dollar on 'em."

"Don't talk to me 'bout Ike; he's worse'en broke; got no karacter. He done niggered me already outen a good hat and a pair of pants."

"How you like an order on boss?"

"'Tatch your wages?"

"Dat's it."

"Done."

Having at length accomplished a comfortable breakfast, the gentlemen sallied out to see the town. At a short distance from the hotel they were accosted by three boys who offered some black bottles at a bargain. The Squire was indignant: "What the devil," said he, "should we want with empty bottles?"

"They'll hold beer," replied the leading juvenile; "and only five cents."

"Go about your business," said the Squire, with an impatient gesture. "I perceive, Robert, we are in a nest of speculators, where any thing may be had at a bargain, ranging from a man's soul down to a beer-bottle."

"Well, mister," persisted the merchant, "if you don't like beer, they'll hold whisky jist as well."

The Squire turned fiercely and shook his cane; at which the smallest boy took to his heels, but the others, being better physiognomists, only drew back a little.

Larkin now begged permission to take them in hand, and, under the pretense of trading, enticed them over to a little knoll where the stumps afforded convenient seats. Here he made a ragged sketch, and dismissed the pertinacious speculators with a dime each, and still in possession of their merchandise.

As they departed, shining with contentment, the junior observed to his friend, "Wasn't Jack a fool to get scared and turn back when he might have made ten cents jist as easy?"

Chattanooga is a new place, apparently just cut out of the woods. It has lately sprung into importance as a point on the great railway thoroughfare connecting the Mississippi River at Memphis with the Atlantic Ocean at Charleston, South Carolina. It contains four or five thousand inhabitants, and has some pretty and substantial buildings dotted about on its straggling and irregular streets, which are often interrupted by stumpy fields, ponds, and patches of forest timber. Such towns usually can not boast of many attractions, other than those of a commercial and speculative character; but the site of this place is associated with many of the most interesting incidents in the early history of Tennessee, while the natural beauty of its surroundings make it a spot where an artist would love to linger.

It is situated at the mouth of the Chickamaugua, on the south side of the Tennessee River, at the point where this stream enters the Cumberland mountains. Behind the town rises the imposing form of the Lookout Mountain, from whose top may be obtained one of the most beautiful and varied views in all the West. Below one catches romantic glimpses of that savage pass called the Narrows, through which, for a distance of twelve or fifteen miles, the hitherto quiet and navigable river winds foaming, boiling, and roaring, in its frantic struggles to find an outlet to the lower country—an elysium for the tourist, but a terror to navigators.

The view of the long ranges of grinning precipices marking the course of the stream, and stories of danger connected with the passage, so fired the imaginations of our travelers that they determined, if possible, to make the trip. After many unsuccessful attempts to procure a conveyance and a pilot, they at length chanced upon a rough waterman who promised to take them through in a row-boat; not, however, wtihout bribes and persuasion was the promise obtained. The hour for departure was fixed, and the gentlemen hastened to make preparations for the voyage. The ladies were to remain at the hotel, and the Squire went forthwith to inform them of the arrangement, while Larkin looked about for some boat stores.

At the end of an hour the gentlemen met again on the landing, with their countenances somewhat fallen. The ladies had positively refused to be left alone, in a strange tavern in a strange town.

"If," said the Squire, "I had known what a set of ridiculous, perverse—"

"It makes no difference," interrupted Larkin. "The boatman is as drunk as a fool, and now says he won't take us; nor is he able to do so if he was willing."

This report the boatman himself presently verified by staggering up to the speakers and inquiring, if they thought he was going to *resk* his life to satisfy the kurosity of a couple of d—d fools? Larkin answered that, from appearances, such a loss would be irreparable both to his family and society in general, and, in consequence, they would excuse him.

"But," continued the boatman, "I can tell you a good story about the first time I ever went through them Narrows."

The artist intimated that, if the story was a good one, he would feel compensated for the disappointment.

"This was the way of it," said the mariner, balancing himself, and looking wise: "There was a man and his family come from

above somewhar, in a flat bound for Arkansaw. He was pretty well
loaded with farm-stock, women, children, and truck; and having
heard tell of the Narrows, he was afeared to go through by himself,
but wanted a pilot. So, after considerin' a while, I agreed to put
him through for two dollars."

"But I thought you were telling of the first time you went
through?" said Larkin.

"So I am, boss! if you'll only let me talk. I never had been
through there, but I had heard people talk about the Skillet, and the
Sleek, and the Bilin' Pot, and all that; and I thought I could shoot
her through, and if I sunk her I'd lose my money—that's all. So we
tuck a few drinks and put off, and I takes the steerin'-oar and put
her head down, and let her rip. Night come on pretty soon, but that
was all the same to me; so we tuck a few more drinks, and let her
slide. And we went over some rough places, and, after while, come
to a pretty smart current runnin' smooth. 'Now she goes it slick as
goose-grease!' says he to me. So, by-and-by, we see lights on the
shore, and passed by a house where a feller was playin' 'Old Zip
Coon' like a saw-mill, and people dancin'. 'Here's good fun to you!'
says he, and we tuck another dig. So we went on pretty sprightly:
and, by jingo! before we got well out of sight and hearin' of that house
we went past another, whar they were dancin' to the same tune.
'Success to 'em!' says I. 'Hand us that bottle; while fun is goin',
we might as well have our share.' So we drank a mouthful, and
before we were done talking about it we went past another place,
fiddlin' and dancin' like the rest.

" 'Mister,' says he to me, 'this here's the jolliest settlement ever I
traveled through—all agoing it to the same tune.' ' 'Pears to me,' says,
I, 'I hear another fiddle and fellers a laffin';' and, presently, sure
enough, we streaked past another house whar they ware goin' it a
leetle more extravagant than the others—tune about the same. 'Mister,'
says the boss to me, 'this rather beats my time. Do the people along
this river mostly spend their nights fiddlin' and dancin'?' 'Certain,'
says I; 'that's their reg'lar business.' But now, I tell you, I was be-
ginnin' to get bewildered and oneasy myself. So, pretty soon we
passed another house, and another, and another, all dancin' and
fiddlin' like blazes. The boss he set quiet, and didn't say a word

for a while, but tuck a swig now and then. Next house we passed
they were goin' it on Old Zip Coon with a will. Then the boss
spoke up. 'Pilot,' says he, 'there's one of two things—either we're
drunk, or there's hell's doin's goin' on along this river to-night!'
'What time o' night is it?' says I. 'About two o'clock in the mornin'
by the stars,' says he. 'How many houses have we passed?' 'I've
counted nine,' says he, and his voice began to shake a little. 'Now,'
say he, 'it might be that the hellish thing is a follerin' of us.' 'Nine,'
says I, 'is the devil's number,' says I, pretty badly skeered! 'if the thing
appears agin, go call your wife, and if she can't see it, we're drunk,
certain.' 'Listen!' says he; 'don't you hear 'em? thar's the lights! ten
times! we're drunk, sure. Katy! Katy! sweet-heart, wake up!'

"This time I headed the flat a little in nearer shore, and we could
hear 'em plain, cussin' and swearin'.

" 'Katy,' says boss, 'do you see or hear anything over there on
shore?'

" 'I see lights,' says she, 'and hear a passel of drunken boatmen
dancing Old Zip Coon.'

"I wanted to put in, but boss says 'No; but sure as I'm a man,
if they're carrin' on at the next house we pass we'll tie up and make
out the night with 'em!'

"In about half an hour, as I expected, we come upon another spree.

" 'Head her in!' says he. So we tied up at the landing, and went
in the house.

"Now, stranger, how do you think it was? Why, this was old Jack
Cogles's house, down thar fornense the Bilin' Pot, whar some fellers
and some gals were dancin' all night; and we went bilin' around and
around, passin' by the same place over and over agin! Now at fust
it came to me like a sort of a dream; then it was all clare; and without waitin' to be cussed or laughed at, I streaked it. But it's all true,
jist as I tell ye."

Obliged to abandon the idea of passing through the Narrows,
the travelers consoled themselves by planning a visit to the Nick-a-Jack
Cave. This was accomplished by taking the Nashville cars next
morning and going to Shell Mound station, a point about twenty miles
distant from their starting-place. The station is immediately upon
the Tennessee River, and is named from the immense banks of

fossil shells found on the spot. From this point the travelers proceeded on foot across a cultivated flat called the Old Fields, and, at the end of a half or three quarters of a mile, found themselves at the base of the Racoon Mountain, which rises abruptly to the height of twelve or fifteen hundred feet above the low grounds. In the face of a perpendicular cliff immediately before them appeared the yawning mouth of the Nick-a-Jack Cave. It is not arched, as these subterranean passages usually are, but spanned by horizontal strata resting on square abutments at the sides, like the massive entablature of an Egyptian or Tuscan temple. From the opening issues a considerable stream, of a bright green color, and of sufficient volume to turn a saw-mill near at hand. Having neglected to provide themselves with lights of any kind the gentlemen procured some pitch-pine boards from the sawyer, and, splitting them into strips, made torches sufficient to serve for the intended exploration.

The height of the cliff is about seventy feet, that of the opening forty feet, and about one hundred in width immediately at the entrance, and of this the stream occupies about one-third. The roof of the cave is square and smooth, like the ceiling of a room, but below the passage is rough and irregular, with heaps of earth and huge angular masses of rock, making the exploration both difficult and dangerous. There are no incrustations of any kind upon the walls; and, altogether, the appearance of the cavern is gloomy and repulsive, and well calculated to give effect to the dark traditions connected with its name. It is said in early times to have been the resort of banditti, composed of Indians and desperate white men, whose crimes and bad passions had induced them to join with the savages. Their favorite pursuit was plundering the boats of the emigrants and traders, as they descended the Tennessee River, murdering and making captive the unfortunate whites who fell into their hands; and this cave was a convenient hiding-place for the booty.

"And if any one doubts it," said Larkin, stooping to pick up something from among the rocks, "here's proof positive. I've found a piece of their money."

"Bless me!" cried Annette. "It doubtless belonged to some poor emigrant who was murdered by the robbers! Let me see it. Is there blood on it?"

"There's mud on it, cousin. Come, now it's bright."

"I should like to wear it as a charm," continued the young lady; "a coin so full of historic interest, dark and bloody associations."

"Humph!" said Squire B., "it is a five-cent piece."

"Now I've punched a hole in it, Cousin Netty, let me hook it to your bracelet, and you'll wear it as a remembrance—"

"Of the cave and the robbers," said she, significantly.

On a level spot near the entrance was a blacksmith's forge, where they kindled a brisk fire to keep off the damp air while the party lunched. When this was over the gentlemen took their torches and started for the interior, leaving the ladies at the forge.

THE LANDLADY

Outside, the day was balmy and beautiful; and lingering by the way, they at length found their way back to the station. Here it occurred to them that their lunch had been rather a light one; for exercise in the fresh air is a marvelous appetizer. As the train by which they were to return to Chattanooga was not due for two hours, their attention was directed to a shanty opposite the station-house, where "Cheap Boarding" was advertised in white chalk letters. As the occupants of the establishment, an old black woman and a pup, appeared to be well nourished, the Squire ventured over to explore the premises, and in a short time a meal of bacon and eggs, biscuits and coffee, was prepared—smelling so savory, and so neatly served withal, that the whole party, even including Madam B., were glad to go over and partake.

Aunt Hannah seemed to appreciate the honor done her, and flew round with the sprightliness of a maid of sixteen. She informed her guests that she was quite at home in good society, as she had been brought up in Huntsville, Alabama, and had formerly belonged to some of the high folks in that place. Having become dissatisfied with her position, she scraped together a hundred dollars, bought her time, and was now keeping tavern on the Nashville road.

Larkin drew her portrait, and the travelers took leave, promising to recommend her establishment to all their friends.

Bibliographical Appendix

The libraries of Duke University, of West Virginia University, and of the Peabody Institute and the West Virginia archives are important depositories of Strotheriana. However, by far the most valuable collection of letters, drawings, and journals relating to Porte Crayon is owned by his grandson, D. H. Strother of Milwaukee. Thirty diaries, which chronicle Strother's life from 1861 to 1888, are among this collection of papers.

TEXT

A checklist of Strother's prewar publications which have to do with the Old South is given below. Those which have been included in this book, either entire or in part, are marked with an asterisk, and the nature of omitted material is noted.

* *Virginia Illustrated: Containing A Visit to the Virginian Canaan, and The Adventures of Porte Crayon and His Cousins, Illustrated from Drawings by Porte Crayon.* New York: Harper & Brothers, Publishers, Pearl Street, Franklin Square, 1871. First published in book form in 1857 by Harper's, the 1871 version reproduced in this anthology is a reprint of the 1857 book. The following passages do not appear in this anthology: Chapters I-IV, pages 55-119, of "The Adventures of Porte Crayon and His Cousins," describing the planning and first steps of the trip of Crayon and the girls through western Virginia; Chapter VIII, pages 160-78, of "The Adventures," White Sulphur and Rockbridge Alum Springs; part of Chapter XI, pages 230-35, of "The Adventures," describing "that old time boating on the James"; Chapters XIII-XVI, pages 251-300, of "The Adventures," describing the Loafer and the

Squire, Berkeley Springs, the Bear and the Basket-Maker, and the arrival home.

*"The Dismal Swamp," *Harper's New Monthly Magazine,* XIII (September, 1856), 441-55. This is reproduced in full.

*"North Carolina Illustrated: I. The Fisheries," *Harper's New Monthly Magazine,* XIV (March, 1857), 433-50. In full.

*"North Carolina Illustrated: II. The Piny Woods," *Harper's New Monthly Magazine,* XIV (May, 1857), 741-55. In full.

*"North Carolina Illustrated: III. Guilford," *Harper's New Monthly Magazine,* XV (July, 1857), 154-64. Section from pages 159-62 describing Revolutionary battle of Guilford is omitted.

*"North Carolina Illustrated: IV. The Gold Region," *Harper's New Monthly Magazine,* XV (August, 1857), 289-300. Section from pages 289-98 describing processes of gold-mining is omitted.

"A Winter in the South: First Paper," *Harper's New Monthly Magazine,* XV (September, 1857), 433-51. This essay describes the travels of Bob Larkin with Squire Broadacre's family to Richmond, on the James River and Kanawha Canal, to Saltville, and back to Abingdon, Va.

"A Winter in the South: Second Paper," *Harper's New Monthly Magazine,* XV (October, 1857), 594-606. This describes further travels of Larkin and the Broadacres in East Tennessee.

*"A Winter in the South: Third Paper," *Harper's New Monthly Magazine,* XV (November, 1857), 721-40. In full.

"A Winter in the South: Fourth Paper," *Harper's New Monthly Magazine,* XVI (January, 1858), 167-83. This describes Larkin and Broadacre at Bald Mountain, and a mountain family is sketched.

*"A Winter in the South: Fifth Paper," *Harper's New Monthly Magazine,* XVI (May, 1858), 721-36. In full.

*"A Winter in the South: Sixth Paper," *Harper's New Monthly Magazine,* XVII (August, 1858), 289-305. Section from pages 298-99 giving an "improvised" poem called "Song of Emigration" is omitted; section from pages 303-5 describing Nick-a-Jack Cave excursion is omitted.

"A Winter in the South: Seventh Paper," *Harper's New Monthly*

Magazine, XVIII (December, 1858), 1-18. This describes Larkin and the Broadacres in Alabama and, briefly, in New Orleans.

"Rural Pictures," *Harper's New Monthly Magazine,* XX (January, 1860), 166-80. This describes a visit to a Virginia manor and a village nearby.

It should be noted that *Virginia Illustrated* first appeared as a series of five papers in *Harper's,* 1853-56. When the series was reissued as a book in 1857 the text was substantially the same except that some introductory mottoes in the articles were removed and chapter titles for the book were supplied. The type was reset. Both "The Virginian Canaan" and an inferior and irrelevant article, "The Bear and the Basket-Maker," were added.

BIOGRAPHY AND CRITICISM

Short biographical sketches of David Hunter Strother are fairly numerous, but for the most part they are inaccurate and repetitious. By far the best and most reliable are those in Thomas C. Miller and Hu Maxwell, *West Virginia and Its People* (New York, 1913) and in *Dictionary of American Biography* (New York, 1936). The account of Strother in John S. Hart's *A Manual of American Literature* (Philadelphia, 1874) is particularly valuable because it was one of the first, written in the third person by Strother himself. My article, "A West Virginian in Europe: The Apprenticeship of 'Porte Crayon,'" *West Virginia History,* XIX (July, 1958), 266-79, discusses a limited portion of his career, his study and travels in Europe during the forties.

Although many of Strother's drawings and writings have been reprinted in books and periodicals, critical evaluations are almost nonexistent. Daniel B. Lucas, who wrote an introduction and edited Strother's work for the *Library of Southern Literature* (New Orleans, Atlanta, and Dallas, 1909), praised his treatment of the Southern Negro and made other perceptive remarks. Ella May Turner's *Stories and Verse of West Virginia* has helped to keep Strother's writings before the public. A brief discussion of *Virginia Illustrated* can be found in Van Wyck Brooks, *The Times of Melville and Whitman* (New York, 1947). Professor Jay Hubbell mentions

Strother several times in his *The South in American Literature* (Durham, N. C., 1954). One of the most enthusiastic appraisals of Strother's work was written by Elmer Davis for *Harper's Magazine,* CCI (October, 1950). My article, "'Porte Crayon' and the Local Color Movement in West Virginia," *West Virginia History,* XX (April, 1959), 151-62, traces his efforts to encourage an indigenous literary tradition in that state after the Civil War. The University of North Carolina Press will publish in 1960 my biography of Strother.